Right to Be
HOSTILE

Right to Be
HOSTILE

SCHOOLS, PRISONS, AND THE MAKING OF PUBLIC ENEMIES

Erica R. Meiners

Routledge
Taylor & Francis Group
New York   London

Routledge
Taylor & Francis Group
270 Madison Avenue
New York, NY 10016

Routledge
Taylor & Francis Group
2 Park Square
Milton Park, Abingdon
Oxon OX14 4RN

International Standard Book Number-10: 0-415-95712-5 (Softcover) 0-415-95711-7 (Hardcover)
International Standard Book Number-13: 978-0-415-95712-0 (Softcover) 978-0-415-95711-3 (Hardcover)

Library of Congress Cataloging-in-Publication Data

Meiners, Erica R.
    Right to be hostile : schools, prisons, and the making of public enemies / Erica Meiners.
        p. cm.
    Includes bibliographical references.
    ISBN 978-0-415-95711-3 (hb) -- ISBN 978-0-415-95712-0 (pb)
        1. Critical pedagogy--United States. 2. Discrimination in education--United States.
    3. Educational equalization--United States. 4. Social change--United States. I. Title.

LC196.M435 2006
370.11'5--dc22   2006031607

Visit the Taylor & Francis Web site at
http://www.taylorandfrancis.com

and the Routledge Web site at
http://www.routledge.com

Contents

Acknowledgments

This book was shaped through a number of projects and by working alongside people. Without the support and the challenges of these encounters and movements this book would not have been possible.

I thank the participants, teachers, and other community members at the St. Leonard's Adult High School that I have worked with over the last six years for their humor, commitment, and labor including Mary Zangs, Kevin Glover, Robyn Clark, Renny Golden, Ajitha Reddy, James Hoskins, Bob Dougherty, Ken Addison, David Rutschman, Carla Lewis, Tanitha Dale, Willie Sallie, Roberto Sanabria, T. Manning, Mike Fitzgerald, Jitu Brown, and more recently, Mary Bandstra, Phyllis Porche, Eric Reyes, Karen Biegel, Erica Brown, Toussaint Losier, and Shelley Bannister. This community has been invaluable and sustaining, in particular Jean (Patricia) Hughes, who continues to show me that pragmatism can be radical and visionary and also full of humor and grace.

A number of other organizations in Chicago continue to be places where I learn, and all kinds of change happens, including Beyondmedia Education, Critical Resistance, Chicago Legal Advocacy for Incarcerated Mothers (CLAIM), and the Coalition for Education on Sexual Orientation (CESO). In addition, I have learned from people who resist prisons in a variety of ways including Yaki, Naoma Dye, Joanne Archibald, and Shaena Fazal.

I benefited from opportunities to workshop parts of this project in 2006. Specific thanks to Stephen Hartnett, Alison Bailey, Dawn Beichner, Char Hill, and the Education Graduate Student Association at Simon Fraser

University, and to Leslie Bloom and Valerie Polakow. I thank David Gillborn and Bill Pinar for their support of my academic work over the years.

Therese Quinn, Leslie Bloom, Suzanne de Castell, and Ken Addison all offered smart feedback on parts of this manuscript as did reviewers from Routledge/Falmer and Susan Seals Giroux. If I did not take their suggestions, it is all my error, but their contributions enhanced this project. In addition, Catherine Bernard offered many generous but firm suggestions that improved the book, and, with kindness, Prudy Taylor Board and the staff made my writing better. Wajiha Khan and Anne Seveska provided invaluable research and bibliographic assistance.

Tim Barnett, and then Tyler Barnett Steinkamp, Scott Steinkamp, and now Erik Bataller, Mollie Dowling, and Nic McClellend make a joyously chaotic queer household. David Feiner and Laura Wiley continue to illustrate the value of a fierce, risky love and that art can be astonishing. Conversations and friendships with many made this project possible: Megan Bangs, Katherine Biers, Salome Chasnoff, Chris Cuomo, Marvin Garcia, Fong Hermes and family, Derrick Higginbotham, Nicole Holland, Francisco Ibáñez-Carrasco, Jodi Jensen, Katherine Lieber, Eleni Makris, Cage McCall, Fran Royster, Ann Russo, Karen Schlanger, Susan Tilley, Joan Varney, and Dave Stovall. Denise Meiners and Elena, Heather, Holly May and Stacia Middlemass continue to remind me of where I come from and the possibilities the future holds. Laurie Fuller offered her editing prowess, critical questions, reminders to get over myself, and crazy love.

This book is written in the early morning hours before my paid job at the university, before teaching, or when I place a note on my office door that I am in a conference call. I write between other commitments I have outside the university, on public transit, at the coffee shop on those beautiful mornings I am free, in my red room when there are no friends, or friends of friends, sleeping. I write this not to be special. I know people who are far busier than I, including my sister who has a traditional 8:30 a.m. to 5:30 p.m. job with less than two weeks of vacation a year. I am sure readers have similar, if not more compelling, constraints. My plea is not that I am special or extra busy, but rather this work is partial, and it reflects ongoing commitments to people and to projects that are always in progress. I fully expect and want next year to have new questions, to take new risks, and to learn more.

Finally, this book is for those hundreds of men and women with whom I have interacted who struggle to survive and to flourish and to make political and personal change amidst systems designed to annihilate.

Introduction

On March 19, 2004, at the Los Manos gallery in Chicago, site of Beyondmedia's Voices in Time installation on gender, race, and incarceration, we were preparing for a 6 p.m. community forum on barriers to reentry for those formerly incarcerated. A group of African American students from Percy Julian High School finished their guided tour of the installation. The students were clearly engrossed by the video testimonies of women who survived and resisted prisons and jails in Illinois, the re-creation of the prison cell, and the materials such as uniforms and food that Beyondmedia Education had gathered. Also the data on the poster boards that charted the gendered and raced rising incarceration rate, the location of prisons in Illinois, and the boost to the local economies that prisons are purported to invigorate. An activist former prisoner and staff member of Chicago Legal Advocacy for Incarcerated Mothers (CLAIM) facilitated questions and led the group through this small exhibit. One female voice, toward the end, said:

"The uniforms are just like the ones we had to wear in elementary school. Same white shirts and blue pants. When I look at these I can't help thinking, what were they preparing us for?"

The clarity of analysis possessed by these students moved me. I felt an acute sense of accountability and anger—and also a realization of my inability to hold the profession I am paid to participate in accountable.

With the highest incarceration rate for any Western industrialized country, over two million and growing in prisons and jails, the United States has 5% of the world's total population yet possesses 25% of the world's incarcerated. The number of people under state control in the United States jumps to almost seven million if the four million on probation and the 750,000 on parole are included, and still this figure does not include those housed in Immigration and Naturalization detention facilities or U.S. prisons that are not in the United States. African American women are 8 times more likely and Latinas are 4 times more likely to be imprisoned than white women, and 75% of all women are incarcerated for nonviolent offenses. This addiction to prison expansion has individual and national consequences beyond the abject warehousing of our nation's poor. One in 50 citizens are barred from voting as a result of their incarceration and in southern states nearly one third of African American males cannot vote (Bureau of Justice Statistics, 2005; Critical Resistance Publications Collective, 2000; Mauer & Chesney-Lind, 2002).

For the past decade, activists and researchers have used the term *prison industrial complex* (PIC), first used in *The Wall Street Journal* in 1994, to refer to a multifaceted structure in the United States that encompasses the expanding economic and political contexts of the corrections industry: the political and lobbying power of the corrections officers union; the framing of prisons and jails as a growth industry in the context of deindustrialization; the production, marketing, and sales of technology and security required to maintain and expand the state of incarceration; the racialized and hyperbolic *war on drugs*; the legacy of white supremacy in the United States; and more (Davis, 2003). The PIC devastates communities of color in particular, as a 2003 editorial in the *New York Times* identified:

> The population of the nation's jails and prisons passed two million last year, for the first time in history. The United States has one of the highest incarceration rates in the world, and one that falls unevenly. An estimated 12% of all African American males between 20 and 34 are behind bars, more than seven times the rate for white men of the same age. Our overflowing jails and prisons come at a high price, in dollars and in wasted lives. (*New York Times*, April 9, 2003, A20)

Whereas the PIC typically refers to connections between jails and the economy, this book builds on recent research to expand the definition of the PIC to include relationships between schools and jails. These linkages are physical and grotesquely evident in urban schools with the increased use of surveillance and incarceration tools: metal detectors, surveillance cameras, school uniforms, and armed security guards. Schools look an awful lot like prisons, and sometimes schools look more like prisons than do real detention centers. The connections are also built into the organization of everyday life within schools through the establishment of policies that integrate juvenile justice laws into school disciplinary codes, and the establishment of public military and prisonlike "boot camp" schools. As the interlocking relationships between schools and the judicial system increased in the 1990s, select schools in the United States not only resemble prisons and apply the same disciplinary and surveillance technologies, but they also use the same language, "pedagogies," and philosophies espoused by prisons and jails (Saltman & Gabbard, 2003).

Global changes in trade and industry have also facilitated the movement of youth into jails. Macroeconomic shifts in the last 30 years have restructured the welfare state and have participated in the creation of prisons as a growth economy in an era of deindustrialization. The demise of small family farms due to the rise of corporate agribusiness and the loss of U.S.-based manufacturing industries and jobs created geographic and economic problems for the nation that the development of a rural prison industry appeared to address. These economic and social changes that shape prison expansion, and subsequently participate in the naturalization of prisons as inevitable, are frequently not linked to education, yet the development of our incarceration-nation clearly impacts education. When California, Illinois, and other states build more prisons than schools or colleges, this shapes academic options for youth. When budgets for corrections balloon and funding for higher education contracts, the state's priorities about the future of *select* youth are clear. Understanding how and why prison expansion is possible necessitates connecting schools to prisons and the criminal justice system, and redefining "what counts" as educational policy (Anyon, 2005).

In addition to reframing the landscape related to what is a relevant educational issue, school-based policies and practices that are perceived to be *outside* of a direct relationship to incarceration require reassessment. As school suspension and expulsion are "moderate to strong predictors of future incarceration" that disproportionately impact youth of color (Skiba et al., 2000), it is vital to demonstrate to educators how these policies intersect with the incarceration-nation. As classification in some special education categories again targets African American students (Harry & Klingner, 2005; Losen & Orfield, 2002; and Reid & Knight, 2006) and results in undereducation, and potentially incarceration, the processes through which students are identified as "special education" require scrutiny. Analyzed through a framework of the PIC, these educational practices become linked directly to practices of racial profiling that are endemic in state structures. As early as preschool, these educational policies and practices ontologically disqualify increasing numbers of students of color who are produced through schools as undereducated, underunemployable, and frequently "dangerous" and in need of surveillance and containment (Gilliam, 2006).

Adding the institution of education into the PIC asks researchers, activists, and educators to consider not just how our schools' physical structures resemble prisons—metal detectors or school uniforms—but also the tentacles *in policies, practices, and informal knowledges* that support, naturalize, and extend relationships between incarceration and schools. Naming the processes inside and outside schools that confer this civil and physical death of incarceration on vast populations is imperative because it is, literally, a matter of life and death. I take the term *civil death* from Ruth Gilmore's work, and it refers to the reality that those in prison cannot vote and have diminished rights (Gilmore, 2004). Civil death also refers to consequences of conviction and incarceration that extend beyond life in the prison. In some states those with felony convictions are barred from voting for life and are prohibited from accessing welfare and housing benefits. They are denied access to careers and employments formally, through prohibitions on licensure, and informally, when employers simply discriminate on the basis of disclosed histories of conviction and incarceration.

> A survey of employers in 5 large cities found that 65% would not knowingly hire an ex-convict. Many would not be able to do so legally anyway. . . . In Illinois ex-felons are banned from some 57 different professions, including such jobs as manicurists and barber. (*The Economist*, August 8, 2002, 26)

There are numerous other consequences of incarceration and conviction that illustrate the diminished basic rights of those convicted; for example, the 2005 decision of the Illinois Supreme Court that found Detra Welch to be an unfit parent, terminating her parental rights, *based only on her history of incarceration* (Marlan, 2005). Gilmore also suggests the use of the term *physical death* to refer to the reality of hazardous and inadequate conditions in U.S. prisons and jails including overcrowding in unhealthy facilities, substandard health (including dental) and mental health care, and more (Cooper, 2002; von Zielbauer, 2005). The consequences of these relationships between schools and jails are not simply school failure and underemployment, but potentially a lifetime of diminished basic human rights, or loss of life. By reproducing ways of knowing that contain significant blindspots, and animating a disciplinary framework that frequently erases its gendered and white supremacist origins, the profession of teaching, myself included, is complicit in the construction and maintenance of systems of structural violence, and a kind of "soft extension" of the security or the prison state (Rodriguez, 2004).

This role of schools, and by association teacher education programs, as sites of ideological management is well documented. Schools traffic in all kinds of artificial constructs and launder ideologies for a variety of social institutions. This process is blatant in curricula where textbooks and course materials naturalize ideologies of meritocracy and erase white supremacy (Loewen, 1995), and it is more diffuse in classroom teaching and organization that distributes cognitive and behavioral skills by social class (Anyon, 1980). From the 19th-century *McGuffey Readers* that chastised boys against idleness and girls against the sins of gluttony (Spring, 2001), to the expensive and ineffective 1980s Drug Abuse Resistance Education (DARE) federal program that attempted to scare and to "educate" youth away from drug use (Kane-Willis et al., 2006, Sec. 1:17), curricula support our nation's cultural and social anxieties. As curriculum too often reproduces racialized fears that too neatly map onto histories of white supremacy, and too conveniently manages to scaffold inequitable wealth distribution, this book project also extends this conception of public enemies to examine, more broadly, education's investments in producing "public enemies."

Ideological management extends beyond what gets taught and what gendered, or racialized, identities are offered to students and teachers, as schools also work in concert with other social institutions to legitimize and to shape artifacts that have value in everyday life outside schools. For example, schools naturalize and legitimate the very units of analysis that they are organized around, the constructs of the child and the adolescent (Lesko, 2001; Walkerdine, 1988). The child, and by association also the nuclear family and the adult, possess enormous traction and power outside schools. These artifacts, by definition, signify normal and abnormal modes of association and development, and, in this project on public enemies, clearly delineate who is in need of and worthy of state protection, and consequently, what and who is to be feared. These fears and vulnerabilities translate into powerful rationalizations for the expansion of the PIC. Select, innocent, and vulnerable children need to be protected from sex offenders and drugs, even when the dangers of heteropatriarchy and poverty are much more prevalent and perhaps equally damaging. Schools legitimize these artifacts and processes that also have value and power in other institutions. For example, I argue that schools attempt to naturalize racial profiling, endemic in school discipline and special education categories, and simultaneously function to normalize constructs of discipline and punishment as "logical" and "just" social practices.

The transition of youth of color from schools to jails is further facilitated, not just by the perception of the neutrality and the integrity of school-based practices, but through mass media's explicitly racialized representations of crime and criminals, and its preoccupations with youth, in particular, African Americans and Latinas/os in urban spaces, as inherently dangerous. Television news shows, with an aura of objectivity, take seriously the discourse of the youth as "superpredator," disproportionately use images of street crime that highlight African Americans or Latinos as perpetrators, and sensationalize those participating in any youth violence as inherently violent "gangbangers" capable of spontaneous and unpremeditated violent attacks, or "wildings" (Schiraldi & Ziedenberg, 2001). These representations all contribute to and naturalize discourses of violence as biologically determined and as inherently dangerous, and in need of containment. These erroneous images of rising crime from out of control and dangerously *bad* kids supported juvenile justice policy changes in the 1980s and 1990s, such as lowering the age at which one can be culpable of a crime or making transfers of youth into adult courts easier (Rapping, 2003). Mass media sutures the transition between schools and jails with hyperbolic representations of youth of color as defective and in need of management.

With this analysis of the intersecting relationships between the PIC and education, the title of this book plays on the multiple meanings of the expression "right to be hostile." Those disenfranchised, for example, the youth who see this connect between schools and jails and the correspondingly narrow discussions of what counts as an educational issue, have a right to be hostile. Anger, an "outlaw emotion" (Jaggar, 1989), is a legitimate response to injustice or violence. But what happens when individuals who are racially profiled and tracked toward special education, undereducated in low-resource schools that possess metal detectors and have drug searches conducted by the on-site school police stations, one guidance counselor for 500 students, and a low track record for graduation or for placing students in a community college or university, *get angry*? Who possesses the "right" to be hostile? What mechanisms, built into the expanding PIC, transform these legitimate responses of anger and critique into a dysfunction or a pathology? The response and the analysis of someone who clearly has the moral right but not a legal right to be hostile, gets translated from a critique into a youth with an anger management problem. In the school to jail nexus, the pathologization of dissent is a powerful tool.

> These students leave school in no position to seriously challenge the institutional narratives and media images that represent them as violent and uneducatable and that contribute to the notion that imprisonment is a reasonable, if not natural, option in their lives. (Duncan, 2000, 39)

As youth who are caught up in the intersections between schools and jails are simultaneously constructed as dangerous, uneducable public enemies, requiring containment, schools actively contribute to the privatization of what are essentially public issues.

With this awareness about the economic costs of prison expansion, in conjunction with research that documents the intersections between education and the PIC, the question of the obsolescence of prisons and working toward a future *without prisons* appears less utopian. Prison abolition, or working toward a future that encompasses reinvigorating old models of restorative justice and supporting local community economic development and more, is a necessity for those invested in educational equity. Whereas the term *prison abolition* literally means to work to abolish prisons and it is a small movement (supported through organizations like Critical Resistance, centered in Oakland, California, and other small networks of anti-prison activists such as the Anarchists Black Cross), prison abolition, for most of these organizations, doesn't mean that there will be no crime or violence. Rather, prisons are not a just, efficient, or moral solution to the problems that lead folks to commit crimes. Prison abolition means working to ensure that communities have at least viable living wage jobs that are not dehumanizing; working to establish mechanisms for alternative dispute resolution and other processes that address conflict, or harm with mediation; ensuring that our most vulnerable populations, for example, those that are mentally ill or undereducated do not get warehoused in our prisons and jails because of the failure of other institutions like healthcare and education; and practicing how to communicate and to live across differences and to rely more on each other instead of the police. Working toward a horizon of abolition means an acknowledgment that prisons have been used, as Davis writes, as "a way of disappearing people in the false hope of disappearing the underlying social problems they represent" (Davis, 2005, 41). Our prison and jail cells fill up with high school dropouts, the homeless, those self-medicating with alcohol and street drugs, and people with mental illness.

Expanding what counts as education reform is central to prison abolition, not solely because of my location as a preservice teacher educator, but because schools are "feeder institutions" for jails and prisons. Architecture, curriculum, socialization processes, and literally the presence of police or other structures that serve only punitive functions at specific schools results in the outcome that select youth are prepared through schools to be institutionalized.

When children attend schools that place a greater value on discipline and security than on knowledge and intellectual development, they are attending prep schools for prison. If this is the predicament we face today, what might the future hold if the prison system acquires an even greater presence in our society? In the nineteenth century, antislavery activists insisted that as long as slavery continued, the future of democracy was bleak indeed. In the twenty-first century, antiprison activists insist that a fundamental requirement for the revitalization of democracy is the long over-due abolition of the prison system. (Davis, 2003, 38–39)

Davis's suggestion is that education reform is not just a central component of rethinking our systems of punishment and justice, but also our democracy. This book is written for educators in order to consider our collusion, active and passive, in maintaining practices that perpetuate relationships between schools and jails and to start conversations that imagine futures without overflowing punitive institutions.

Locations for Questions

I reflect on my learning process to offer readers insight into where the questions for this book originated, because this project is grounded in my work in communities that continue to struggle and work toward justice and social change. For the past eight years in Chicago I have moved between two sites: community-based work surrounding the epidemic of incarceration, predominantly people of color, and work as a university educator with a predominantly female and white preservice teacher population. The gendered racialization and economic disparity between these two sites is so central and hypervisible that it was easy to mask. For the first few years I kept the labors separate. I worked at a high school for those formerly incarcerated, which I started under the vision and leadership of Renny Golden and Sister Jean Hughes. There I taught English and Social Studies and participated in a number of small, community-based public pedagogy projects surrounding race, gender, and incarceration. I facilitated domestic violence workshops for women at the Cook County Jail. I started to monitor prison and jails for a nonprofit association in Illinois. I had a relatively separate life teaching pre- and in-service teachers at the university. I did not know how to translate between these two sites that seemed too disparate. I was not exposed to any literature that made connections between these spheres. In addition, I realized quickly that I did not know enough about the history of race, class and gender in the United States to do anything except observe and read and work alongside people who knew more than I did.

I started reading material that I thought provided access to possible intersections of schools and jails, and subsequently writing on this issue because I had questions to work through. As Nadar suggests, questions from my everyday practices and conversations drove this work.

> It was the search for higher levels of understanding that inspired me to move from local to global. My methods took on more in the style of a natural science approach: *the questions were driving the methods.* (Nader, 2005, 31; emphasis original)

Initially these were what I would term clarity or factual questions. For example, I was in a meeting and someone used the term "C number" (a criminal code classification for people who are given de facto life sentences) and I did not want to interrupt to ask what this term meant, so I asked people in quick conversations after the meeting and I worked to educate myself. Most of these lines of inquiry were connected to my observations from being in the Cook County Jail in the late 1990s and in my initial work with people who had been incarcerated. *Why the disproportionate number of people of color in the prison system?* I read Mauer's *Race to Incarcerate* (1999). *Why don't prisons offer drug rehabilitation and educational programs?* I explored articles that outlined the "tough on crime" policy initiatives in the United States. As years passed these lines of questioning became more complex as my experiences deepened. *How are mass media representation such as the HBO TV series OZ connected to public sentiment around crime and how does this shape public policy? What is the relationship between the institution of public education and the prison system?* I searched for responses in books and in quiet side conversations with people who were patient (and gracious) because I wanted to change my everyday practices. Also, my work alongside people directly impacted by the prison system provided me with intimate exposure to the incredible pain and violence, often from the state, that the prison system works to conceal.

In 2004, I read Angela Davis's *Are Prisons Obsolete?* (2003) and had the opportunity to hear women from Critical Resistance, Rose Braz and Ruth Gilmore, discuss the concept of prison abolition. Even though I had been reading and working in relation to prison issues for almost six years, abolition was a new idea for me and it was a significant learning moment to consider how prisons are naturalized as an inevitable social institution. These ideas moved me to locate work with those formerly or currently incarcerated within a larger political context and to consider more broadly the relationships between reform, service providing, and structural change. The concept of prison abolition seemed not just feasible, it seemed so logical, it reframed all of my other projects. How could I consider continuing to participate in the high school without working to change the annihilating systems that produce participants for the high school? I had often joked that I do not want to be running or teaching at this high school in 10 years. Yet, what am I doing to make sure that this doesn't happen? Showing up at the occasional protest rally against police brutality or in support of the moratorium on the death penalty is important, but seemed too fragmented. The framework of abolition moved me to think concretely about participating in a movement that has the real possibility to alter how our nation (and others) has naturalized the role of prisons.

I believed that reading as much as I could about this prison-nation from a variety of sources, and talking to those with more experiences, would make me a more useful worker. Most specifically, my relationships with *people* propelled me to read and to think more, to be able to live up to their expectations, even if these were merely my interpretation of their expectations. The men and women who sat in my classes at the adult high school had so much faith in me as a teacher that I owed it to the students to know as much as possible about how they came to be sitting in my Social Studies or English class. When I looked out, semester after semester, I felt that at the least, I owed it to the students to know the most about black history and the intersections between race, gender, ethnicity, and class and our criminal justice policies. And, I didn't want to let Sister Jean Hughes down, one of the savviest women I have ever worked with. These relationships, and witnessing the often exploitative and "missionary" tours of other academics through my community networks, made me think clearly about what kind of academic work I could do and projects that could be of use, and to whom and how I would be accountable.

Also, I began to recognize the connections between my two major teaching sites: a high school program for formerly incarcerated men and women, and a teacher education program in a university. The gender, race, and class discrepancies between these two sites moved from being so consistently stark that they were easy for most, including myself, to ignore or repress, to clearly understanding these two sites as *interconnected processes* of explicitly racialized and gendered systems. Bringing my writing and reading on prison-related issues back to my teaching with teachers sharply illuminated the roles schools play in producing public enemies; for example, how schools legitimate and enhance select fears that in turn require the intervention of the PIC, and how schools enact a kind of racial profiling that anticipates the work of other state institutions. An urgency developed to write something that could connect these spheres, to illustrate the role the profession of teaching plays in producing the students who sit in my high school classes. A deepening awareness moved me not just to write about one of the central themes in this book, how my work in preservice teacher education is directly linked to our incarceration-nation, but to consider the processes inside and outside schools that assign this civil and physical death on vast, yet specific, populations.

Epistemologies and Methodologies

Outlining the intersections between education and the PIC requires the use of multiple, often overlapping, theoretical frameworks acquired through my teaching, research, and organizing. Feminist policy analysis, media analysis, and institutional ethnography are some of the methods, or theoretical tools, that have been instrumental in shaping this book project. I am deeply influenced by feminist policy analysis, which meticulously reviews policies and attempts to hold the government accountable for its propagation of "hate" toward marginalized populations that becomes codified in policy (Polakow, 2004; Roberts, 1997). By linking sex offender registries and drug-related laws to school-based policies and practices, this book attempts the rigorous work of this policy analysis. Media analysis, including deconstruction, considers the role of mass media in suturing the movement of youth of color into prisons. And this analysis requires deconstructing stereotypes and simultaneously linking these representations to larger changes in the movement of capital and to histories of race and gender in the United States (T. Rose, 1994; Rapping, 2003). I borrow from Smith's practice of institutional ethnography, which emphasizes a rigorous examination of the discursive practices within institutions that disqualify women (D.E. Smith, 2005). Her focus on how the textual relations of ruling names and frames the feelings and experiences of marginalized vulnerable communities is a central framework. Understanding the complex relationships between schools and jails requires tools from a variety of disciplines, and I use these multiple methods and theoretical frameworks throughout this book.

Yet, as one whose intellectual work and analysis is grounded in practice, and because I have been moved by many qualitative research projects, I initially considered collecting narratives to document the movement from prisons to jails. My experiences directly working for and with those formerly or currently incarcerated demonstrated that those who have been directly impacted by the system are often powerful advocates and analysts, and they have the right to speak and to advocate for themselves. In a system that actively attempts to eradicate or contain the voices of those impacted, self-representation is not just a significant methodological issue for academic research, it is a human right. As antiprison activist, educator, and criminologist Karlene Faith writes, "The first human right is to speak in one's own voice. Only someone who has been imprisoned can speak subjectively of this experience. Advocates can only report on what they have been told" (Faith, 2000, 160). When I considered methodologies that could incorporate or include the "voices" of those directly impacted, not only did practical tensions emerge between my roles as educator, ally, administrator, and the potential new role of researcher, but other questions about how research methodology debates cloak deeper epistemological doubts developed. Is doing interviews really permitting those impacted by the intersections of schools and the PIC to speak for themselves? Who, exactly, is empowered or benefits by writing or "being included" in an academic book project, aimed at educators?

Representing the voices and experiences of others is tricky. For example, a significant portion of the literature on women in prison in the academic sphere tends to "depict women in psychological and individuated terms," and this focus on the individual can render the woman, and her "personal failings," hypervisible, where the structural forces, such as public policies, that directly shape her "failures" are sidelined (Sudbury, 2005, xvi). Perhaps an emphasis on a particular line of research has contributed to this kind of representation of women and incarceration.

> Ironically, feminist preferences for qualitative and hands-on research methods and interests in the personal and psychological realms tend to contribute toward this problem. Interviews with incarcerated women run the risk of simply replicating the discourse of individual responsibility and the language of correction that prisoners learn (and sometimes internalize) as they are processed by the system. Unless researchers step back from the ideas that circulate within the domain of dominant prison discourse, we will become distracted by discussion of familial dysfunction, childhood abuse, drug addiction, and alcoholism. (Sudbury, 2005, xvi)[1]

In part, I agree. Qualitative research can reproduce the dominant frameworks, and narratives about women and prison, or school "drop-outs," frequently highlight stories of violence in the home, of drug and alcohol problems, school failure, and more. Clearly, the trauma women testify to is significant, but as Sudbury notes, a focus on these events can often obscure attention from larger structural issues, most specifically the public policies that actively shape the incarceration or undereducation and how and why these policies are perpetuated. Those who read interviews with women in prison or who have been incarcerated can be seduced by the narratives because they are in part much more compelling than reading public policy. At its worst, research that focuses on representing the voices of those

---

[1] Sudbury replays, in part, Judith Stacey's 1988 question about qualitative research: *"Can There Be a Feminist Ethnography?"* (Stacey, 1991).

impacted by punitive institutions and policies can actively reproduce discourses of deviance and pathologies.

Further complicating the possibility of qualitative practices, people on the margins develop healthy survival skills to navigate the institutions that work to regulate their lives (these resistance tactics are also the focus of qualitative work!). For example, some of those on welfare or on parole learn the valuable skill of ventriloquation to not disclose certain facts. These are key skills if you negotiate governmental structures, such as social workers, parole officers, or educators, on a daily basis and when people have the power to assess you, to determine your mobility, and whether or not you are fit to access your own children. As Suzanne de Castell often reminded me, there is an inverse relationship between power and documentation; those with the most power have the ability to protect themselves from documentation. As a fundamental survival skill, those with less power cannot afford *not* to participate in structures that organize and shape their lives, and cannot afford *not* to know how to navigate institutional discourses and systems. Academic research that prioritizes the voices and the experiences of those impacted may simply reinscribe academic constructs of the knower and the known, and experience may become simply, as feminist historian Scott notes, "evidence for the fact of difference, rather than a way of exploring how difference is established, how it operates, how and in what ways it constitutes subjects who see and act in the world" (Scott, 1999, 82).

More broadly, locating social science research questions at the methodological level, which generally encompasses rules, procedures, and methods of inquiry is, I argue, an attempt to contain fundamental questions about making knowledge and to place the researcher somewhat outside of these questions. Methodological questions such as *What is my role as a researcher? Did I acquire informed consent? Should I do interviews or surveys?* may tweak or challenge the practices, but they simultaneously reify a research paradigm that possesses the preset positions of the knower and the known. The questions the researcher elects to investigate and the tools used to pursue these questions shape the knowledge that gets produced. Reframing the discussion from methods to epistemology, literally knowledge production (or the nature and grounds of knowledge), raises the ethical stakes and shifts the focus from developing the right methods or procedures to the mechanisms involved in knowledge production, and it is this process that I find more useful to address in a book written for educators. In particular, I argue that what is also vital, in this political moment, is not just concrete evidence of the consequences of our public policy or institutional failures, but scholarship that illustrates for *us*, teachers, teacher-educators, and others in the profession, how our practices and our profession are complicit in the movement of bodies from schools to jails.

As educational activist and theorist Fine writes, perhaps research, "the cultural gaze of surveillance" (1997, 64), requires some recalibrating. She suggests a move away from a focus on those disempowered and marginalized toward the systems and structures that shape, name, and legitimate the oppression.

> My work has moved towards institutional analysis because I worry that those interested in qualitative inquiry and critical "race" theory have focused fetishistically on those that endure discrimination. (Fine, 1997, 57)

Researching the intersections between school and prisons means addressing the life experiences of deeply marginalized individuals who are *always and already* scrutinized and under systems of surveillance. These individuals are already objects of research and voyeurism, and not in control of how they are perceived or documented, even if these practices of documentation and research are executed with the best of intentions. Even if more focus on the lives that endure these intersections between schools and jails is required, what is equally vital is work that unpacks and meticulously documents the movements between schools and prisons and moves us, those in relative positions of power and privilege in school- or university-based contexts, to identify and then *to change* our collusion with these institutional processes. For me, this move both reduces the likelihood of more school-based surveillance, and perhaps, invites new questions.

> Defensively, we wish to protect those who are subjected to the School from any further action by the School—particularly from anything that starts with an identification of the child as a person with qualities to be discovered by the agents of the School. . . . It is certainly a call for those acquired by positions of authority—teachers, counselors, psychologists, and researchers among many others—to work at becoming aware of the practical consequences of their own actions: What do they make for others? (Varenne & McDermott, 1998, 215)

The *School* is the site of the production of so many debilitating identities for students. The move from those affected, the subject as a natural object of inquiry, to the relations that shape and produce the subject, is motivated and intentional. This is not a call for educators to cease qualitative work, rather a push for those of us who have been "acquired" by institutional authority to investigate how our profession participates in the creation and maintenance of educational practices and categories that contribute to the disqualification of communities.

However, despite this push to examine the sociocultural contexts that shape the movement of youth from schools to jails, and the emphasis on the relations of ruling that participate in this movement, this book does prioritize the experiences and the testimony of those incarcerated and uses writings by women (and men) who are in or have exited prisons and, in some cases, assumed leadership roles in the prison reform or prison abolition movement. This grounding reflects my work in communities, with and for those formerly incarcerated, acknowledging the deep impact that voices and experience, however textually mediated, continue to make on my life. In addition, I incorporate theoretical and biographic work in parts of this project written by those formerly incarcerated, not just because it validates the agency of those most impacted by the epidemic of incarceration, but because it is the smartest analysis available.

Although writings by those currently and formerly incarcerated might be difficult to access as the Internet is often not a viable medium to circulate writings for impoverished or incarcerated populations, there is no shortage of material available. I benefited enormously from reading newsletters in and outside prison, for example, *Stateville Speaks* from Statesville penitentiary in Illinois and *The Fire Inside*, a series of writings put together by the California Coalition for Women Prisoners. Works such as Paula Johnson's *Inner Lives: Voices of African American Women in Prison*, the articles, poetry, and interviews on Beyondmedia Education's *Women and Prison: A Site of Resistance*, and the writing and research of Kemba Smith and Linda Evans in Julia Sudbury's *Global Lockdown* all offer intimate portrayals and analysis of the experiences of women in the prison system. Joy James's anthology *The New Abolitionists* provides writings and research from current and former political prisoners, and Jimmy Santiago Baca's *A Place to Stand* is a compelling memoir of literacy. These writings offer concrete empirical evidence of how the state maintains misogyny and white supremacy. Just as the questions that fueled this book are generated from my everyday experiences and are not merely abstract or theoretical examples, this analysis and testimony, by those directly impacted, are also part of the foundation for this work. This process of using published analysis and testimony by current and formerly incarcerated men and women does not guarantee authenticity, nor does this process ensure lack of exploitation or better data. As noted in Scott's quotation earlier, experience is textually mediated. However, in the economy of citations and textual production, women are not reproduced as research subjects in someone else's project, but as agents of knowledge production.

More pragmatically and personally, I also make this move because I do not have the relationship of "researcher" with the women (and men) I know who have exited prisons and jails, and I don't want to have this identity. I inhabit other roles: teacher, administrator, professor, acquaintance, ally, means-to-an-end, "the white Erica," and, very occasionally, friend. To solicit testimony would require shifting to researcher and I am unwilling to inhabit this identity, in part because I care, perhaps too deeply, about the people and the projects to shift into a research role. When working with individuals and in communities impacted by mass incarceration and punitive public policies that actively support the future of incarceration for youth, I cannot duplicate the same mechanisms of institutional violence. *Our incarceration-nation attempts to disappear those that are poor through the technologies of making them hypervisible: confession, surveillance, and objectification.* Using these same tools, even in the name of empowerment or policy change, will not alter the relations of ruling. I haven't figured out how to reappropriate these same tools. The individual is clearly my "unit of concern," but not my unit of analysis (McDermott, Goldman & Varenne, 2006, 13).

Overview of the Project

Trapped in failing schools that are often physically deteriorating, disciplined and moved into juvenile justice systems through violations of punitive zero tolerance policies, failing to pass high-stakes standardized tests and channeled into special education programs, youth of color are, materially and conceptually, moved from schools to jails. This chapter tracks the links between the public schooling system and the prison industrial complex to chart how this movement takes place. Chapter 1, *Surveillance, Ladies Bountiful, and the Management of Outlaw Emotions,* reviews contemporary research with a focus on the role the profession plays in participating in this movement through perpetuating racialized surveillance in schools.

Chapter 2, *Strange Fruit: Prison Expansion, Deindustrialization, and What Counts as an Educational Issue,* builds from this discussion of the nexus between schools and jails to outline how the PIC constitutes a geographic and economic solution to socioeconomic problems while maintaining the state's commitment to white supremacy. With changes in the welfare state and the public sphere, this chapter illustrates how prison expansion is a natural outcome of economic shifts in the past three decades. This chapter also argues that definitions and conceptions of educational policy and urban school reform must "realign," as Anyon (2005) suggests, to encompass prison policy in order to adequately theorize, and shift, urban school failure.

From *COPS* to *Law & Order, CSI,* and *Court TV* and the network news, mass media creates "common sense" surrounding prisons (and crime), which includes actively creating cultures of racialized fear, representing crime as street crime—not white collar crime, advancing discourses around victim's rights that naturalize the role of prisons and incarceration, and supporting frameworks about innocence and evil, victim and perpetrator, that do little to address actual violence, or the realities of those impacted. Chapter 3, *Life After OZ: Policies, Popular Cultures, and Public Enemies,* illustrates how mass media supports the movement of youth from schools to jails. By linking popular culture to arguments that advance regressive PIC policies, such as the eradication of the Pell grants for those in prison, this chapter demonstrates how mass media circulates old stories of race and crime in new masks.

Chapter 4, *Awful Acts and the Trouble With Normal,* uses the creation of sex offender registries within the prison industrial complex to illustrate how schools participate in scapegoating and how schools legitimate concepts, such as the child, that require protection and expansion of the PIC. Examining sex offender registries offers a unique and timely opportunity to unpack the relationships between schools and the PIC. Even though acquaintances or family, not strangers, perpetrate the majority of assaults on children, the popularity of sex offender registries grew in the last decade with highly specific restrictions. This chapter offers a preliminary discussion on registries for those convicted of sexual offenses and how these policies emerged in an era characterized by a moral panic surrounding (white) youth and (hetero)sexuality. In addition, these registries require and subsequently produce specific understandings of "the child" that require the expansion of the PIC, and exploring the efficacy of these policies to reduce violent crimes unearths important cultural anxieties about the racialized constructs of the child.

Chapter 5, *Political Recoveries: "Softening" Selves, Hard Experiences, and Organized Resistance,* argues that a major component of the PIC is its ability to recast what are essentially social problems as private issues. With two interrelated discussions, on schools and special education, and on the recovery movement, this chapter investigates how institutions shape and name experiences that have the potential to radically challenge the effectiveness of institutions and even to call into question our democracy. I select these two lines of analysis because of my locations in teacher education and working with those formerly incarcerated. The prevalence and the widespread acceptance of both of these discourses and practices, special education and recovery, at each of the sites I work at, instigated questions. Further research led me to suggest that the interrelationships between these discourses are important to unpack. With the examples of the Boarding School Healing Project, and Beyondmedia Education's *Women and Prison: A Site for Resistance,* this chapter also offers ideas for politicizing experience and for movement building.

Chapter 6, *Horizons of Abolition: Strategizing for Change Through the Good, the Bad, and the Innocent*, examines some contemporary strategies that are working to interrupt the school to jail track, and considers these strategies in the context of prison abolition work and in relation to investments in *the good, the bad, and the innocent*. With a discussion of solidarity and movement building for change, the emphasis in this chapter is on strategies for change, to complicate practices that have had limited success, and for mobilizing "us" educators in elementary, secondary, and university classrooms to participate in movements that work toward abolition.

The lines of inquiry that shape each chapter are directly linked to my everyday work. Whereas what compels me to write is not necessarily what compels others to read, as my editor politely reminded me, the bases for this project are my everyday experiences, and contradictions, and the questions that emerged from these experiences. I have incorporated the origins of the questions in a confessional vignette at the start of some of the chapters, intending to locate my relationships and the geography that influenced the questions that frame each chapter. For example, I started thinking about sex offender registries (chapter 4) from casual conversations with men who were having serious housing difficulties because they were registered sex offenders. I began to think about the prevalence and the limitations of "recovery narratives," the immense role 12-step programs play in prisons, and the privatization of public issues, from my work at the Cook County Jail cofacilitating workshops on domestic violence (chapter 5). I started to consider the role of mass media in producing public enemies when I was in New York City and saw that a popular gay bar had a screening night for the problematic HBO TV show, *OZ* (chapter 3). I examined the intersections between the Immigration and Naturalization Service (INS) and the Department of Corrections (DOC), and the changing role of the welfare state in the context of the rise of the racialized surveillance state, when I talked and read the research and the experiences of an undocumented graduate student who illustrated to me clear relationships between the punitive functions of the INS and the DOC (included in chapter 2). I wrote the last chapter, which critically examines several contemporary strategies that work to interrupt the school to jail nexus, in the context of prison abolition, because I wanted to respond to the frequent question, "what about the really bad people?" that emerged in the majority of my discussions, inside and outside of classrooms, about prison abolition (chapter 6). These lines of thought did not emerge in a vacuum. Conversations with a range of folks, most of whom knew more about the subject from their lived experiences, or from their own work, made me ask these questions and offered insight into the discussions and arguments in the following chapters.

White Supremacy, a Racial Contract, and the Epistemology of Ignorance

Threaded throughout this project on public enemies are overlapping themes. A central theme is tracking and naming how white supremacy is maintained in public policies through willful public ignorance, and how it intersects with gender and sexuality. Charles Mills's concepts of the *Racial Contract* and the *epistemology of ignorance* offer a useful framework for me to understand the persistence of the relationship between incarceration and education in the United States. Mills writes that Western scholarship and (white) disciplinary ways of knowing have largely failed to account for the structured role white supremacy plays in shaping what counts as knowledge and who counts as fully human, a citizen, and an agent of knowledge production. Mills names this political system, central to contemporary social practices, institutions, disciplinary ways of knowing, and more, the *Racial Contract.*

The utility of Mills's analysis, for me rested on a strong foundation of scholarship that addresses issues related to white supremacy, systemic ignorance, and heteropatriarchy. For example, Frankenberg's feminist analysis, *White Women, Race Matters,* which offers complex narratives of how white women participate and resist the racial order; and Sedgwick's *The Epistemology of the Closet,* which first enabled me to theorize on the significance of ignorance "as the result of a careful education" (1990, 5) and warns against invoking simply ignorance, "from which the heroics of human cognition can occasionally wrestle facts, insights, progress" as ignorance too frequently "appeals too directly to the redemptive power of simply upping the cognitive wattage on any question of power seems, now, naïve" (7). Concepts from these authors, and others, provided frameworks for me to consider the interrelationships between numerous trajectories and moved me to investigate not just the history of the relationships between schools and prisons and how systems were, and are, overtly structured to produce the natural by-product of school failure or incarceration (McDermott, 1987), but how a very particular kind of *willful public ignorance* is produced that maintains the inevitably of school failure and incarceration.

Language

Language functions throughout this book as a barrier because the terms at stake participate in masking reality and rarely represent the interconnectedness of issues. The term crime, for example, often presupposes a *real* or a natural category, but what counts as crime, however, is hardly static, as political prisoner Muntaqum notes:

> When talking about the "greatest robber" it seemed particularly appropriate in the midst of the biggest financial rip-off in the history of this country to think about the billions of dollars the Savings & Loan criminals stole, and about how most of them have gotten away with it. I thought about the complete insanity of how this country defines crime in a society. If you steal $5 you are a thief, but if you steal 5 million—you are a financier. (Jalil Muntaqum, in James, 2000, 29)

Researchers have documented that in terms of harm Muntaqum is accurate. Street crime is hardly the most damaging. More centrally, his point is that crime, including what is defined by law as a criminal act and who is criminalized, is a result of interlocking institutions, histories, and forces: racial, political, economic, and more. Untangling these constructs is difficult because communities and individuals have naturalized these categories, institutions and experts are built around studying and measuring these practices, and, frequently, these categories do function to address a "harm" or a "problem" and they can be used to access resources.

Therefore, one of the difficulties of this work, not unlike any other work on "deviance," or even on identity, is that it is important to deconstruct the terms at stake at the same time as these terms are used for excavation or analysis. Language gets in the way. In this project on public enemies, the process is tricky, to carefully unpacking the terms and preset conceptions of who is dangerous, or disabled, or a disciplinary problem. Whereas this deconstruction is valuable, I am also invested in exploring what these categorizations make visible and what they cloak. What kinds of relationalities are made possible by these names, and what are masked? A significant part of the work of this project is to reframe the terms of the debate and determine how, and possibly why, terms and language mask particular experiences.

Interlocking Ontological Choreographies

The interlocking relationships between schools and jails, and the production of this civil and physical death, is not a linear or a discrete process. Haraway and Cussins use the term *ontological choreography to* describe the process of species creation that is neither biological nor humanist. "Ontological choreography" describes what I outline in this book, how individuals come to be viewed as disposable bodies, public enemies that threaten "our" way of life, for whom civil and physical death is viewed as a natural outcome of independent individual choices. Or, to augment and rephrase:

biologically deterministic or psychological discourses cannot adequately describe how we arrived at this economic, social, and political moment or *how to move away from this place*. This process, the production of these bodies as both highly disposable and simultaneously valuable, is not, as Haraway and Cussins suggest, a neat, linear process. Haraway writes:

> Charis (Cussins) Thompson suggested the term "ontological choreographies." The scripting of the dance of being is more than metaphor; bodies, human and non-human, are taken apart and put together in processes that make self-certainty and either humanist or organicist ideology bad guides to ethics and politics, much less to personal experience. (Haraway, 2003, 8)

While acknowledging an allegiance to philosopher Louis Althussar's concept of interpellation, entities are *hailed into being* through ideology and through the modern apparatus of the state, at the same time I elect to use Haraway's term as I want to acknowledge the increasing role scientific discourse plays in literally naming and shaping bodies. *Organicist or scientific discourse is a bad guide to ethics or politics.* What I encounter in this project are legitimate discussions and "scientific facts," either from experts in psychology (educational, developmental, or other) or experts in criminology, which state that certain people are just born bad, or dangerous, or have bad genes, or are not able to be rehabilitated. Children and youth *are* learning disabled or behavior disordered. These science discourses shape bodies, and it is a struggle to develop useful ways to undercut this production, especially when these stories about science and bodies are espoused by the individual and enable resource acquisition, at the same time they are marginalized by these discourses. The term *ontological choreography* captures a part of this encroachment of science and forefronts this difficulty.

Feminist Frames

Whereas race, gender, class, sexual orientation, and nation/country of origin are central to the prison system, women, specifically low-income women and women of color, are the fastest growing population in prison (Johnson 2004). Research and writing that do not explicitly name this, or that lose the blackness in the broad term "women of color," are dangerous. Gender structures our prison system and our educational system. Again, the prevailing terms and tools used in academic projects that address women in the PIC frequently, not always, are limiting. Frequently due to the constraints of language, paradigms address gender, or race, or sexual orientation, thus further marginalizing, or even erasing, African American women. Ritchie, writing specifically about black women, says:

our capacity to understand them, build prevention or intervention programs to support them, let alone organize antiprison struggles around them is limited by the dominant paradigms we use to study incarceration and the ways we understand gender violence among young people. . . . Our intellectual and political agenda will not accommodate the challenges that their reality poses: they threaten both the gender-neutral analysis of racism that characterizes much of the antiprison work and the race-neutral analysis of patriarchy and sexuality that many feminist scholars and activists rely upon. (Ritchie, in Sudbury, 2005, 76)

Ritchie asks that feminist scholars not reproduce the same dichotomies, *woman* and *African American*, that characterize many of the traditional research projects that address gender in the PIC. I take seriously intersectionality, and this project rigorously starts with and from the reality that race, ethnicity, sexual orientation, age, ability, socioeconomic status and gender are interrelated.

On a more pragmatic level, the majority of my work, at the high school, in the university, in social justice nonprofit organizations, and in loose neighborhood and community initiatives, has been possible because of women, some of whom identify as feminists and some of whom identify as queer. Generally, when I am at a community justice–oriented event, a fundraiser, potluck celebratory dinner, educational campaign, or a community art installation, the majority of the people who make the event happen, who take out the garbage, hustle to get the word out, and staff the door, are women. Or, I am at a community meeting on over-policing, local school reform, or the militarization of our public schools, and women are making the photocopies, reserving the space for the meeting, and sitting in more than 70% of the chairs. Yet, frequently, women take up less than 50% of the speaking time. These incredible uncompensated hours of women contribute to the maintenance of the spaces that support my acting and thinking, and can be often simply erased in an academic project that focuses on analysis. I work to highlight feminisms and women in this introduction, not to reify a category "women" that exists in isolation from race or class, but to acknowledge the material bodies that make my thinking and writing possible. I owe a significant debt to the writers and activists, mostly women and frequently feminists and queers, who continue to create spaces and audiences for all of my work.

Antidisciplinarity

This book brings together a range of writers: anthropologists who work in prisons (Rhodes and Britton), philosophers and literary theorists who investigate how white supremacy underpins epistemology (Mills and Sedgewick), media studies scholars (Rapping), interdisciplinary scholars in the field of educational studies and policy analysis that ask that what counts as "educational policy" be widened (Polakow, Duncan, Anyon, Fine), literary studies scholars who investigate the tense dynamics in narrating trauma to have political or personal efficacy (McBride and Sommer), theorists and activists who are working against the prison system (Davis, Evans, K. Smith, Johnson, Sudbury, Diaz Cotto, Mauer), and numerous advocacy organizations that are producing reports on the epidemic of mass incarceration (The Sentencing Project, The Urban Institute) and the state of our public educational system (Civil Rights Project), and may other writers and organizations. I traffic work across the disciplinary apparatuses: Following Clifford:

> I often function as a kind of import-export specialist between the disciplines. Looked at most cynically, the import-export person in the disciplines takes some idea that's outmoded in one field and moves it into another field, where it becomes an exciting new thing. (Clifford, 2003, 55)

Antidisciplinarity means taking ideas that are relatively de rigueur from one space across and into conversations with ideas from other disciplines in an effort to enable new conversations, and to highlight methodological or epistemological blindspots. Addressing the crisis of mass incarceration and the systemic failure of our educational system for the poor requires dialogues that are not trapped within disciplinary trajectories, as the questions clearly are not contained within these boundaries.

I use the term *antidisciplinary* as this project highlights the limitations of disciplinary ways of knowing in addressing pressing, multifaceted social problems, and this process has been both useful and trying. Working on a book project that is squarely aimed at an education audience, both because it is my primary academic home and because it is how the publishing industry shapes academic products (the author has legitimacy and marketability in the field in which she is employed and degreed), has raised my awareness about the disciplinary structure in the social sciences. Or, who has the right to say what, and to whom? And, in the trafficking of ideas across borders, what else is imported?

> We are presently working in an era of interdisciplinary and antidisciplinary moves, and as most readers know, disciplinary transgression is both a blessing and a curse; it can lead to repetition, imaginative thrust, or new knowledge. . . . At the same time interdisciplinary work may result in decontextualized and dehydrated borrowings from anthropology by researchers trained in other fields. (Nader, 2005, 71)

Ironically, the more I operate in academia and I recognize that a coherent professional identity, in any discipline, is quite mythic, I simultaneously view the merits of deep immersion in a particular field—however *not at the exclusion of political and social contexts.* As this project comes to a close I believe the skills and resources I acquired from higher education were instrumental, yet what enabled this analysis was my multiple locations, an incredible privilege, in communities: the alternative high school collaborators and participants, the Beyondmedia Education women, queer educational studies and women's studies folks, the Dominican Sisters from the "mothership," and more. A worry, through this project, is a real risk of the "dehydrated" borrowings from crossing boundaries, even if these borders are fragile or constructed. Although, as Haraway writes, "Anyone who has done historical research knows that the undocumented often have more to say about how the world is put together than do the well pedigreed" (Haraway, 2003, 88), I can't help but feel as I write this book that *I wish I knew more.*

These frameworks of the *Racial Contract,* antidisciplinarity, feminisms, and ontological choreographies, are threaded through this project that explores education's relationship to the maintenance of our incarceration-nation. This expansion requires individual and national consent or active indifference. The isolation and invisibility of this development is not a natural process; a particular public ignorance is actively supported through collusion with other institutions. As the youth who participated in the *Voices in Times* exhibit and forums were beginning to name, many other social institutions, particularly schools, are required to support the production of youth of color as public enemies, requiring containment. Times of crisis may permit an opportunity to examine systems of power and how they reconfigure rather than collapse.

> The object is to figure out what (including "who" i.e. deal with agency in its non-voluntaristic sense) makes oppressive and liberatory structures work, and what makes them fall apart. At the most general level of abstraction, we know that structures change under conditions of power redistribution—i.e. during times of crisis. In times of crisis, dynamics are particularly apparent, and insofar as we can catch historical or contemporary shifts on the fly, we might recognize something powerful about race and freedom. (Gilmore, 2002, 17)

Perhaps it is rhetorically inflammatory to name this moment, the highest levels of incarceration in the United States, as a crisis, but I utilize Gilmore's call in this book project to investigate how the state maintains its commitment to misogyny and white supremacy in moments of shifting economic contexts. Schools are one physical and discursive site, but this book illustrates that mass media and other systems and institutions play central roles in shaping specific bodies as "dangerous," "uneducable," *public enemies*, thus facilitating their natural movement from schools to jails. Starting from the writer Leslie Marmon Silko's perspective: "It seems to me that there is no better way to uncover the deepest values of a culture than to observe the operation of that culture's system of justice" (Silko, 1996, 20), *Right to Be Hostile* examines the social practices and institutions that participate in the production of public enemies.

CHAPTER 1

Surveillance, Ladies Bountiful, and the Management of Outlaw Emotions

Scene: A Social Studies class in a nondescript high school classroom, third floor of a three-story brick building.

Characters: David – 19-year-old African American male. Erica – 35-year-old white woman. Twenty-five other African American students between the ages of 19 and 50 years.

Background: It is halfway through the semester. Both Erica and David are crabby. Erica has had a long day in boring meetings and David has spent the day in court-mandated programs, and trying to find work.

Class starts. David walks in 10 minutes after class starts, right in front of the teacher, Erica, and waves to the group of men his age sitting at the back of the room, who shout back, interrupting Erica's outline of the agenda for the night. David takes his seat in the back left of the room. Puts his headphones on his ears.

Erica: David, don't you want to take those headphones off? Class has started.

David: No. I like them. I am not listening to music. *He slumps over on the desk.*

Other students watch and wait. Erica is getting visibly more crabby. Her face gets a little tinged with red and her voice pitches up. David pulls his hood up over his head and zips up his enormous parka even though it is a good 70-plus degrees in the room. His face is invisible under the faux fur rim of the hood.

Erica: David. You are in class now. Please take the earphones off.

The rest of the class is watching the interchange. The women have their arms crossed. No one makes eye contact with Erica or David. The men David waved to when he walked in are doodling intensely, or staring at their shoes.

David: *No response. A faint electric whir is audible in the room, as David turns the CD player in his Sony Walkman on.*

Erica: Listen, if you are not going to participate – don't take up a seat. Feel free to go. No one is keeping you here.

No response form David but the whir of the CD player gets louder.

Erica: David – it seems like you have better things to do tonight – so why don't you leave.

David: Why are you always picking on me? What have you got against me? Stomps out of the room and the rest of the room can hear him yelling up the hallway.

Rest of class sighs at Erica for mismanaging the event.

Erica sighs at herself for mismanaging the event.

I start this chapter, which focuses on what activists and educators call the "school to jail pipeline" with a brief discussion of anger because I am frequently surrounded by manifestations of anger, myself included. The keen restless rage of young men and women, such as David, whose anaesthetizing and pleasure-producing use of illegal medications often lead to incarceration, and release and rehabilitation (and housing) are conditional upon participation in anger management programs. Anger is a legitimate response to institutions that set you up for failure, or to a political state that systemically denies you the right to participate, but it is dangerous to be angry in public spaces. Yet, if one does not have the right to be hostile, where does the anger go when it is "a grief of distortions between peers, and its object is change" (Lorde, 1984, 129)? Sometimes I am so angry I can't think. There cannot be this much anger, *just because,* and I take this emotion, as feminist philosopher Jaggar terms it, an "outlaw emotion," as a starting place for inquiry:

> Outlaw emotions are distinguished by their incompatibility with the dominant perceptions and values. . . . Outlaw emotions stand in a dialectical relation to critical social theory: at least some are necessary to developing a critical perspective on the world, but they also presuppose at least the beginning of such a perspective. (Jaggar, 1989, 144–145)

Outlaw emotions can provide important insights into structural inequities. Jaggar argues that oppressed people have a kind of "epistemic privilege" and their responses "are more likely to be appropriate than the emotional responses of the dominant class. That is, they are more likely to incorporate reliable appraisals of situations" (Jaggar, 1989, 146). Failing to listen to anger or not interpreting anger as a critical commentary, risks missing fundamentally important critical perspectives on the world.

David and I each have legitimate reasons to be angry, perhaps, but although this is my starting place of inquiry for this project on the relationships between schools and jails, I also heed Lorde's warning that any displays of anger will always be used against those that are marginalized. As Lorde writes, evocatively, in her essay, *Uses of Anger:*

> Everything can be used / except what is wasteful / (you will need/to remember this when you are accused of destruction). (Lorde, 1984, 127)

Anger can be a vital tool to mobilize communities and individuals for change, yet it is simultaneously an emotion that is too frequently used to devalue or to erase the responses or analysis of those that are marginalized. Lorde, speaking to black women, offers a reminder that outlaw emotions are necessary and productive, and will be used to disqualify valuable critiques.[1]

If anger is a legitimate response to an oppressive political state, who has the agency and the political power to be able to name their anger *as* anger? Certainly not youth or any other nonautonomous population, such as those incarcerated, women, the poor, and more. These populations, generally under forms of hyper-racialized surveillance, do not have the power

---

[1] Chapter 5 takes up the issue of how other institutions work to recast these outlaw emotions as pathologies or deviances.

to interrupt how their emotions are named, framed, and interpreted. This chapter examines educational structures and practices that name and shape these outlaw emotions and behaviors, because the stakes of anger in schools are high. Recent literature on what scholars, educators, and activists term the "school to jail pipeline" illustrates that a failure to *control oneself*, to *keep that anger in check*, to *act and learn appropriately*, in particular for those in any way marginalized, might mean school expulsion, criminalization, or pathologization. If you do not have the right to be hostile, anger can be read as violence, disruption, disrespect, or as evidence of inherent deviancy, or cognitive and behavioral impairment.

Of course, the movement from schools to jails is facilitated not just through these manifestations of outlaw emotions. Material inequities create fundamentally different schooling experiences and educational outcomes for students across the United States. The ongoing unequal allocation of resources, in schools and in the neighborhoods around schools, and the corresponding inequities in facilities, curriculum, and teacher qualifications, are well documented in texts such as *Savage Inequalities* and *Shame on the Nation* by Jonathan Kozol, *Beyond Silenced Voices*, by Lois Weis and Michelle Fine, and *Ghetto Schooling* by Jean Anyon. These works and many others highlight that poor students and students of color are offered unequal education in different physical structures and that college and university preparation is not the function of all public schools. These texts clearly demonstrate that tracking based on gender, race, and class is the norm in U.S. public schools. Building on this foundation, this chapter examines two practices of racialized surveillance within schools that create additional interlocking relationships between school and jails.

Zero tolerance and school discipline policies and practices and the category of special education work to shape the movement of youth of color and poor youth into prisons and jails. After surveying recent research on the "school to jail pipeline," notably work from the Civil Rights Project, *Opportunities Suspended: The Devastating Consequences of Zero Tolerance and School Discipline Policies* (2000), and other interdisciplinary research, this chapter discusses the profession of teaching, specifically the feminization of the field, and speculates on the practices of teacher education that, perhaps, participate in this movement. Charles Mills's theoretical frameworks enable a "studying up" (Nader, 1974) to consider the role of the profession to maintain a very specific gendered and racialized contract. I focus on the profession of teaching, in part, because this is the sphere where I and readers of this text—educators—may have direct influence.

Schools to Jails

As youth, overwhelmingly youth of color, who do not complete high school are more likely to enter prison than students who complete high school, pipeline metaphors are increasingly used to describe the school to prison movement of a population that the United States has identified as "superfluous" (Duncan, 2000). This research documents how curriculum, disciplinary regulations, pedagogy, and other educational structures and practices function to normalize an "expectation" of incarceration for youth (Ayers et al., 2001; Davis, 2003; Duncan, 2000, 2004; Wald & Losen, 2003). This analysis asks us to see direct links between the prison industrial complex (PIC) and education. Trapped in failing schools that are often physically deteriorating, disciplined and moved into juvenile justice systems through violations of punitive, zero tolerance policies, demoted or labeled through failure to pass high-stakes standardized tests or through biased assessment materials, and channeled to special education programs, poor and/or youth of color are undereducated. This scholarship tracks links between the public schooling system and the PIC to chart how youth of color are, as Duncan has termed it, "racially profiled" to be materially and conceptually moved from schools to jails (Duncan, 2000).

Although recent educational research does name and deconstruct these intersecting relationships between the prison industrial complex and the education system, this linkage is not new, inviting the question of how some continually forget about these connections. Activists and historians continue to document how schools continue to function as punitive institutions for specific communities. For example, Haig Brown, in *Resistance and Renewal* (1988), charts how the First Nations residential schooling movement in Canada trained aboriginal communities for low-wage domestic labor, less than secondary status in the nation-state, under- and unemployment, and more. And Anderson, in *The Education of Blacks in the South, 1860–1935* (1990), chronicles how public education prepared African Americans for low-wage "Negro jobs," or underemployment, specifically the work that was available after white men were employed. "Far from being novel, today's prison industrial system is a variation on past educational and legal measures aimed at subjugating people of color in the U.S." (Duncan, 2000, 36). In addition, Foucault's *Discipline and Punish* (1977) meticulously described how power manifests in schools and prisons through material apparatuses and the structure of schools: the actual panopticon, the construction of authority, hierarchical structures, and more.[2] Linkages between schools and jails are less a pipeline, more a persistent

---

[2] A panopticon, designed by J. Bentham in 1791, is a circular prison with cells distributed around a central surveillance station.

nexus or a web of intertwined, punitive threads (Simmons, 2004). This nexus metaphor, while perhaps less "sexy" or compelling than the *schoolhouse to jailhouse track*, is more accurate as it captures the historic, systemic, and multifaceted nature of the intersections of education and incarceration. As this chapter illustrates, frameworks that incorporate a history, potentially a "nexus," are perhaps more useful for analysis and intervention.

Researchers have identified two contemporary educational policies and practices as the most significant and destructive for youth of color that facilitate their school-leaving experiences or under-education: contemporary discipline policies and the category of special education.

Discipline

The 1994 federal Gun-Free Schools Act (GFSA) required that each state receiving federal funds for education must have a state law requiring a mandatory one-year expulsion for any public school student who brings a weapon to school. According to the act, the school must refer the child to the criminal justice system. However, each state is free to "allow the chief administering officer of such local educational agency to modify such expulsion requirement for a student on a case-by-case basis" (Gun-Free Schools Act of 1994). Although a weapon is defined by the GFSA as a firearm or gun, bomb, grenade, rocket, missile, or mine, schools have added to the list objects that look like weapons, personal grooming items, and other, normally harmless items (Gordon et al., 2001). The laws have also been extended to include behavior perceived as a threat against a teacher, disrespectful to a teacher, or behavior that is defiant toward authority figures (Gordon et al., 2001).

Not unlike the "tough on crime" policies passed in the United States in the 1980s and 1990s despite a decline in incidences of violent crime, there is no conclusive proof that U.S. schools are becoming more dangerous, or that schools were sites of rampant community violence in the early 1990s to warrant the 1994 passage of the GFSA. Contrary to popular belief, the number of incidences of reported violence actually decreased or stayed the same in the 18 years preceding the GFSA's 1994 passage. According to the National Center for Educational Statistics (NCES) 1998 report, The Condition of Education, "Victimization rates at school for high school seniors changed little between 1976 and 1996, with the exception of small increases in the percentage of students who reported being threatened both with and without a weapon in the previous 12 months" (NCES, 1998, 144). The decline in reported school violence noted in the 1998 report continues into the 2004 report, Indicators of School Crime and Safety, which states that in 2002, students ages 12–18 were more likely to be victims of nonfatal serious violent crime away from school than at school (NCES,

2004).[3] According to the Bureau of Justice Statistics, this decline in crime in schools reflects a similar decline in the national crime rate: "Between 1992 and 2002, crime in the Nation's schools for students age 12–18 fell, a pattern consistent with the decline in the national crime rate" (Bureau of Justice Statistics, 2004a).

Even if zero-tolerance policies are having either no or simply a marginal impact on school-based violence, and the decline in school violence reflects acts that the institution is compelled to report, not actual violence, these policies have other consequences. According to the Civil Rights Project, rigid zero-tolerance policies hurt the developmental needs of students by not allowing students to form strong and trusting relationships with key adults and by creating negative attitudes toward fairness and justice. Suspending already at-risk students may exacerbate the behavioral problems the school is trying to discipline against (*Opportunities Suspended*, 2000). Zero-tolerance policies also target, therefore negatively impact, students of color. School suspension rates for African American students are between two and three times higher than that of their white counterparts (Skiba, 2000; Skiba et al., 2000; Gordon et ala., 2001; U.S. Department of Education, Office for Civil Rights, 2002). For example, in Chicago during the 1998–99 school year, African American students represented 53% of all students enrolled, yet they represented 73% of those students who were expelled (*Opportunities Suspended*, 2000). Starting as early as preschool, this overrepresentation of students of color in school suspensions and expulsions is consistent across the U.S. (Gilliam & Shahar; 2006; U.S. Department of Education, Office for Civil Rights, 2002).

One trouble with school discipline policies is that they are often relatively subjective in their implementation, and, partially as a result of the GFSA, policies have extended to include any action that is seen as a threat against a teacher, as disrespect, or as defiance of authority (Gordon et al., 2001). These highly subjective behavior practices impact African American students, who are disciplined and suspended more frequently than white students for subjective behaviors like disrespect, excessive noise, threats, and loitering (Skiba, 2001, 176–187). For example, two students

[3] "Data on homicides and suicides at school show there were 32 school-associated violent deaths in the United States between July 1, 1999, and June 30, 2000, including 24 homicides, 16 of which involved school-aged children. In each school year from 1992 to 2000, youth ages 5–19 were at least 70 times more likely to be murdered away from school than at school. Trends in school crime over time are also of interest to researchers, educators, and families. Data show that the percentage of students being victimized at school has declined over recent years. Between 1995 and 2001, the percentage of students who reported being victims of crime at school decreased from 10 percent to 6 percent. This included a decrease in theft (from 7 percent to 4 percent) and a decrease in violent victimization (from 3 percent to 2 percent) over the same time period" (NCES, 2003b).

at Hubbard High in Chicago were suspended for break dancing. A white
school official thought that the various break-dancing poses were gang
signs (Gordon et al., 2001). Similarly, a white substitute teacher in Florida was trying to maintain discipline in the classroom. A female African
American student said, "I'm going to whip you." The girl was expelled and
charged with first-degree misdemeanor assault (*Opportunities Suspended*,
2000, 7). The subjective components of these policies (or laws) impact African American youth. Even though African American and white students
have relatively similar referral rates and charges for weapons, and whites
have higher numbers of charges for drug-related offenses, African Americans are referred to the office much more often than whites for subjective offenses such as insubordination, disrespect, and disruptive behavior
(*Opportunities Suspended*, 2000). There is no consensus about what these
terms mean across districts where they are used, or even within schools.

These practices of removing students from an educational setting, the
most dramatic educational sanction available, start in preschools, as a
2005 survey of 40 states' prekindergarten programs indicates.

> Boys were expelled at a rate over 4.5 times that of girls. African
> Americans attending state-funded prekindergarten were about twice
> as likely to be expelled as Latino and Caucasian children, and over
> five times as likely to be expelled as Asian American children. (Gilliam, 2005, 3)

Head start programs and public schools had the lowest rates of expulsions
for this age group, with faith-based organizations at the top. The rate of
preschool expulsion, in all states but 3 in the 40-state survey, *exceeds* the
rate of expulsion in K–12 classrooms (Gilliam, 2005).

When students of color are singled out for less serious, more subjective disciplinary measures, not only does it impact the students' developing sense of justice and self-worth, but, as previously stated, these policies
hurt students' academic achievement. Students may not be given a chance
to make up their missed assignments or to attend an alternative school
during suspension or expulsion. Clearly, students who are not in school
are probably not learning, and suspension or expulsion may develop or
cement negative attitudes toward learning and schools. Children who are
"held back" in a grade may show poor attendance and attitude, which is
a possible result of suspension, or be judged to not have the academic or
social skills required to progress to the next grade level, also a possible
result of suspension. According to the Civil Rights Project

> [S]uspension is a moderate to strong predictor of a student dropping
> out of school; more than 30% of sophomores who drop out have been

suspended. Beyond dropping out, children shut out from the education system are more likely to engage in conduct detrimental to the safety of their families and communities. (*Opportunities Suspended*, 2000, 13)

Socioeconomic status also plays a significant role both in youth perceptions of discipline, and in who gets disciplined in schools. Students who receive free school lunch are at a higher risk for school suspension (Skiba et al., 1997). Low-income students also report that they feel they receive more severe consequences for disciplinary infractions than high-income students (Skiba et al., 2000). Clearly, school discipline policies exacerbate an already problematic race, class, and gender division in the United States. Moreover, these policies criminalize children and, by requiring mandatory referrals to the criminal justice system, remove schools' abilities to implement other consequences for behavioral actions that do not simply rely on the punishment logic. Furthermore, the criminalization of children is detrimental to their developmental needs, and, "The ultimate result is that Zero Tolerance Policies create a downward-spiral in the lives of these children, which ultimately may lead to long-term incarceration" (*Opportunities Suspended*, 2000, 13).

In Johnson's *Inner Lives: The Voices of African-American Women in Prison*, an anthology offering chapters that are authored by women in and out of prison, schooling experiences are significant. Cynthia, who left school in Newark, NJ, in 1977, eloquently identifies the need to consider behaviors in contexts and in histories, and the consequences of schools' punitive responses to "outlaw behaviors." Currently incarcerated, she acknowledges that anger was her persistent response to surroundings that she could not control and that actively harmed her. "Today, I can say that there was just the rage, the anger, everything and I lost my temper" (Johnson, 2004, 76). Her anger is connected to experiences of poverty, abject violence, and more. As an African American attending school in New Jersey in the early 1970s, she liked learning but was not able to get it together.

I always liked math and science. I was in the biology club and the African American history club. A couple of teachers made impacts on my life – a math teacher and my biology teacher. They encouraged me to do things right, to expand. It just wasn't easy. I was considered a problem child. I was suspended from school for getting into a fight. I fought because I felt that I was being picked on because I was real shy. Now that I am older, I realize that I thought fighting was the way because my mother and my father used to argue a lot and fight a lot. (Cynthia, in Johnson, 2004, 65–66)

School had an opportunity to work with Cynthia, to build on that love of math and science and channel the legitimate anger in new ways. Clearly teachers were already attempting this, but the institutional practices won out. She is suspended and "after the disappointment with school and the violence" she starts to self-medicate with alcohol, becomes homeless due to family sexual and physical violence, and continues to be depressed.

Clearly, school suspension did not assist her in any way to address the significant issues that she faced in her community and in her home. Rather, the policies and practices of a public institution, school, move her toward another public institution, the prison. Even if her teachers had the capacity to interpret her anger as a sign of other issues, the school was simply not able to address the larger social problems that shaped her anger. Significant, however, is that the school policies, suspension, actually make her situation worse. With a suspension, Cynthia is not in school, her professed interest in math and science is further diminished, and her trust and time with teachers that she perceives actively care about her, is restricted. The school is not a neutral space as it mirrors the treatment she received in other institutions: family and government.

Special Education

Frequently overlapping with school discipline policies, another school practice that negatively impacts youth of color is the special education category. Since the Supreme Court's desegregation order in 1954, African American students have been filling up special education classes at an alarming rate. This rise warranted both an investigation by the Office of Civil Rights (OCR) and two formal investigations (1982, 2002) by the National Academy of Sciences. African American students constitute approximately 17% of national total student enrollment and 33% of those labeled mentally retarded or cognitively disabled as of 2003. They are three to four times more likely to be identified as mentally retarded than white students and nearly twice as likely to be labeled emotionally disturbed (Losen & Orfield, 2002; Blanchett, 2006). In Chicago, the most recent data from the U.S. Department of Education document that 71.40% of those identified with an emotional disturbance are African American (3,320 students; 2,670 of these are male), and yet only 13.84% (1,510 students) of the total number of students registered in gifted classes are African American males (OCR Elementary and Secondary School Survey, 2002).

In *Why Are There So Many Minority Students in Special Education?* Harry and Klingner document the significant overrepresentation of minorities in special education, in particular in classifications defined as "soft" or reliant on assessment practices that are perceived to be much more subjective.

When these data are disaggregated by disability category, it becomes clear that the risk rates for African Americans and Native Americans are actually much higher in three of the "judgment" categories— those that depend on clinical judgment rather than on verifiable biological data. There are four such categories – Mental Retardation (MR), specifically Mild Mental Retardation (MMR), also referred to as Educable Mental Retardation; Specific Learning Disability (SLD), also referred to as Learning Disability (LD); Emotional Disturbance (ED); and Speech and Language Impairments (SLI). (Harry & Klingner, 2005, 2–3)

Each of these "soft" special education categories is differentially interpreted across states, and researchers have found that these categories are clearly applied differently within schools and districts. The use of each of these categories also shifts across time, a further indication of "a sign of the instability and ambiguity of the categories themselves" (Harry & Klingner, 2005, 4). For example, the number of students classified as EMR declined from 1.58% to 1.37% between 1974 and 1998, whereas the category LD increased from 1.21% to 6.02%, and ED increased from 1% to over 5% during this same time period (4). The growth in the category of LD, viewed by some as a less stigmatizing category, is in part a response to the charges of racial bias in the earlier overrepresentation of African Americans in the EMR category, a category viewed by some as more stigmatizing than LD. Significantly, this shift from EMR to LD is also a response to the number of lawsuits that charged that African Americans were disproportionately and erroneously classified as EMR, such as the *Larry v Riles* decision (1979/1984) "in which the courts supported the plaintiff's charge that the IQ tests being used to place children in the EMR category were biased against African American children" (3). The category of EMR, under scrutiny after this and other decisions, illustrated the racial bias inherent in classification, and resulted in the expansion of other categories, where bias is more difficult to concretely highlight.

Not unlike the subjectivity of school-based disciplinary actions, where *disrespect* or *acting out* move children into the category of a disciplinary problem, Harry and Klingner document that a number of factors that have little to do with objectivity are responsible for placing youth in the category of special education.

When a child's referral actually got to "the table," it was clear that neither "rationality" nor "science" were in control. Rather, we noted six "soft places" that either informed, influenced, and at times distorted the outcomes of conferences on eligibility and placement: school personnel's impressions of the family, a focus on intrinsic deficit rather than classroom ecology, teacher's informal diagnoses, dilemmas of disability definitions and criteria, psychologists' philosophical positions, and pressure from high stakes testing to place a student in special education. (103; see also Losen & Orfield, 2002)

These imprecise processes enable soft decisions where bias is less readily visible; however, this research clearly identifies that the classification process is porous and can be impacted by a number of factors that are clearly not relevant to the students' potential academic abilities. The Individuals with Disabilities Education Act (IDEA) requires that if a child is overly disruptive or requires special attention in class, they cannot be referred for special education until an intervention team first investigates and recommends strategies to deal with the problem in a regular classroom. Only after all possibilities have been exhausted can a child be seriously referred for special education evaluation. Unfortunately, many teachers do not even know that there should be a prereferral intervention (McNally, 2003b; Harry & Klingner, 2005). Furthermore, "It is clear that in many circumstances, school officials are ignoring the law and that parents and students are probably unaware of their rights or unable to enforce them" (*Opportunities Suspended*, 2000, 10).

Classification within some of these "soft" special education categories has lasting implications for students. Mentally retarded and emotionally disturbed special education students have the lowest graduation rates: 41.7% of students with mental retardation and 41.9% of emotionally disturbed children. These children also have the highest drop-out rates; and half quit school (U.S. Department of Education, 2002; Blanchett, 2006). Although African American students are three times more likely than whites to be given short-term suspensions, they are 67% more likely than white students with emotional and behavior problems to be removed from school on the grounds of dangerousness and 13 times more likely than white students with emotional and behavior problems to be arrested in school. This pattern continues as 58% of the African American students with emotional and behavior problems leave school and 73% of all students with emotional and behavior problems who do not finish high school are arrested within three to five years of leaving school (McNally, 2003a). Young adults without a high school diploma are more likely to be unemployed and underemployed, and to earn less when they get a job than those with a high school diploma and to be incarcerated (Petit & Western, 2004). While over represented in K-12 education, students of color with disabilities are notably under represented in post-secondany education (Reid & Knight, 2006).

Clearly, it is important to remember that this analysis of the production, interpretation, and application of categories of special education does not mean that children, or adults, do not learn at differential rates. Children do need services or interventions. Children have problems learning, problems paying attention, and they develop at rates that vary. There is a difference between stating that Erica has problems learning, and Erica has a learning disability. The category of Learning Disability is perhaps "a *product* of America, not something that is *revealed in* America" (Varenne & McDermott, 1998, 11) and the associated meanings attached to the child are reified through the acquisition by a child of an educational disability.

> Learning Disability is not a destiny, but it is one of the roads open to children. Worse, now that it has become institutionalized, the livelihood of many well-educated people is dependent on a goodly number of children walking down this road. (Varenne & McDermott, 1998, 42)

The consequences of these categorizations are evident at the individual level, as those classified have, as previously stated, lower graduation rates and other negative consequences, and yet they also may receive needed services or resources, a very positive outcome. As increasing numbers of youth, frequently African Americans, are educationally disabled, this can function to disqualify these youth, as classification as special education decreases a student's possibility of graduation and his or her probability of meaningful employment, and increases his or her probability of incarceration. The entry points into these classifications are not racialized nor are these consequences highlighted.

Racialized Surveillance

Significantly, what the data on school discipline and special education also illustrate is that schools naturalize surveillance that is centered on racial categories. Disproportionately targeting African Americans for entry into educational disability categories in middle and elementary school, and sanctioning them for anger, "disrespect," or "loitering" in middle school, is intimately connected to the surveillance and racial profiling of adults by police and other enforcement bodies. The practices that start in schools, and that are not discussed or named as racial profiling, are directly connected to practices that continue outside of schools.

Racialized surveillance is a pattern throughout major punitive and "security" institutions: schools, police, government, customs, and immigration. Racial profiling by police forces across the nation is a persistent problem, as the Department of Justice (April 2005) study found that nationally "blacks and Hispanics are roughly three times as likely as whites to be searched, arrested, or threatened or subdued with force when stopped by police" (American Civil Liberties Union, 2005). Surveillance persists despite routine evidence that illustrates that African Americans and Latinos are no more likely than whites to possess drugs, or to speed, or to break the law or norm. They are even under surveillance when they are statistically documented to be the least likely to be culpable.

> African-American women were stopped at customs at a rate eight times greater than that for White males, even though white males far outnumber any demographic group of travelers. Customs' own study revealed that in 1997, an incredible 46 percent of African-American women were strip searched at O'Hare airport. Even so, Black women are found to be the least likely to be carrying drugs: at 80 percent, the percentage of negative searches was greatest for African-American women. (Johnson, 2004, 43)

Clearly, safety or the public good is not the motivator of this increased surveillance on select communities of color because there is no evidence that suggests that Latinos are more likely to speed, or black women are more likely to smuggle drugs.

One clear consequence of this hypersurveillance is that communities of color are tracked into further state control and management. If the rate of drug usage or speeding is relatively equal across all racial groups yet police and enforcement is not examining one group and is targeting another, a higher percentage of those targeted will be caught.

> Although African-Americans only represent 13% of all monthly drug users (consistent with their proportion of the population), they account for 35% of those arrested for drug possession, 55% of drug possession convictions, and 74% of those sentenced to prison for drug possession. Latinas and African-American women are disproportionately incarcerated for drug offenses compared to their white, and male, counterparts. In 1997, 44% of Hispanic women and 39% of African-American women incarcerated in state prisons were convicted of drug offense, compared to 23% of white women, and 34% and 26% of African- American and Hispanic men, respectively. (Allard, 2002, 26)

This surveillance by punitive institutions invariably tracks people into the criminal justice system. The grotesquely high numbers of African Americans and Latinos in prison is not an indication of their great proclivities toward crime or illegal activities, but in particular for drug-related offenses, they are targeted at every level of the system—surveillance, prosecution, sentencing, and so forth. More frequent searches of Latinos and African Americans result in a higher rate of arrests and subsequent convictions.

Surveillance persists across institutions. Poor mothers are watched for signs of bad parenting. Black children are scrutinized for signs of behavior and learning disabilities. Latinos are suspended for wearing shirts that are suspected indicators of gang affiliation. Indigenous people shopping in stores are watched for shoplifting. Brown (not black or white) people are asked to produce citizenship papers in southern border towns when shopping or paying bills or enrolling their child in schools. After assessing the linkages between contemporary special educational practices and the intimate history between education and eugenics in the United States, Baker states that if we inverted these relations of surveillance, there would be a significant number of "special" educators.

> If the degree of surveillance that is directed at children who are so labeled were to be turned on the adults in the school, then perhaps there would emerge many teachers, administrators, and psychologists whose observed behavior might be thought of as disturbing and emotional. (Baker, 2002, 685)

Baker's observation is humorous partially because her prognosis is accurate, but it is an unlikely occurrence. Those with power are generally able to protect themselves from punitive surveillance that has significant consequences. Surveillance means that people get caught up in systems and tracked into the disciplinary apparatus, but also people get worn down. They get exhausted, and justifiably angry and hostile. People unjustly targeted by legitimate and powerful institutions such as schools or police forces, as documented, will not behave "appropriately."

Both expulsion or suspension and "special education" classification have serious effects on the life chances of students. Clearly, the grotesque overrepresentation of youth of color caught up in school discipline policies and in the category of special education illustrates that educators and educational institutions are not exempt from a kind of "racial profiling" endemic to our police systems. Rather, racialized surveillance *prefigures* the practices undertaken by police, customs, and other punitive institutions, and I argue that the establishment of these practices in schools functions to seemingly launch, for individuals caught in these punitive practices and for those who participate and observe, the processes of racial profiling. The educational terms used to describe this movement can foster a kind of simplistic neutrality masking that these school-based practices—discipline and special education—are deeply racialized. Because of the perceptions of schools as *ahistoric* and *apolitical* institutions in the United States, education-related practices are often imbued with integrity and perceived as value-free (Apple, 1979). Despite the staggering data that illustrate disproportionate representations in special education and in school-based suspensions and expulsions, *and* the data that illustrate the disproportionate numbers of African Americans and Latinos targeted by police or theDepartment of Homeland Security, we rarely make this connection.

Stopping the numbers of youth of color caught up in racial profiling requires a number of responses. Schools must examine behavioral policies and expectations to ensure that "differential discipline is not applied to any group of students based on their ethnicity, gender, ability, socioeconomic status, or an intersection of those variables" (Townsend, 2000, 385). Blanchett argues that perhaps more effective teacher training in conflict resolution can help educators create more supportive, inclusive classroom environments. In particular, understanding how youth resist criminalization through criminality is key (Rios, 2006). For example, Richard Rutschman and Victor Montanez from the Chicago Teachers Center at Roberto Clemente High School are implementing new models of in-school suspension that try to empower youth. Richard and Victor work with the youth who are "sentenced" to in-school suspensions for behavior, truancy, or other violations and sent to "serve" their in-school suspension in a large basement room at the school. Generally in-school suspension means that a student sits blankly and stares off into space for one hour in what youth term "the Dungeon" in silence with 50 to 60 of his (or her) peers. Victor and Richard have the youth who are assigned to this form of detention talking together, participating in team-building group activities, in an attempt to reframe their anger into community and youth leadership and also to use the time in detention productively. It is a small project, but it is an intervention that is attempting, with all youth of color, to interrupt the flow of youth into disciplinary processes at the school and to reframe the anger they possess.

Beyond these responses, it is important to step outside of the classroom to examine other factors that shape these school practices. If schools do the material and conceptual work to prepare bodies for incarceration, and they practice racialized surveillance, the feminization and the whitening of the teaching profession is not a coincidence or simply a "random" outcome. Clearly, teachers' attitudes and classroom management skills are responsible for placing African American children, especially boys, in the school disciplinarian's office on referrals more often than white children. The teaching force is predominantly white women. To understand this movement of youth of color from schools to prisons, how racial profiling happens in schools, it is important to consider the profession of teaching and our complicitness in these practices of structural violence.

White Ladies and the Profession

Language and contexts shift, necessitating concrete empirical evidence of exclusionary educational practices. For example, after *Brown v Board of Education* in 1954, the work of the formerly de jure segregation is now done through special education. Laws are no longer needed to mandate segregated classrooms. Whereas evidence of these new manifestations of old practices is required, it is also central to be able to consider the structures that are complicit in the reproduction of these old stories. I argue that it is increasingly important to study up or "to study the colonizers rather than the colonized, the culture of power rather than the culture of powerlessness" and to look at the role that the profession of teaching plays to mask racist and sexist exclusionary educational practices (Nader, 1974, 289). Clearly, it may be debatable how much power teachers have in a context of governmental regulations, parental "choice", and principal or leadership oversight, but teachers still possess more formal, institutional power than their students. Shifting the gaze from the students to the teachers, and the contexts that shape the profession of teaching, may offer new opportunities to view the nexus of relationships between schools and jails, and options to interrupt this movement.

I use the work of Charles Mills as a starting place in this discussion about disciplines and the profession. Mills offers a critique of the discipline of philosophy, for its studied erasure of the systemic role of white supremacy from the apparatus of philosophy itself. Mills writes that Western scholarship and (white) disciplinary ways of knowing have largely failed to account for the structured role white supremacy plays in shaping what counts as knowledge and who counts as fully human, a citizen and an agent of knowledge production. Mills names this political system, central to contemporary social practices, institutions, disciplinary ways of knowing, and more, the *Racial Contract*. Mills argues that this contract is "obvious" because there is irrefutable historic evidence—colonialism, racist tracts debating the humanity of nonwhites, and miscegenation laws. For example, real estate companies still blatantly "steer" or discriminate against nonwhite house purchasers and renters. National Fair Housing Alliance's (NFHA) 2006 report states that there are about "3.7 million instances of housing discrimination every year" (fewer than 1% are reported) and "one of the most blatant findings of NFHA's 2006 investigation was the use of schools as a proxy for the racial composition of neighborhoods" where white families are steered away from neighborhoods with predominantly nonwhite schools. In 2005, NFHA "filed nine complaints against real estate companies in Atlanta, Chicago, Detroit, Mobile, AL, and Westchester County, NY. Seven of these complaints involve franchisees of the national companies of Coldwell Banker, Century 21, or Re/Max" and the majority of these complaints involved racial steering practices (NFHA, 2006 Report, 2–3).

The Racial Contract is also embedded in "commonsense" ideas about resource allocation, use of space, and more.

> The Racial Contract continues to manifest itself, of course, in unofficial local agreements of various kinds (restrictive covenants, employment discrimination contracts, political decisions about resources allocation). But even apart from these, a crucial manifestation is simply the *failure to ask certain questions*, taking for granted as status quo and baseline the existing color-coded configurations of wealth, poverty, property and opportunities, the pretence that formal, juridical equality is sufficient to remedy inequities created on a foundation of several hundred years of racial privilege, and that challenging that foundation is a transgression of the terms of the social contract. (Mills, 1997, 74; emphasis original)

Mills argues that white supremacy, a powerful political system, is so pervasive it is unremarked in certain spheres. "It is just taken for granted; it is the background against which other systems, which we are to see as political, are highlighted" (Mills, 1997, 2). In particular, the discipline of philosophy, overwhelmingly white ["surely this underrepresentation itself stands in need of an explanation" (2)], has actively colluded in this process to erase the systemic role of white supremacy to shape the field.

> Philosophy has remained remarkably untouched by the debates over multiculturalism, canon reform, and ethnic diversity racking the academy; both demographically and conceptually. It is one of the "whitest" of the humanities. (Mills, 1997, 2)

Mills highlights the erasure or dismissal of the white supremacist practices, political tracts, and writings from the canonical figures of Western analytic philosophy from Aristotle to Kant and beyond, and corresponding dismissal of writings by people of color from the canon, as an obvious example of the limitations of the discipline or an example of outright collusion of the discipline with the Racial Contract. His project is not unlike the work of Carol Pateman (1988) in the "Sexual Contract" that illustrates the gendered (patriarchal) foundation to the field. Pateman's work, Mills writes,

> [R]eveals and exposes the normative logic that makes sense of inconsistencies, circumlocutions, and evasions of the classic contract

theorists and, correspondingly, the world of patriarchal domination their work has helped to rationalize. (1997, 6)

Building from Pateman, Mills directly names the role the disciplinary apparatus plays to maintain the Racial Contract and to secure an epistemology of ignorance. He offers a harsh critique of the discipline of philosophy. The studied erasure of the Racial Contract from the foundational apparatus of philosophy itself through the dismissal of the white supremacist practices, political tracts, and writings from the canonical figures of Western analytic philosophy and corresponding elimination of writings by people of color from the canon, and provides an obvious example of the limitations of the discipline, or an example of outright collusion of the discipline with the Racial Contract (Mills, 1997, 1).

Although the same cannot be said about the profession of teaching, we have been "touched" by debates about multiculturalism, and gender and race are topics within teacher education. Mills' work in the discipline of philosophy challenges me to analyze the "discipline" of teacher education, and to ask questions about our disciplinary ways of knowing and their limitations. What do we learn when frameworks of a Sexual Contract and a Racial Contract are placed on the profession of teaching?

Starting from the obvious might be a useful way to unravel possible ways to understand the logic of a system in practice. One obvious manifestation of race, gender, and heteronormativity is the overrepresentation of women in the profession of teaching. Although the feminization of the field, historically, was in part because "male teachers no longer could enjoy validation of their manhood as they worked in schools filled with women and children," the public body of the teacher persists as a white woman (Blount, 2005, 25). For example, a cursory look at contemporary data regarding gender and race for K–12 public school teachers in Illinois and in the United States offers a representative snapshot. According to the Illinois State Report Card for the year 2003, Illinois had 129,068 teachers of which 84.6% were White, 10.2% were Black, 4.1% were Hispanic,1.0 % Asian/Pacific Islander, and 0.1% Native Americans. 76.6% are female teachers, and the remaining 23.4% are male. Nationally, as of 2005, teachers are predominantly white (86%) and female (79%) (Education Commission of the States, 2005), and students of color account for approximately 27% of the student population. Clearly, there is an increasingly white and female teaching population and a school population that is increasingly not white (Toppo, 2003).

Following the frameworks of Mills and Pateman, this gendered and racialized discipline or profession is not merely an inconsistency, but is a result of an expressed logic or a system. When considering the role the profession of teacher education plays to regulate the Racial Contract in education, gender is central. Empire building had always required control of institutional education, and white women, historically, have functioned to mask the Racial Contract in education. Scholars from a range of fields such as cultural studies, education, anthropology, women's studies, and history have documented the work of white female teachers to disseminate, at a cheaper price, the ideologies of the state. Helen Harper writes:

> The image of "Lady Bountiful" is particularly salient in terms of the teacher or colonial governess who was seen as having a unique duty to bring civilization to the "uncivilized." Initially, in the early 1800s, her role was to educate British working class women in religion, morality, and hygiene. However her sphere expanded with imperialism to anywhere the British flag was flying. . . . The specific image of the white lady teacher is one of a spinster headmistress, intelligent but thwarted in her academic pursuits by her gender and possibly her social class, whose maternal instincts and academic interests have been directed towards her "Native" charges. Embodied, she was the sponge or mediating agent between subaltern and the colonial state. (2000, 131–132)

Harper illustrates that the white lady teacher is charged, implicitly, with colonizing her "native" students and molding them into good citizens of the republic. From Harper, I borrow the term *White Lady Bountiful* (WLB) to describe the roles white female teachers played in empire building. The white lady bountiful teacher archetype is not the only iconic representation of "teacher" available, nor is it the case that there are no other archetypes or representations of female teachers. For example, in the United States the black woman teacher (Mary McLeod Bethune, Sarah Mapps Douglas) is another significant "teacher archetype." I focus on the WLB as I view this often-unacknowledged identity as a prevalent and persistent icon with significant consequences related to the linkages between schools and jails.

White women educators worked to educate but simultaneously to "civilize" others. Canadian historians document, in early nineteenth- and twentieth-century Ontario, Canada, that women were the ideal bodies to reproduce patriarchal values and colonial epistemologies but not to challenge these frameworks.

> Young and socialized to obedience in a patriarchal family setting, they were the ideal people to fill the growing number of jobs in schools that were increasingly governed by rules and regulations from above, whether from immediate superiors such as principals and trustees

or from more distant authorities such as state or provincial departments of education. (Danylewycz, Light, & Prentice, 1991, 36)

The foundation of the profession is gendered, sexualized, and racialized, and "school teaching became work that was feminine, or fitting for women" (Blount, 2005, 15).

The role of teaching (and social work) was to execute class-based surveillance and monitoring. Female social workers and teachers were not trusted to create the template for this surveillance, but they were viewed as cheap, malleable, and relatively unthreatening mechanisms to execute this work. Built into the foundation of these "semi-professions" is the work of surveillance designed to identify "outlaw" behaviors and emotions. These professions are intimately linked to the economy and to the political needs of the nation-state. Modes of production shape identities and the industrialist Henry Ford was at the forefront of social work when he sent investigators into workers' homes to regulate "morality", which clearly meant monogamous heterosexuality and Christianity, in the name of productivity (Martin, 1994).

This relationship between white women, the profession of teaching, and the aims of the nation is also apparent in the United States where young, single, white women were appealed to as "republican mothers" to go west as teachers to civilize the new frontiers (Kaufman, 1984; Martusewicz, 1994). Unmarried women moved into a limited role in the public sphere through their expanding roles as common school (elementary) teachers. Catherine Beecher extolled in 1846:

> [S]oon in all parts of our country, in each neglected village or new settlement, the Christian female will quietly take her station, collecting the ignorant children around her, teaching them the habit of neatness, order, thrift, opening the book of knowledge, inspiring principles of morality and awakening the hope of immortality. (Catherine Beecher, 1846, as cited in Martusewicz, 1994, 177)

White women were essential to the survival and development of the nation and the dissemination of particular ideologies. As stated by the Boston school board in 1841, white women were recruited into teaching as they were constructed as naturally more suited to childcare, their minds were less likely to be occupied by worldly issues such as economics, politics, or science, and because women were in possession of purer morals (Spring, 2001, 139). Unstated, of course, was that women were significantly cheaper to employ than men. The intersection of ideologies and the role of the *White Lady Bountiful* is eerily represented in the 1872 painting *American Progress*.

George A. Crofutt. American Progress. Chromolithograph, ca. 1873, after an 1872 painting by John Gast, Library of Congress.

Reproduced throughout the turn of the century, *American Progress* vividly captures mainstream beliefs and policies. With the "star of empire" on her forehead, schoolbook in one arm and telegraph wire in the other, the hyperstaticized white lady is *progress*, moving westward and transforming that which is dark to light, and that which is savage (animals, Indians, and nature) into civilized order and industry. Gast's painting, reproduced in Wallace Adams's article "Fundamental Considerations: The Deep Meaning of Native American Schooling, 1880–1900" (1988), which examines how federal education policy aimed to wage the quiet war on Native Americans through control of education, perfectly depicts the intersections of the ideologies that the residential school movement worked to disseminate— imperialism, individualism, republicanism, capitalism, and Protestantism. Gender is not central to the analysis offered by Wallace Adams; therefore, although he includes the image he does not discuss the implication (or it is outside the scope of his work) that the central figure in the painting is the white lady holding a schoolbook. The very body of the white woman attempts to mask particular ideological practices, and, as I argue, aims to neutralize the explicitly Racial Contract. Intersectionality is central to an analysis as the WLB is produced through the overlapping frames of white supremacy, imperialism, heteronormative patriotism, and capitalism. This is also not a new practice, as Gast's work illustrates.

With this analysis, I aim not to dwell excessively on the ontological choreography that produces the White Lady Bountiful (WLB) as this usually serves to re-center white women and (white) theorizing, and forefronts (white) guilt. The WLB image is critically discussed in spaces as varied as the fields of nursing and social work, the discipline of anthropology, and feminist and postcolonial theory. There is considerable dialogue about whiteness and femininity in the field of teacher education, and whereas these texts circulate at the theoretical level I am skeptical about how successfully these works have infiltrated teacher education programs or professional development initiatives in North America.[4] WLB is well represented in North American popular culture, perhaps most vividly in the tousled blonde head of Michelle Pfeiffer, who saves "at risk" students (urban youths of color) by taking them out for expensive dinners in the Hollywood film *Dangerous Minds* (1995).

More significantly, I return to the first part of this chapter where I outlined the disproportionate number of youth of color suspended for outlaw emotions such as anger or disrespect and the movement of African Americans into "soft" special education categories such as LD through subjective practices such as "school personnel's impressions of the family, a focus on intrinsic deficit rather than classroom ecology, teacher's informal diagnoses" (Harry & Klingner, 2005, 103). Teachers, predominantly but not at all exclusively white women, are responsible for implementing these practices. If the foundation of teaching is intimately connected to forms of race-, class-, gender-, and sexuality-based surveillance, it seems more than plausible that we continue to reproduce versions of this surveillance today. Teachers, scaffolded by institutional policies and norms that work to mask how schools support other systems and attempt to erase race, move youth from schools to jails.

I do not suggest that the aforementioned intentions are those of every white lady teacher that sets out into the world or that every teacher edu-

---

[4] For example, Vivian Paley's 1979 book, *White Teacher*, chronicles the experiences of a white female teacher in a black school in the United States; Valerie Walkerdine's *Schoolgirl Fictions* (1990) deconstructs femininity and pays critical attention to the ways that female teachers reconstruct gendered categories; and anthologies such as *Women and Education* (1991), edited by Jane Gaskell and Arlene McLaren, examine the wide range of relationships women have to the practice of education. More recently, texts in education and cultural studies such as *Race, Identity and Representation in Education* (1993); *Off-White: Readings on Race, Power, and Society* (1997); *Dismantling White Privilege: Pedagogy, Politics and Whiteness* (2000); *Latinos and Education: A Critical Reader* (1997); and *White Reign* (1999) include sections that attempt to address intersections between race/whiteness, femininity, and the practices of teaching.

cation program in North America energetically sets out to achieve these goals. In teacher education contexts, the invisibility of this icon, the fact that for some faculty or staff she is not perceived as problematic, or, she is often not even visible, is a significant part of the problem. As Mills suggests, the Racial Contract requires a corollary, a specific kind of ignorance, so that "whites will be unable to understand the world they themselves have made (Mills, 1997, 18). Deviating from this ready-made mold will require a little self-deconstruction, and a recognition of this history of teaching as the explicit manifestation of a gendered and racialized contract and that whites are, perhaps, as Mills writes, "a cognitively handicapped population," unable to see the systemic nature of white supremacy because:

> (i) *motivationally*: whites benefit from the existing order, and so have a vested interest in not seeing it; (ii) *experientially*: whites don't experience racial oppression themselves and live in a largely segregated white lifeworld—raised in white families, growing up in white family/school/social circles, hanging out with other white people, dating and marrying their fellow whites—thereby having little opportunity to gain access to non-whites' divergent perceptions. (Mills, 2003, 157)

If teachers are "cognitively impaired" (rather than handicapped), this is a limitation that has significant repercussions. Whites live in predominantly white life worlds. As Gary Orfield documents in his 2001 study of school segregation, white students are the most segregated. "Whites on average attend schools where less than 20% of the students are from all of the other racial and ethnic groups combined. On average, blacks and Latinos attend schools with 53% to 55% students of their own group" (Orfield, 2001, 1). In addition, whites interpret integration very differently (Frankenberg, 1993).[5] This segregation is rarely publicly viewed as embarrassing for whites, or as leading whites to be disadvantaged.

The profession of teacher education maintains and advances these gendered and racialized contracts. The disciplinary parameters of what constitutes the *education canon*—unformulated but at the same time deeply regulated—mask profoundly problematic ideologies (and often this does not need to be masked). In particular, the conventions of the profession of education, what constitutes core texts to educate pre- or in-service teachers'

---

[5] Frankenberg's study documents complicated and skewered interpretations about the realities of geographic segregation. For example, her study identifies white women who perceive that they live in an all white neighborhood but do not see the labor of the non-white people or include them in their definition of community, and white women who live in deeply segregated communities but never perceived their communities as segregated (Frankenberg, 1993).

training, masks sets of power relations.[6] College and departments of education, although frequently viewed as professional programs, not disciplines, by universities, possess parameters. Although these borders may appear (or even be) more fluid that "traditional" disciplines, for example, History or English Literature, there are still conventions. Stacey writes about disciplinary organization being as anachronistic as "19th century political maps" and yet this organization possesses power.

> For disciplines are not merely knowledge maps and circuits, but social institutions with accumulated organizational resources, status, cultural capital, social networks, constituencies, and publics. (Stacey, 1999, 695)

Those in the field of educational studies are "disciplined" in a *discipline*, however recently packaged and murky its canon may be, and these disciplinary practices shape our professional landscape, or our "consequential quotidian geography" (Stacey, 1999, 693). Disciplinary practices shape our ways of reading and knowing, our image and a sense of a professional identity, and our understanding of what we can and should do with the tools we acquire.

Does the canonical flexibility and the professionalization in the field of education make the Racial Contract less visible? For example, although I usually have a lot of latitude in course reading selections for an undergraduate philosophy of education class, I frequently hear grumbles or questions from students or from colleagues that the readings selected for the course are not relevant to education or to teaching. Occasionally these are outright questions, and often they are comments. Where are these expectations or norms structured? Where have expectations or understandings of what is relevant to education been shaped? Why might it be relevant for preservice elementary educators to read Davis's *Are Prisons Obsolete? What kind of relationality is denied, shut down, seen as epistemically impossible, in the current professional and disciplinary construction of "education"?* Or do the seeming advances we have made in multiculturalism, or in making gender an issue (in comparison to the discipline of philosophy, for example) make it more difficult to identify and track the Racial Contract?

---

[6] I argue that even the formal and informal dispositions that certification programs ask preservice teachers to exhibit mask sets of relations. For example, does a teacher have to "love children" to want to be an educator? What kinds of gendered relations are implicit in this question? If she elects not to marry, or not to have her own children, is her love for children suspect? Historically, women were only permitted to be educators if they did *not* marry, and in contemporary contexts, I wonder if marriage, or other signs of domestic heteronormativity confer "fitness" on both male and female teachers (Blount, 2005).

I argue that it is not terribly useful to speculate on what a teacher education curriculum that takes seriously the Racial and Sexual Contract might resemble as the scope of the contract exceeds teacher education. In addition, as this chapter works to point out, education is one of the central vehicles preparing bodies to participate in the economy and in the prison industrial complex. Too often, "more education" is perceived as the response to inequitable and systemic structural problems.

> In particular education is an organ that can be transplanted into the "sick" society so as to somehow make it well again. This is unproven; more often than not we find that new institutions installed alongside the old ones do damage more quickly and efficiently (Acey, 2000, 210).

Yet, one step, beyond enumerating or highlighting the overrepresentation of African Americans in school suspension or expulsion and in the category of special education is simply to name this foundation, as Mills does, explicitly, as a contract that is actively maintained through the "cognitive impairment" of the majority of bodies in the profession. Acknowledging this systemic ignorance in the profession and in teacher education programs might open up curricular discussion in different kinds of ways to conceptualize teacher education through different trajectories and languages. The endurance of this lady-icon image as it is subtly and often not so subtly reinforced in popular culture, in teacher education programs, and beyond, actively prohibits certain bodies from entering the field. White teachers with little exposure to youth of color are more likely to rely on mass media sterotypes and be fearful of African-American boys as early as in the elementary grades (Ferguson, 2001). For example, any man interested in elementary education is still rendered slightly sexually suspect. In my own context, I do not find much data to contradict the statement Acker wrote in 1983: "Men who wish to teach such children [young children] run the risk of being branded as sexually deviant" (Acker, 1983, 134). The Racial Contract, then, is reinforced through the maintenance of the feminization of the field and through compulsory heteronormativity. This does not mean the presence of women's bodies, rather, the association of the field with characteristics stereotypically attributed to women. "Feminine" is a social construct. As masculinity is still perceived as antithetical to elementary education in particular, continual work is needed to link and interrupt how homophobia continues to regulate gender inside and outside schools.

Recruiting and retaining new bodies, those that do not slide into this construct so neatly, to be teachers will not disengage the Racial Contract but may provide a more critical mass to acknowledge its existence. The lack of Latino and African American teachers and school leaders translates into fewer role models for the students of color in the classroom. Whereas race is clearly a factor, cultural competence is also relevant. White teachers can be proficient cross-cultural practitioners, and African American or Latino educators are not exempt from contributing to the overrepresentations of youth of color that are in school disciplinary processes. Harry and Klingner ask, "Is cultural consonance between teachers and students a requirement for success in schools?" and whereas they respond, "*No*" (2005, 43), I am less sure of this response. When a teacher lacks fundamental competencies in cross-cultural interactions, or simply lacks exposure to any other cultures (is "cognitively impaired"), this will result in more verbal, physical, or behavioral "misunderstandings." White teachers with little exposure to communities of color are more likely to rely on mass media stereotypes and be fearful of African American boys as early as elementary school (Ferguson, 2000).

Shifting the foundational idea of the concept of the teacher, drawing on other archetypes not the lady, and highlighting teachers and educators whose work, identity, and definitions of teaching radically expose the sexual and racial foundation in education, is one possibility. The field can take responsibility for initiating change is to actively challenge the archetype that is currently shaping the profession, and work to recruit new bodies into the profession.

For example, friend and colleague Dr. Therese Quinn's recruitment strategy developed at the School of the Art Institute, an expensive and private program that focuses on art education in Chicago, is a sample of one teacher certification program's attempt to draw attention to a public resignification of the body of the profession. Framed by the slogans *Be an Activist / Be a Teacher*, or *Change the World / Be a Teacher*, their posters broaden the images of the teacher to include educators such as Miles Horton or Kathleen Cleaver, and the recruitment tools directly work to reconstruct the profession, not by reinvention, but through acknowledging that we can draw on other archetypes, other foundations. Under a photo of Kathleen Cleaver speaking to a crowd, is a quote from the Black Panther Party's 1966 *Ten Point Plan* that emphasizes education: "We want decent education for our people that exposes the true nature of this Decadent American Society. We want education that teaches us our true history and our role in the present day society." Or, next to a photo of Miles Horton with a scruffy beard is a quote from *We Make the Road by Walking* (1991), "A good radical education . . . wouldn't be anything about methods or techniques; it would be loving people first. And that means all people everywhere, not just your own family or your own countrymen or your own color." Politicizing the language of teaching, fronting the work of teaching as a public and a justice project, and using archetypes such as the Black Panthers as exemplars of educators, creates a different public construction of the teacher.

I juxtapose this recruitment strategy with a brief discussion I had in 2004 with the coordinator of the small new cohort "urban education teacher education program" at my university. Recruiting students of color for this program, which was still relatively new, was a significant priority, and men of color were relatively nonexistent in the first cohort. The poster inviting candidates to apply for this elementary or secondary certification program that offered a lot of useful perks such as additional advising, cohort classes, and automatic registration, was very "friendly" with a crayon-esque font and text that emphasized a love of working with children, and used the traditional education graphics such as the apple, chalkboard, and the ABC icon. Despite the reality that this program wanted to recruit older more "nontraditional" students, and those with an interest in secondary math and sciences, the poster was clearly geared to a stereotypical conception of an "average" elementary school teacher. When I casually mentioned that the flyer would probably not appeal to secondary educators, and might not target the desired "new" audiences, the hardworking coordinator responded to this discussion that he had never considered how the recruitment flyers might impact who participates. Although anecdotal, juxtaposing these two recruitment strategies, one clearly appealing to other histories, other intellectual trajectories, and one recycling all too familiar images, illustrates that interrupting these professional foundations is difficult because they are embedded in our everyday identifications.

The profession plays a role in shaping the movement of youth of color into prisons and jails. Not only are the structures and the pedagogies of specific schools moving toward resembling prisons and jails and conditioning the behavior of the youth to be institutionalized, schools also naturalize and enact the racial surveillance that materially tracks youth of color into prison. Through the educational practices of special education and through school disciplinary practices, schools enact surveillance practices that track low-income students and African Americans and Latinos. The ontological disqualification of populations and individuals perceived to be superfluous to the economy, and to the ideologies at the core of the nation-state, has long been the purview of the profession of teaching, specifically the work of white women teachers. Used as decoys, white women have "softened" the exploitation at the core of empire building. Connecting this history of teaching as a practice of both ideological management and colonialism to the current movement of youth of color into prisons and jails illuminates the role of the profession to collude in the production of youth of color as public enemies. The contract at the core of the profession reproduces our own disciplinary ignorance surrounding these practices.

These school-based practices exist in concert with other systems that currently impact these populations that the state has designed as extraneous, dangerous, or incapable. Restricting the discussions to schools does a disservice to teachers and to schools as it once again locates the origins of social problems in the failures of schools or teachers. From the national "crisis of youth obesity" to the moribund economy, it is an impotent fix to point to the school as the cause of and the solution for endemic social and economic problems. Mainstream media and politicians decry schools that sell soft drinks and eliminate physical education programs as responsible for obesity, or teachers who do not teach a rigorous math and science curriculum as causing our economy to stagnate. Schools are, without a doubt, a powerful social institution, but it is also important to illustrate how schools are *interconnected* with other forces, the economy and mass media. Just as this chapter analyzes how white women are used as "decoys" during westward expansion to acquire land and to disseminate ideologies compatible with nationalism and industrialized capitalism the contemporary relationships between schools and jails are also framed by economic changes.

CHAPTER 2

Strange Fruit

Prison Expansion, Deindustrialization, and
What Counts as an Educational Issue

I travel hours across Illinois to monitor prisons and to visit people incarcerated. Generally located in rural environments, often inaccessible to public transportation, and occasionally foreshadowed by signs admonishing drivers to "not stop for hitchhikers," prisons in Illinois have sprouted up in former family farmland: medium-security Lawrence, opened in 2001, where the average age of men inside is 33, and the average annual cost per person incarcerated is $28,326; medium-security Decatur, which opened in 2000, and in 2006 is just over its capacity of 500 women, average age 36, at a cost per person of $36,164; supermax control unit, Tamms, which opened in June 1995 and houses approximately 500 men, average age 36, at a cost per person of $58,994 a year (Illinois Department of Corrections, 2006). Eerily prescient, the "strange fruit" of the Midwest (also other regions) is now soy plants and the increasingly more valuable black or brown *urban* bodies imported to fill these new fortresses.

As one whose paid employment is in public higher education, a field that has faced three decades of significant cutbacks, I find the nation's extraordinary *public* investment in incarceration to be striking. The cost of incarcerating one adult in Illinois is about "four and a half times the cost of one child's annual education" (Kane-Willis et al., 2006, Sec. 1:13). An examination of the Illinois Department of Corrections (IDOC) website indicates that Illinois has built over 20 prisons in the last 25 years and no new institutions of public higher education.[1] In 2003 Illinois spent $22,627 a year to incarcerate an adult (IDOC, 2003), and the appropriation for a full-time student in higher education per year was $6,968 (National Center for Higher Education Management Systems (NCHEMS), 2006).[2] In Illinois, between 1985 and 2000 the state appropriations for higher education increased 30% and appropriations for corrections increased over 100% (Kane-Willis et al., 2006, Sec. 1:13).[3] Similar to most states, in Illinois prisons are an expensive, and expanding, institution.

> Between 1970 and 2001, the Illinois prison population increased more than 500 percent, from 7,326 to 44,348 people. By the end of calendar year 2000, Illinois had the eighth highest prison population in the United States and had an incarceration rate of 371 prisoners per 100,000 residents. (La Vigne et al., 2003)

Illinois' exponential growth in prisons and prisoners is mirrored in other states. Obscured in this data is that women, specifically women of color, are the fastest growing population, and African American men are eight times more likely than white men to be in our nation's prisons (Bureau of Justice Statistics, 2005). Currently, in Illinois there are more African Americans in prison than in college, and in 1999, 992 African American males were awarded undergraduate degrees whereas approximately 7,000 were released from prisons and jails for drug-related offenses. In 2001, Illinois had approximately 20,000 more African American men in prison than in college or university (Kane-Willis et al., 2006, Sec. 1:13).

When the public and the politicians appear to continue to cry "no new taxes", and fiscal restraint and accountability is the frequent response to any demand for public educational expenditure, I am stymied at the public endorsement and the corresponding tax dollars that support our incarceration-nation of over two million. Although correlation does not imply causation, and there is no clear direct indicator that government resources allocated for incarceration are directly from public education, numerous studies track the decline in resources for education, specifically higher education, and the increase in resources for prisons, surveillance, and policing. Fine and her colleagues chart a relationship between funding for (higher) education and prisons:

---

[1] The number of prisons in Illinois jumps to 34 if work camps, transition centers, and other centers are included (IDOC, 2006).

[2] Illinois is not an exception. For example, for the 2001–2002 school year, California spent $7,324 per student on education (Ed Source, 2006) and for the 2002–2003 fiscal year, California spent $49,200 per youth on incarceration (California Department of Corrections and Rehabilitation, 2006).

[3] By 2005, the educational appropriations per full-time student had decreased to $6,851 (NCHEMS, 2006).

Nationally, from 1977 to 1995, the average state increased correctional funding by two times more than funding for public colleges. In 1988 New York's public university funding was double that of the prison system. Over the past decade, New York reduced public higher education spending by 29 percent, while state corrections enjoyed a 76 percent budget increase. During that same time period, SUNY and CUNY tuition rates were raised and remediation programs were withdrawn from the senior CUNY campuses. Tuition rates rose to account for 25 percent of White families' incomes and a full 42 percent of Black or Latino families'. As public education moves out of reach for poor and working-class families, the long arm of prison moves close in. (Fine, Torre, Boudin, Bowen, Clark, Hylton, Martinez, "Missy", Roberts, Smart, Upegui, 2001.

The Justice Policy Institute has completed similar studies on other states. In California, during "1980–81 higher education accounted for 9.2 percent of the state's General Fund expenditures while corrections was only 2.3 percent of General Fund Expenditures... in 1996–97 higher education is only apportioned 8.7 percent of the General Fund while corrections received 9.6 percent" (Justice Policy Institute, 1996, 5). In Ohio, "from 1985 to 2000, Ohio increased spending on corrections at five times the rate that it increased spending on higher education. Higher education spending increased by 38 percent or $670 million while corrections spending skyrocketed by 200 percent or $1.026 billion" (Justice Policy Institute, 2002, 1). This increase in corrections spending and a corresponding decrease in higher education funding is apparent in all states and the District of Columbia, where between 1984 and 2000 state spending on prisons was six times the increase of spending on higher education (Justice Policy Institute, 2002, 2).

Despite mounting evidence that clearly indicated that this allocation of resources was inefficient, throughout the 1980s and the 1990s funds for education, generally higher education, stagnated as funds for corrections rose. Research from the Joint Center for Poverty Research by Lochner and Moretti clearly documents that supporting students to persist in education and to increase their educational levels would reduce the need for prisons and jails and cost taxpayers less. Just *one more year of high school* would significantly reduce incarceration (and crime) rates. They conclude that one more year of schooling would decrease the likelihood of imprisonment for white men by .1 percentage points, and for black men by .37 percentage points. Although this may appear a small fraction, the economic benefits, raising the male high school graduation rate by simply 1%, would result in the nation saving $1.4 billion dollars (Lochner and Moretti, 2004;

see also Kane-Willis et al., 2006). In an era where the call is to shrink big government and to make cuts in spending, the increase in resource allocation for corrections and the concurrent decline for education, most notably postsecondary education, warrant closer scrutiny. This is particularly vital when research clearly identifies that this public policy is not only inefficient, but is also harmful to citizens as it increases their likelihood of incarceration, and the subsequent risk of physical and civil death associated with incarceration.

Researchers who work on urban education attend to the development of prisons, as youth, overwhelmingly youth of color, who fail to graduate are more likely to be unemployed and underemployed and to earn less when they get a job than those with a high school diploma, and are more likely to enter prison than students who complete high school. Petit and Western identify the risks of incarceration to be "highly stratified by race and education" and that those without a high school education are more likely to be incarcerated.

> High school dropouts are 3 to 4 times more likely to be in prison than those with 12 years of schooling. Blacks, on average, are about 8 times more likely to be in state or federal prison than whites. By the end of the 1990s, 21 percent of all young black poorly educated men were in state or federal prison compared to an imprisonment rate of 2.9 percent for young white male dropouts. (Petit and Western, 2004, 160)

The dramatic number of low-income men, particularly African Americans, without a high school diploma who are in prison indicates that prison is, not unlike joining the military or parenting, a "life stage" event for low-income, undereducated, men *and women*. Those without a high school diploma or college education are the most vulnerable and "the novel pervasiveness of imprisonment indicates the emergence of incarceration as a new stage in the life course of young low-skill black men" (Petit and Western, 2004, 151).

Schools participate in the preparation and naturalization of this life-stage event as they shape bodies for institutionalization at prisons in Illinois such as Pontiac and Kankakee where approximately 14.2% of state prisoners have no more than an 8th-grade education and 43.1% of state prisoners do not have a high school diploma or GED. Of the prison population 19% are illiterate, compared to 4% of the total U.S. adult population (and 40% of the prison population are functionally illiterate, meaning they would be unable to write a letter explaining a billing error, compared to 21% of the total U.S. adult population) (Bureau of Justice Statistics, 2003b; Wagner, 2003). As outlined in the previous chapter, *pipeline metaphors* are increasingly used to describe this movement of youth from school to prison. This is relatively well documented, in particular by recent interdisciplinary research; for example, the conference and subsequent publication (2003), *School to Prison Pipeline: Charting Intervention Strategies of Prevention and Support for Minority Children*, Polakow's *The Public Assault on America's Children* (2000), and Ayers, Dohrn, and Ayers's *Zero Tolerance: Resisting the Drive for Punishment in Our Schools* (2001) concretely document the overrepresentation of youth of color in our nation's juvenile justice systems and in school-based disciplinary actions.

This research highlights that schools are increasingly a "major feeder of children into juvenile and adult criminal courts" (Dohrn, 2000, 162) and suspension or expulsion is a "moderate to strong predictor of a student dropping out of school" (*Opportunities Suspended*, 2000). Whereas examining how schools enact and simultaneously seek to mask surveillance offers a central example of how schools and prisons are interconnected, examining the stagnation of education-related funding in the context of skyrocketing resources for incarceration, and reviewing the enormous growth in the detainment facilities and then connecting these economic, geographic, and political shifts to education, illuminates other links in how and why youth are moving from schools to jails. This analysis illustrates how the prison industrial complex (PIC) constitutes a geographic and economic solution to socioeconomic problems while maintaining the state's commitment to white supremacy (Gilmore, 1998–1999).

These economic and political lines of inquiry are frequently not perceived to be related to educational policy or practice. Definitions and conceptions of educational policy and (urban) school reform must "realign," as Anyon suggests, in order to adequately understand and shift urban school failure. A focus on school-based practices as a mechanism for educational improvement and reform is useful, but those invested in high educational outcomes for all students may need to widen the framework to examine the interconnected relationships between schools and other institutions.

> If, as I am suggesting, the macro-economy deeply affects the quality of urban education, then perhaps we should rethink what "counts" as educational policy. Rules and regulations regarding teaching, curriculum, and assessment certainly count; but perhaps policies that maintain high levels of urban poverty and segregation should be part of the educational policy panoply as well—for those have consequences for urban education at least as profound as curriculum and pedagogy. (Anyon, 2005, 3)

Examining policies that contribute to, if not create, poverty and segregation should "count" as educational policy. Building from Anyon's argument, connecting urban school failure to prison expansion expands the landscape for educational reform. When states expend more resources on incarceration than on education, and build more jail cells than classrooms, ignoring prisons as an educational policy issue is dangerous.

Expanding what counts as educational policy to encompass new sets of relationships invites new questions. What is the relationship between urban education policies and the expansion of the prison system? What roles do prisons and incarceration fill in the U.S. economy that is seemingly transnational and fluid? How and why did predominantly white rural communities in Illinois transform to lobby hard in the state capital, Springfield, to open prisons? Why does the state permit and naturalize sending young black men, and increasingly women, far from urban centers such as Chicago, where they did not finish high school at their segregated schools, to expensive and new prisons?

This chapter starts with an examination of trends in the reframing of the welfare state. Reviewing the push in the last 30 years to "downsize big government" illustrates the rise of the punitive arm of the state and the contraction of the social services once provided by government. This discussion is then linked to a global context, outlining concurrent transnational economic changes, partially because modes of production impact modes of association. Economic shifts necessitate corresponding social and cultural changes, including modification in public space. The overview of changes in the nature of the welfare state and in larger transnational modes of production is required in order to contextualize the growth in the PIC in the last several decades. Prison expansion needed public policy, and transnational economic shifts actively support the prison expansion. Finally, I return to educational policy, to outline why knowledge of this landscape is imperative for educators.

Big Government

A prevailing bipartisan public sentiment in the last 30 years is to reduce the financial burden of government on the people, or to have smarter government. Although this drive to shrink big government may, for some advocates, be motivated by a desire to lower taxes or to reduce the role and the cost of government in everyday life; for others it is also an ideological framework (Blackmar, 2005; Harvey, 2005). However, when politicians and some citizens describe shrinking big government they frequently mean specific components of government services, typically *social services*, as the shift in the last 30 years has been the downsizing of some government services and the inflation of other areas. In the last 30 years, budgets of the Drug Enforcement Agency, the Bureau of Prisons, and the

Immigration and Naturalization Services (INS) have swelled at least 10% a year (Bohrmann & Murakawa, 2005, 110), while funding for social welfare programs, for example, housing, unemployment compensation, and food and nutrition assistance, has decreased significantly since 1975. For some of these agencies, the budgets may have grown, but it is important to attend to how the focus of the agency has shifted. The enforcement arm of the INS has grown, but not the service or the assistance components.

> Over the last twenty years the biggest increases in federal employ-
> ment have been within immigration and crime control agencies. By
> 2002, the number of federal law enforcement workers surpassed the
> number of service provision workers. . . . Most of the INS's growth
> has been in the enforcement staff, which has increased by 450 per-
> cent since 1975 and now constitutes 75 percent of the total INS staff.
> (Bohrmann & Murakawa, 2005, 110–112).

The enforcement functions of federal agencies are also overlapping and federal agencies, such as the INS, through the construction of the Department of Homeland Security, are framed as a security force. Bohrmann and Murakawa use the term *interlocking* (115) to also signify the degree to which immigration services and crime enforcement are interconnected. The increase in incarceration and deportation of noncitizens, the increased militarization of border areas to resemble large prisons, the shared uses of punitive tactics, and the overlapping policies, for example, the cross-deputization of personnel, indicate that the federal government views immigration services as a policing function (Bohrmann & Murakawa, 2005).

On the surface, these issues may appear contradictory. How can the rhetoric be to shrink big government, yet the application is to expand select areas of government function, specifically the punitive and surveillance functions? These twin "interlocking" trends in government, the growth of the security state and the shrinking of the support of the welfare state, are related:

> Welfare retrenchment and punishment expansion represent oppo-
> site trends in state spending, but they rely on the same ideology.
> This ideology holds that the liberal welfare state corrodes personal
> responsibility, divorces work from reward, and lets crime go without
> punishment; consequently the lenient welfare regime attracts oppor-
> tunistic immigrants and cultivates criminal values. (Bohrmann &
> Murakawa, 2005, 110)

To be anti–big government, then, is to oppose offering welfare benefits to those with drug felony convictions, but not to oppose the establishment of the Department of Homeland Security. I exclude here "anti–big government" organizations such as Americans for Tax Reform or civil libertarians who tend to be remarkably consistent and want to defund police *and* the welfare state. These twin shifts are not coincidental or arbitrary; rather they suggest the advancement of core U.S. ideologies of individualism and meritocracy.

Demands to reduce "big government" and, more recently, critiques of the welfare state/new deal policies have always been in existence in the United States. These critiques received no traction after World War II, as white males overwhelmingly took full advantage of public federal initiatives, for example, the GI Bill and the federal subsidization of suburban housing, and were not in the position to critique these programs, nor, as they directly benefited, probably desirous of dismantling programs that enabled their educational and economic mobility. Blackmar writes that "political disaffection and economic vulnerability" (2005, 66) from deindustrialization or the "lagging capitalism" of the 1970s and 1980s coupled with the mainstream's growing distrust of government from Watergate and anti-Vietnam politics, enabled this persistent critique of the welfare state to have any traction. The white men who had already benefited from "big government" and the new deal initiatives moved, because of political and economic shifts, to support and advance criticisms. Government morphed into being perceived as antithetical to free individual progress, and this is an important shift. "Common property offered no incentives to labor, and without incentives to labor, society faced the problem of 'free riders' and 'shirkers,' two groups who turned the public domain itself into a wasteful commons by taking something for nothing" (Blackmar, 2005, 70).

More pointedly, this call to shrink big government must be concurrently interpreted through the larger context of the history of white supremacy and race relations in the United States. Most people of color and women were specifically excluded from participation in the *original* structuring of the new deal welfare state. Union membership, social security, and housing markets excluded most communities of color and women, impacting their ability to accumulate wealth and to participate in the public sphere. Movements of the 1960s involved widespread, organized challenges to white supremacy and demands that these programs (and other basic forms of civic life) be extended to groups typically excluded. African Americans wanted access to the Federal Housing Authority's resources, to equal public education, and more. However, as these groups work to remove formal barriers, resistance and white male backlash emerges (Bohrmann & Murakawa, 2005; Fine, 1997; Frankenberg, 1993).

Despite its persistence, the U.S. progress narrative, where the white supremacy formally in place until the Civil Rights Act of 1964 simply vanishes after the 1960s, is mythic. It is a stretch to imagine that the explicit system of apartheid, in place in the United States for hundreds of years, simply evaporated in a few years. What activists and scholars highlight is that white supremacy, after WW II, shifts politically and discursively.

> Since white identities could no longer be overtly depicted as superior, they were now presented in "coded" fashion as beleaguered American individualism, as the hallmarks of a noble tradition now unfairly put upon by unworthy challengers, as the "silent majority" and so on (Winant, 2004, 181).

White supremacy morphs into individualism. The explicit systems of legalized segregation have, in some cases, been eradicated, but the beliefs and the values are embedded and transferred into other systems and practices that sometimes do not use explicitly racial language. Individualism and meritocracy, for example, are terms that work to neutralize or mask explicitly racialized practices in the United States. The backlash to the movements for racial and gender equality take many forms, for example, "campaigns for English only laws in states where public institutions *already* conduct business in English, controversies over educational curricula, and the resurgence of white supremacists political movements" (Frankenberg, 1993, 232; emphasis original).

White supremacy has not been erased, and the dismantling of the social welfare programs and the expansion of the surveillance and punitive functions of the state over the previous 30 years turn on the maintenance of particular tropes about race and gender. Downsizing of the welfare state is required because of all the freeloaders and the shirkers that take advantage of the state's generosity, and concurrently the subsequent expansion of the punitive functions of the state is required to contain threats of imminent violence and chaos. This anger and fear is deeply racialized. These are old stories in the United States.

> Categories like "black woman," or particular subsets of those categories, like "welfare mother/queen," are not simply social taxonomies, they are recognized by the national public as stories that describe the world in particular and politically loaded ways—and that is exactly why they are constructed, reconstructed, manipulated, and contested. They are, like so many other social narratives and taxonomic social categories, part of the building blocks of "reality" for many people; they suggest something about the world; they provide simple, uncomplicated, and often wildly (and politically damaging) inaccurate information about what is "wrong" with some people, with the political economy of the United States. (Lubiano, in Morrison, 1993, 330–331)

Welfare freeloaders manifest in mass media as the "lazy black mother" or the "illegal alien families" although data consistently illustrate the same rates of welfare use across race at every socioeconomic level and that "less than 1 percent of surveyed immigrants move to the United States primarily for social services," and "fear of deportation" and confusion about eligibility mean that immigrants are less likely to use state resources (Bohrmann & Murakawa, 2005, 119). An imminent threat, also reproduced by mass media, is the hyper-violent black man and the dangerous, darker, alien foreign nationals, even though violent crime is on the decrease and violent crimes across racial groups are infrequent. As political prisoner Gilbert points out, this is a classic strategy of scapegoating where those that are really culpable are masked and others are blamed.

> The genius of the rulers since 1980 has been the classic but still highly effective reactionary strategy of scapegoating: to shift white working people's focus from the corporations and government causing the anxiety and frustration to "despised others" of even lower social status—welfare mothers, immigrants, and prisoners. This disdain is built on the U.S. bedrock of white supremacy but without the indelicacy of using explicitly racist terms. (Gilbert, 2005, 315)[4]

Scapegoating is the simplistic but highly effective move to identify the wrong perpetrator or enemy and to make this person or persons take the fall for someone else's mistakes. Gilbert suggests that the restructuring of the welfare state that has occurred since the 1980s in the United States produced (and required) the construction of an enemy. Rather than focusing on economic shifts or looking at employers' or corporations' culpability and greed, or on the government's focus on expanding punitive and enforcement practices, the blame is placed on communities and individuals that represent old anxieties about race, gender and power in the United States.

These shifts do not, for this writer, indicate that the state is "withering"; rather, the state's responsiveness to capital is strengthening (Gilmore, 1998–1999). I argue that perhaps the restructuring of big government has resulted in government playing a greater role in the lives of the poor and marginalized. Far from reducing big government, these shifts

---

[4] Aaron McGruder, creator of the comic strip *The Boondocks*, offered a salient analysis of how white supremacy shapes working-class whites' ability to view how these changes in the welfare states hurt whites. McGruder, in response to the rapper Kanye West's 2005 remark after Hurricane Katrina that Mr. Bush doesn't care about black people: "If you're black and you don't know that by now, you're in trouble. I think it's time that poor whites start realizing that George Bush doesn't care about them either and he will let them die too" (Ogunnaike, 2005, 29).

have translated into a dramatic increase in the state's role in the lives of those poor. Even if welfare roles have shrunk, government responsibility for education or health services has been reduced with the Bureau of Justice predicting that 1 in every 15 persons will experience incarceration in his or her lifetime (6% of the population), the government is intimately regulating the lives of men and women, especially those most marginal (Bureau of Justice Statistics, 2006).

White supremacy is reproduced through this restructuring as these interlocking trends continue to marginalize people of color and women, but simultaneously, race and gender are central to the development and rationalization of these very policy initiatives. The remaking of the state also negatively impacts the poor, women, and communities of color; therefore this expansion of surveillance and punitive institutions, from schools to jails, aggressively signifies race.

> [T]he overgrown carceral system of the United States has become a major engine of symbolic production in its own right. It is not only the preeminent institution for signifying and enforcing blackness, much as slavery was doing during the first three centuries of U.S. history. (Wacquant, 2002, 57)

Although it may be more attractive to use progressive public policy changes such as affirmative action as a means to assess the success of race relations, the growth and shifts in prison policy offer another clear indicator of race relations in the United States, in particular when African Americans and indigenous communities, increasingly women, are represented in prisons rather than in universities or colleges.

*Post-*Fordism

What are the larger transnational economic changes that impact these very local practices and that have corresponding social and cultural consequences? How and why have modes of production shifted so that communities view *prisons* as an attractive commodity? To respond to these questions, it is imperative to sketch a global landscape of changes in modes of production and the movement of capital. In the 1920s and 1930s, the United States developed a system of mass production that economic geographers and economists term *fordism*. Fordism describes not only the physical system of production, but for some theorists it also refers to the resulting sociocultural shifts that this connection between worker and consumer fostered, for instance, Fordism's *mode of accumulation* had a corresponding *method of regulation* (Esser & Hirsch, 1994, 74).

These modes of production encouraged the development of specific kinds of cultural and domestic arrangements that correlate with increased consumption and worker productivity. In order to monitor and maintain these ways of living, systems of surveillance are required. For example, Henry Ford wanted a stable workforce and saw the enforcement of the practices of heterosexual Christian monogamy as the way to ensure a stable worker and a stable consumer (Gramsci, 1971; Martin, 1994). He gave bonuses to married employees and implemented surveillance, and he used social workers to regulate his employees' personal habits and practices in the name of productivity (Martin, 1994). The social shifts that arose out of this mode of production were wide and deep:

> The image of the Fordist town was characterized by strong agglomeration processes, the standardization and industrialization of construction, the nuclearization of the family and far-reaching processes of social disintegration, resulting in the erosion of the traditional socio-cultural milieux (e.g. worker's settlements). Supported by the large scale imposition of the car, extreme spatial-functional differentiations developed, characterized by suburbanism, the formation of satellite towns, the depopulation of inner cities, the dying out of smaller production and business operations, whilst at the same times stores and discount supermarkets blossomed in parts of the inner city. Life in the nuclear family, standardized labor, television and cars became the basis of a new model of life and consumption and structured urban spaces. (Esser and Hirsch, 1994, 79)

A "Fordist town" produced very specific leisure practices and domestic arrangements, and created particular uses of space. All of these spatial and social developments were interconnected with consumption and productivity.

In the 1970s sectors of industry and manufacturing moved to nation-states where labor was cheaper than in the United States, raw materials were more abundant, or host governments/political regimes provided attractive incentives for industry—relaxed environment standards, little regulation of labor force and human rights. These changes in production had significant consequences for the social practices and spatial organization that had developed to scaffold earlier modes of production. These "new" modes of production are frequently global, decentralized, and flexible. Gone is the "company" town with the employee society.

> On the world scale, a new international division of labor is developing. This is characterized by an internationalization of production which is driven by the multinational concerns. Production processes, man-

agement and control operations can become extremely fragmented on the basis of new production, information and communications and transport technologies, allow varying aspects of location to be exploited flexibly (cheap or qualified workforce, "highest" capacity environment – "worldwide sourcing"). Capital becomes more flexible, major spatial heterogenization processes mark this: enforced industrialization in former peripheral regions ('threshold countries' or 'new industrializing countries') go along with the deindustrialization of metropolitan regions. (Esser & Hirsch, 1994, 79–80)

New information technologies change the physical process of production and create much more flexible economic processes. Although consumer goods are manufactured outside Western postindustrialized nations, largely by women, Western postindustrialized nations' regions continued to meet the challenge to consume. Sociologists, cultural geographers, and political scientists all use different terms to refer to this shift from neocolonialism to post-fordism, but the term encompasses not just economic changes. Hall writes: "If post-fordism exists then, it is as much a description of cultural as of economic change. Indeed that distinction is now useless" (as cited in Amin, 1994, 31).

In addition to producing and requiring flexible workers, these changes in modes of production use and produce new sets of spatial relationships. With the demise of the company town and changes in the welfare state, there have also been corresponding shifts in the definition of the public and public space. For example, one significant shift in public space in the last 30 years is the proliferation of gated communities and the expansion of private homeowner associations. Cultural geographer Low offers some conservative figures of the growth of the gated community in the United States: In 1998, 4,013,655 households (or 3.4%) of the U.S. population lived in communities that require entry codes, keys, cards, or security guard approvals. By 2001, 16 million lived in gated communities where rights are based on property ownership, not on citizenship; and public services—roads, sanitation, and so on—may be paid for in part by the state but access is tied to ownership. Low also documents that "one-third of all new communities in Southern California are gated, and the percentage is similar around Phoenix, Arizona, the suburbs of Washington, DC, and parts of Florida" (Low, 2005, 86). The number of homeowners' associations has also grown (Low does not differentiate between cooperatives and homeowners' associations).

In 1962 there were only 500 homeowners associations in the US . . . and by 1992 there were 150,000 housing over 32 million people. . . . Today in major metropolitan areas, 50 percent of all new housing units are being built and sold as a part of a collective housing regime. (Low, 2005, 88)

This growth in homeowners' associations, gated communities, and walled urban compounds is notable as these private associations frequently do the work that the state once did—pick up trash, organize security, and maintain the association's common property.[5] These once public services are not only being absorbed and regulated by private associations, but are offered only to property owners. These spatial shifts with corresponding new modes of association, such as homeowners' associations and walled components, overlap with changing modes of production.

"Flexible" workers are also required for these spatial and economic shifts. Research often focuses on women of color and children outside the borders of the United States. A successful multinational corporate model is "white models + brown workers = mega profits" (Pintado-Vertner, 2002, 36), or as Korzeniewicz states more politely in relation to the NIKE company, "overseas subcontracting and domestic marketing" (2000, 166). In their analysis of *maquiladoras,* economists Martin, Lowell, and Taylor identify the growth of border factories:

> There were twelve maquiladoras employing 3,000 workers in 1965, almost 600 maquiladoras employing nearly 120,000 workers in 1980, almost 2,000 maquiladoras employing 472,000 workers in 1990, and about 4,000 maquiladoras employing just over 1 million workers in 1998. . . . Most maquiladoras prefer young women workers, a preference that has been ascribed to the willingness of women to work for low wages, their dexterity, and their willingness to perform tedious and repetitive tasks. (Martin, Lowell, & Taylor, 2000, 143)

As modes of production also produce and require different kinds of relationships between consumers and producers, if earlier modes of production were characterized by linking of producer and consumer, in current economic contexts the last thing contemporary clothing companies want consumers to be pondering is the lifestyle of the women in Honduras, Mexico, or Korea who produced the $100 boot-cut stonewashed jeans. The 1999 Kathie Lee Gifford public relations fiasco aptly illustrated to industry across North America that the nimble fingers that assemble those cheap T-shirts need to be rendered carefully invisible in the playful, colorful *queer*

---

[5] There has been a move to be able to deduct these fees from your taxes (Low, 2005, 98) but as of yet this has not met with widespread success. An irony (or not) of the establishment of suburban, gated communities (as opposed to urban walled ones) is that they both require urban tax dollars and use their resources, but frequently benefit from lower taxation rates in nonurban contexts.

advertising campaigns of mainstream clothing brands such as Calvin Klein and Old Navy. Gifford was a popular mainstream American TV show host and erstwhile singer. In 1995 it was revealed in the mainstream media that teenage girls/women made her line of clothing, sold at the American mega-chain Wal-Mart, in Honduran sweatshops (Fishman, 2000).

Although this global analysis is critical, intolerable labor conditions also exist in the United States, and it is equally important to acknowledge the myriad of ways the United States also produces flexible and cheap labor within its own borders, specifically through the increasingly interlocking educational, immigration, and criminal justice systems and through the prison industrial complex. From the Chinese Exclusion Act of 1888 to the current HI-B "foreign guestworker" regulations, the Immigration and Naturalization Service (INS) plays an important role in regulating the labor force (Salazar-Parrenas, 2001; Yoon-Louie, 2001–2002). New immigrants, "illegal" foreign nationals or those disenfranchised by our criminally unjust system—largely people of color—often do the low-paid labor work/service industry work in the United States.

Prisons

Despite the enormous numbers of people required to work in the prison-nation and in supporting industries, prisons have always been an economic engine and oddly erased from the national landscape.[6] The exploitation of the labor within prisons is not a new occurrence, and it is intimately connected to slavery. For example, the convict lease system in U.S. prisons emerged as a mechanism to control black labor after the abolition of slavery. As Davis documents in "From the Convict Lease System to the Super Max Prisons," laws written after the Civil War, Black Codes of the southern states that essentially reworded the Slave Codes, specifically targeted African Americans and criminalized their activities (Davis, 2000). Once incarcerated "in conditions far worse than slavery" these men constituted a ready supply of "free black male laborers in the aftermath of the Civil War" (Davis, 2000, 68).

The foundation of the U.S. penal system is intimately connected to slavery, white supremacy, and capitalism. From the post–Civil War Black Codes, which essentially reworded the Slave Codes to criminalize actions such as vagrancy and possession of a firearm only when the person charged was black, to the 1986 Anti–Drug Abuse Act that disproportionately targets nonwhites and those less affluent, "government sanctioned racially discriminatory" laws and practices persist.

---

[6] This erasure is addressed in chapter 5.

As southern and northern colonies adopted comprehensive race-based criminal law regimes, the notions of people of African descent as being naturally criminal was further inculcated into the evolving national consciousness. Such government-sanctioned racially discriminatory treatment also further legitimized the subordination of people of African descent in all areas of American society, not just within the criminal justice realm . . . *increasingly race became the sine qua non for determining criminality and punishment.* (Johnson, 2004, 20; emphasis mine)

The justice system (or known as *Just Us* to African Americans as my colleague Ken Addison frequently reminds me) is intricately and intimately connected to white supremacy.[7] What counts as a crime, who counts as a criminal, what are the consequences of violating laws; all of these policies, laws, and structures developed in relation to the political and economic system of white supremacy.

Punitive immigration, employment, and citizenship laws, laws not typically viewed as "criminal," also historically functioned to criminalize certain populations and deeply shape their participation in labor markets. Examining the history of other nonwhite populations in the United States illustrates that criminalizing communities was a strategic mechanism to control and to cheapen labor both inside and, equally important, outside of prisons. As Stormy Ogden, formerly incarcerated in California, has stated, numerous laws have targeted Indigenous Peoples, criminalized their behavior, and subsequently framed them to be cheap, or free, labor.[8]

In 1850 the California legislature passed the Government and Protection of the Indians Act, which can only be described as legalized slavery. The act provided for the indenture of "loitering, intoxicated, and orphaned Indians" and forced regulation of their employment. It also defined a special class of crimes and punishment for these Indians. Under the act, California Indians of all ages could be "indentured or apprenticed to any white citizen." (Ogden, 2005, 63)

---

[7] Outlining the history of the justice system and its interrelationship with white supremacy (and also heteronormativity and misogyny) is beyond the scope of this project. For excellent discussions of this, see James's *States of Confinement* (2000), and Steelwater's *The Hangman's Knot* (2003).

[8] I choose to use the term "Indigenous Peoples" instead of Native American or American Indian. I take seriously the critique of the latter terms offered by Pewewardy, which links the terms with a distorting narrative of "discovery and progress." This change in language signifies "the cultural heterogeneity and political sovereignty of Indigenous Peoples in the western hemisphere" (1999, fn. 3).

Illinois is not an anomaly. As of 2001 "about 350 rural communities have acquired new prisons since the start up of the prison boom began in 1980" (Huling, in Mauer and Chesney Lind 2003, 199). The constant threat of incarceration of select communities functioned to render their labor, outside prisons, cheaper. By making it difficult to be in select public spaces without cause or reason, being affiliated with a white citizen could be interpreted as a matter of protection. The law results in both the economic exploitation of Indigenous Peoples outside of prisons, and continued discrimination in every aspect of everyday life. This practice continues today and is evident in our immigration laws which effectively function to criminalize populations (Bohrmann and Murakawa, 2005; Salazar-Parrenas, 2000).

In the 1980s prisons emerged as *one* response to the previously outlined changing economic forces, post-fordism, on at least two levels. Perhaps the most obvious form of economic exploitation transpires as a direct result of Amendment 13 (1865), *Neither slavery nor involuntary servitude, except as a punishment for crime whereof the party shall have been duly convicted, shall exist within the United States, or any place subject to their jurisdiction.* Amendment 13 clearly permits slavery-like working conditions in U.S. prisons and jails and creates the category of highly exploitable prison labor and thus ensures that crime and incarceration are linked to the economy. Labor within prisons is contracted out to for-profit companies such as Victoria's Secret for often as low as 26 cents a day. In U.S. prisons minimum wage laws do not apply, overtime and healthcare benefits are not an issue because companies simply do not offer them, and profits are to be made. UNICOR, the federal prison industry corporation, employs approximately 22,000 workers in U.S. federal prisons, and their sales of office furniture and textiles in 2001 totaled $583.5 million. Prisons create legal sites where labor can be exploited. While marginal, Parenti suggests that about 3% of U.S. prisons participate in private for-profit industries (Parenti, 1999). Former prisoner Linda Evans writes:

> Companies that use prison labor include IBM, Motorola, Compaq, Texas Industries, Honeywell, Microsoft, Boeing, Starbucks, Victoria's Secret, Revlon, and Pierre Cardin. . . . They are paid pennies per hour—in UNICOR, the prison industry operated by the federal prison system, wages start at twenty-two cents per hour. (Evans, in Sudbury, 2005, 217–218)

This is not a new practice, but it is important to highlight that the maintenance of legal physical sites of exploitable and highly contained labor pools within U.S. nation-state borders creates precisely the kind of flexible *but concurrently highly immobile* labor. As Joyce Ann Brown, who served 10 years in a Texas prison falsely convicted of murder, writes, those incarcerated are "state property." When Brown attempted to avoid eating in the mess hall because she was trying to stop herself from becoming institutionalized and objected to the way women were fed, the major at the prison told her that she would be written up for starving herself, which was destroying state property. Brown writes: "That is when I realized that I was only a piece of property, a piece of property that belonged to the state" (Brown, in Johnson, 2004, 155).

The issue of employment in prisons is complicated, because when I visit people in prisons and jails in Illinois, most incarcerated would like to work. They desperately need money and they have little else to do, yet there are few positions available. People talk about waiting years to acquire a janitorial job in the prison, or work in one of the outside industries: the soapmaking factory, the furniture shop. This work is generally hard labor that pays pennies, but in institutions of 2,000 people, where there are 45 slots a year for GED classes and perhaps 150 jobs in industry, and few programs, employment translates into resources and something to do during the day.

Perhaps more central than the possibility of exploiting the labor of those incarcerated, the construction of multibillion-dollar prisons and the subsequent staffing and maintenance of these institutions is perceived to function as an economic engine for depressed rural communities, where those incarcerated, from one vantage point, are commodities. Kemba Smith, now released, wrote from inside prison: "The government gets paid $25,000 a year by you (taxpayers) to house me (us). The more of us that they incarcerate, the more money they get from you to build prisons. The building of prisons creates more jobs" (Smith, in Sudbury, 2005, 106). Although the vast majority of prisons in the United States are public institutions, prisons, prison management, services such as a healthcare, and construction can also be privatized further, facilitating profit, as Evans writes:

> Increasingly, private corrections companies are building and running prisons. One of the largest private prison companies, Corrections Corporation of America (CCA), operates internationally with more than sixty-eight facilities in the United States, Puerto Rico, Australia, and the United Kingdom. Under contract by state and federal governments to run jails and prisons, corporations such as CCA are paid a fixed amount per prisoner, so they operate as cheaply as possible in order to make the greatest profit. (Evans, in Sudbury, 2005, 217)

Public or private, prisons are perceived as development. Mauer cites a call to potential investors "while arrests and convictions are steadily on the rise, profits are to be made, profits from crime. Get in on the ground floor of this booming industry now" (Mauer, 1999, 10).

Rural communities across the United States that were hard hit by the closing of manufacturing plants, the consolidation of farms, and other shifts this chapter narrates, lobby for prisons to replace or sustain economies. Illinois is no different. For example, in 2001, the maximum security Thomson Correctional Center was built near the city of Lanark in Illinois but as of 2006 it remains partially closed and waits for the state to appropriate money necessary for it to open. Thomson has 1,600 cells, 8 cell houses, and a separate 200-bed minimum-security unit. A letter to the Editor in the *Chicago Sun-Times* from Lynn Kocal, a resident of Lanark, connects employment and economic development to prison development. She asks the state why, when other prisons are overcrowded, does the new Thomson Correctional Center only have 600 inmates "instead of the 3000 promised by the state?" Kocal continues: "We have never asked for much, and this time, when we have asked the state for help with our 11 percent unemployment, we have, once again, been forgotten" (Kocal, 2003, 42). The letter is accompanied by a photo that chronicles a demonstration over the "empty prison" and demonstrators carry signs that read "We Want Your Felons" and "Jobs Not Empty Jails." As prisons are perceived as economic development, citizens in towns such as Lanark that are 99.76% white appear to believe that a prison will revive or sustain their town.

Illinois is not an anomaly. The 1980s was the decade of prison construction and expansion across the United States. In the last 25 years the state of Illinois has opened 34 centers of detention: prisons, work camps, adult transition centers, and more (Illinois Department of Corrections, 2006). Of the 20 new prisons that Illinois has built in the last 25 years, half of these institutions were constructed between 1980 and 1989. The prison construction boom in the 1980s corresponds starkly to the creation of educational spaces. Cultural geographer Katz offers a stark contrast.

> Over 70 percent of the prison space in use in the United States by the mid-1990s, for instance, was built in the previous decade, while only 11 percent of all classroom space in use by that time was built in the 1980s. (Katz, 2005, 114)

Communities lobby for these prisons because they need jobs. The mobility of capital has frequently translated into manufacturing moving to nation-states where labor is cheaper. Big agribusiness has swept through the Midwest, gobbling up government subsidies, and further reducing the economic viability of the small family farm. "In 1969, the total farm count in the USA was 2.7 million. In 1992, the total had dwindled to 1.9 million.

At the same time, "large farms" ($100,000+) jumped from 51,995 in 1969 to 333,865 in 1992" (Bureau of the Census, 1996).

Prisons are perceived as a viable economic solution to the problems incurred by economic shifts, but they do not deliver on their promise. Most new jobs that prisons provide do not go to local workers (Huling, in Mauer and Chesney-Lind, 2003, 201). Construction and higher-wage jobs go to outside firms. Those incarcerated may even take jobs away from low-wage workers in the region, and the establishment of a prison may discourage other industries from opening in a "prison-town" (Huling, 2002, 203–204). However, there is a clear advantage for the community: prison inmates are counted for the U.S. census in these towns and not in their home locations. These once small, once rural, and once predominantly white communities benefit from the reallocation of resources from urban centers due to larger census counts although those in prisons cannot vote. Illinois has built many prisons in the past 25 years, and most released prisoners do not reside in these small communities once they are released. In Illinois most of the approximately 30,000 or so folks that were released from the state's prisons and jails each year (2002–2004 data) return to 6 of Chicago's 77 neighborhoods—Austin, Humboldt Park, North Lawndale, Englewood, West Englewood, and East Garfield Park. These neighborhoods are among the most economically disadvantaged communities in Illinois (La Vigne et al., 2003). These communities lose the resources and representation attached to the Census. Despite an inquiry in 2006 that prisons inflate the numbers for small communities and direct resources away from needed urban centers, the 2010 census will continue to count those in prisons in the frequently rural communities where the prisons are located, increasing population counts by the thousands and impacting the corresponding resource allocations (Goldfarb, 2006; Ohlemacher, 2006). For example, in Franklin County, New York, the 2000 Census documented a rapidly growing African American population, yet 91% of the African American population is housed in the five prisons in the county (Heyer & Wagner, 2004, 1).

What Counts as Educational Policy

I have worked in this chapter to suggest that incarceration, scaffolded by white supremacy, fills a needed geographic and economic gap created by changing modes of production. Public policy actively supports this increase in incarceration. In addition, educational policies do not operate in a vacuum. Building from the previous chapter, this chapter suggests that educational policies be considered in the context of changes in prison policies. As Anyon suggests, *"macroeconomic mandates continually trump urban educational policy and school reform"* (2005, 2; emphasis original).

Whereas the practices of racialized surveillance in schools require exposure and discussion, the practices of racial profiling outlined in the previous chapter will not change by shifting teacher certification requirements or adjusting the school calendar or contracting out schooling to for-profit companies. This chapter argues that schools and prisons are intimately connected, not just through education-related practices, but through larger economic forces that are frequently not perceived as being school related. No amount of teacher certification reforms, standardized testing, or curriculum changes will improve urban education because "low achieving schools are not primarily a consequence of failed educational policy, or urban family dynamics, as mainstream analysis and public policies continually imply" (Anyon, 2005, 2). Anyon suggests a realignment of what counts as educational policy:

> What *should* count as education policy would include strategies to increase the minimum wage, invest in urban job creation and training, provide funds for college completion to those who cannot afford it, and enforce laws that would end racial segregation in housing and hiring. (Anyon, 2005, 13; emphasis original)

To this list I would add, reforming regressive criminal justice policies, such as those that blatantly discriminate on the base of class and race, or in application dramatically disproportionately impact women, many from the 1986 Anti–Drug Abuse Act; or, changes in welfare laws that deny housing and welfare benefits to those convicted of any drug-related crime but not those convicted of murder, rape, or any other crime. Specifically, the 1996 TANF reforms (Temporary Aid to Needy Families), section 115, states that anyone convicted of the sale of drugs is subject to a lifetime ban on receiving aid. These are just two of the many drug policies that impact urban communities.

In the previous chapter I made a similar point about the role of the profession of teacher education to regulate the body of a teacher, and this chapter raises similar questions: what role does the profession play to regulate what counts as an educational issue? Initiatives do occur, in pockets, and are supported locally by teachers' unions, or professional associations, and national organizations such as American Educational Studies Association (AESA). Faculty who teach in teacher certification programs, such as myself, do interpret our accreditation agencies' goals to prepare teachers for diverse communities and workplaces, through our own frameworks and in the "best" light possible. For example, the National Council for Accreditation of Teacher Education (NCATE) Standards for Professional Development Schools, Diversity and Equity (Standard IV) requires that we "reflect issues of equity and access to knowledge by diverse learners" and "draw on the histories, experiences, and diverse cultural backgrounds of all people (NCATE, 2001,14). This standard could clearly encompass what is perhaps, ironically, the most difficult material to include in teacher certification programs, thoughtful and detailed work on gender analysis. When the teacher education population is increasingly white and female, our profession cannot afford to ignore, marginalize, or water down feminist theory, or the ongoing work in gender studies that engages with legacies of white supremacy and the intersections between whiteness, femininity, and heteronormativity. In addition, "diversity and equity" can provide leeway to invigorate old practices of community-based restorative justice, and include in teacher education curriculum histories of struggles where communities of color and of whites worked together for economic and racial justice. Or Collaboration (Standard 111) that requires our professional programs to "invite engagement with and critique from the broader education and policy communities" (NCATE, 2001, 13), is a call to include dialogues with economists, community-based organizers, and school counselors that address policy work on the minimum wage, and on universal healthcare, when these policies directly impact the academic achievement of students.

The stagnation of education-related funding in the context of skyrocketing resources for incarceration, and reviewing the enormous growth in the detainment facilities and then connecting these economic, geographic, and political shifts to education, illuminates links in how and why youth are moving from schools to jails. While profit, the state's need to contain superfluous populations, and deindustrialization all scaffold the expansion of prisons, white supremacy, and a corresponding willful public ignorance, has been and continues to be inextricably connected to prison expansion. Clearly, the United States has concrete histories of using immigration and crime policies to contain populations deemed to be undesirable to the state, to cheapen the labor of some communities and to simply work to eradicate or make invisible communities. However, policies are not adequate to mobilize the public. Without the image of the "welfare queen" and the corresponding emotions of disgust that accompany this image, it would not have been possible to move welfare from a right to needless fringe benefit. Without images of youth as "gangbangers" that are inherently violent and remorseless, it would not be possible to change juvenile justice policies. Mass media works to cement these transitions through the creation of representations that exacerbate these "politics of disgust" (Hancock 2005). Mass media works to tell us who is lazy, who is responsible for our nation's economic stagnation, and who is dangerous. Mass media is a glue that holds deindustrialization to prison expansion—as specific representations convince the public that it is not just acceptable, but necessary for safety, to house-poor urban youths, undereducated and underemployed, in warehouses far from their home. Understanding how youth of color move between prisons and jails requires an analysis of mass media, and how mass media impacts public sentiment.

CHAPTER 3

Life After *OZ*

Policies, Popular Cultures, and Public Enemies

I am in New York City on a snowy February day. After a breakfast in the neighborhood I walk, with my friends that I am staying with, back to their apartment along a busy commercial strip past small groceries, hip boutiques, and more. My eye is drawn to a local queer bar that has flashy posters depicting cellblock bars and a nude torso of a handcuffed man advertising an upcoming prison theme night. On closer inspection, the prison theme is a weekly event that coincides with a screening of the HBO television prison series *OZ*. It is a big deal—my hip NYC friend tells me, the place has a line-up around the block and the gay boys dress up as characters from the show or even in prison uniforms. I peer in the window and sure enough there is a drink special set for the night, a trivia question, and a request to come in costume. Living in a household without a TV for the past five years, I am a little out of the loop. I am not sure how to feel, although I am certainly for pleasure, and for the queer appropriation of all kinds of institutional practices, but I have known too many folks who were (or are) in these hellish spaces to view it as a site of pleasure. I went to Stateville Prison, in Illinois, and went into the last roundhouse, panopticon, in the nation on a ninety-degree Fahrenheit day and it was so loud and hot and painful I almost vomited. My NYC pal tells me to lighten up. "It is just for fun," he tells me. "It is just a TV show. When did you turn into such a prude?"

With gritty shows featuring racial violence, rape, and murder, HBO's *OZ* propelled prison dramas to be the new *hot genre* in the late 1990s, according to cultural and media studies watchers. Firmly ensconced in all three of the film genres that impact the body—horror, melodrama, and pornography—*OZ* moved up the ratings charts during a decade when privatization and supermax prisons are posited as conscious solutions to rising incarceration rates (despite declining crime statistics) and flagging rural economies in the United States (Mauer & Chesney-Lind, 2003; Herivel & Wright, 2003). Prior to *OZ*, popular representations of crime such as the *Law and Order* franchise on television offered images and narratives of "good cops" and "bad guys" but hid images of prison from public view. Movies offered images of prison that portrayed the system as inherently just, or the criminal as honest amidst a system that was unjust (*Cool Hand Luke* in 1967, *Hurricane* in 1999), or the film was set in the past exempting a comparison between contemporary incarceration and freeing the filmmakers to use old stereotypes (*Shawshank Redemption* in 1994).

Offering audiences the *feeling* and *belief* that they know what life is like in a maximum security institution, *OZ* departs from this history of the representations of prisons as the show is centered on a gendered and racialized spectacle of punishment within a maximum security institution. The majority of plots on *OZ* revolve around Emerald City, "Em City," an experimental section of the Oswald State Correctional Facility, where the white, ineffective, and liberal unit manager works to promote a philosophy of rehabilitation that is generally represented on the show as impotent. Utilizing documentary cinematic techniques to convey realism—for example, close-ups, characters speak directly to camera, the use of a narrator— the show works to give off effects of the real, *verisimilitude*. Examining *OZ* is central, not just because it is the first time mass media represents prison life, but because this representation occurs simultaneously with "tough on crime" policies. With the significant absence of other representations of prison life in the public sphere, *OZ* functions as a teaching machine, offering dramatic "real life" representations about the site of prison, and subsequently offering de facto meanings about crime, punishment, rehabilitation, and criminal policies.

Mainstream mass media, an umbrella term I use to describe a variety of sources including print journalism, television shows, and Hollywood movies, actively facilitates the movement of youth of color into the prison industrial complex (PIC). By mainstream, I refer to popular or readily available sources in North America and I use alternative terms to refer to small, generally community-based or not-for-profit media entities.[1] Depictions of youth in mass media as violent, and prisons as spaces for deranged and hyperaggressive predators, are one soundtrack that justifies the expansion of our prison nation. Television news shows take seriously the discourse of the youth as "superpredator", disproportionately use images of street crime that highlight African-Americans or Latinos as perpetrators, and sensationalize those participating in any youth violence as inherently violent "gangbangers" capable of spontaneous and unpremeditated violent attacks, or "wildings" (Mauer, 1999, 173–174). These representations all contribute to and naturalize discourses of violence as biologically determined and youth as inherently dangerous, and in need of containment. These erroneous images of rising crime from out of control and dangerously *bad* kids, supported juvenile justice policy changes in the 1980s and 1990s, such as lowering the age that one can be culpable of a crime or making transfers of youth into adult courts easier (Rapping 2003, Dohrn, in Polakow, 2000).

Understanding the linkages between prisons and schools requires not just connecting the technologies of surveillance and punishment used in both institutions, or the larger economic relationships between the prison expansion and education, but also an understanding of how select populations come to be perceived as "superfluous" to education (Duncan, 2000), and in need of surveillance and containment. I argue that mass media reproduces an active public racialized *ignorance* about crime and prisons, and ignorance is not a benign force; it can be "harnessed, licensed, and regulated on a mass scale for striking reinforcements" (Sedgwick,1990, 5). Just as punitive welfare reform was ushered in through mass media representations of those who use welfare as lazy, irresponsible, and "overly fertile," and just as these themes correlate with public opinion polls

---

[1] In 2006 five multinational companies controlled access to the majority of mass media in the United States. Viacom, News Corporation, General Electric, CBS Corporation, Disney, and Time Warner control access to the largest media outlets: magazines, TV and radio stations, newspapers, music, and more. Diversity in media ownership is generally perceived to be a "good" for a democracy as the more media outlets, the wider range of perspectives on an issue will be in the public sphere, educating the general population. However, as Amy Goodman writes in her description of the "access of evil," the consolidation of media producers and distributors was facilitated by changes in government regulations, specifically the 1996 Telecommunications Act, which permitted companies to acquire a greater share of the market. Goodman argues that this reduction in the diversity of media outlets has significant impacts on the representations we receive, and Goodman cites George Gerbner, former dean of the University of Pennsylvania Annenberg School of Communication, who in 1997 "described the media as being 'driven not by the creative people who have something to tell, but by global conglomerates that have something to sell'" (Goodman, 2006, 16).

where those surveyed identify that welfare "doesn't work" and it is an impediment (Hancock, 2005), representations of prisons, and crime and criminals, work to shape public sentiment surrounding criminal policies. Investigating the relationships between mass media products and the active expansion of the PIC offers insights into how representations such as *OZ* coincide with the explosion in the establishment of supermax prisons.

This chapter starts with this brief deconstruction of HBO's *OZ*, arguably the most important representation of prison in the public sphere in the last decade, because mass media reproduce representations that function as the "cover stories that shield the text of power" (Lubiano, in Morrison, 1993, 331). With the active absence of other representations of prison life in the popular sphere, *OZ* functions as a teaching machine, offering dramatic "real life" representations about the site of prison, and subsequently offering de facto meanings about crime, punishment rehabilitation and criminal policies. What policies and realities are protected by these mainstream representation of incarceration? In particular for the realm of crime and prisons, we rely almost exclusively on mass media to interpret these categories. Deconstructing contemporary representations of incarceration offers warnings/insights into the current landscape of public sentiment surrounding crime and prisons, and the production of racialized public enemies. For educators, this process of deconstruction is vital. We need to both encourage/ensure that cultural critique and media analysis is perceived as central to teacher education, but also because daily life in the classroom, from the policies that influence educational practices to teacher's everyday actions, is informed by media. The laws and policies that expand our prison nation require the participation of the institution of education and mass media actively works to cement our consent, through managing our ignorance. Starting with a return to Mills' work to offer a theoretical framework for ignorance, and linking this to the work of mass media, this chapter then moves to offer discussions of governmental policies that directly shape the expansion of the PIC. With a clear example of a policy, the eradication of higher education Pell grants for those in prison, this chapter works to illustrate how stories about crime and race, circulated in mass media, impact public polices, and how, correspondingly, a kind of constructed and willful public ignorance about prisons and the PIC is perpetuated.

OZ and Supermax Institutions

Supermax prisons are formally termed "control units," first initiated at the Marion, Illinois, U.S. Penitentiary in 1972, to refer to a prison or part of a prison that operates under a "super-maximum" or a high-security regime, and where those incarcerated are in solitary confinement in cells almost the entire day and night, between 22 and 23 hours a day. The number of these institutions exploded in the 1990s. A 2006 study by the Urban Institute indicated,"Twenty years ago, super-maximum-security prisons were rare in America. As of 1996, over two-thirds of states had 'supermax' facilities that collectively housed more than 20,000 inmates. Based on the present study, however, as of 2004, 44 states had supermax prisons" (Mears, 2006, 1). As *OZ* directly coincides with the 1990s "tough on crime" explosion in the establishment of these new lockdown institutions, how does *OZ*'s depiction of prison life match up with the reality of life in a super maximum institution in the United States? Not surprisingly, *OZ* deviates markedly from reality.

A few examples: The prison population depicted is attractively multi-racial, yet plots focus on central characters who are white. Whereas *OZ* includes violent white gangs (Aryan Nations and Italians), and whereas this explicit rendering, visible of the category of white as a race, is what critical race studies scholars request (Frankenberg, 1993), this representation of whiteness exists parallel to the continued performance of a second kind of erased, neutral, and "everyman" whiteness. Performing this everyman whiteness are two central characters (Beecher and McManus) who are the show's sympathetic characters for whom acts of violence are most frequently depicted as rational responses to irrational situations, and they are most likely to show remorse. The graphic violence on the show is usually racialized or sexualized violence between prisoners, not violence from the institution. Racial violence between those in prison is clearly an issue, but when prisons are in almost all-white communities, with an almost all-white security force, racial violence between those in prisons and officers is prevalent and much more inequitable (Amnesty International, 1998a; *Human Rights Watch*, 1997, 1998). *OZ*'s representation of race also erases a political reality that prisons are among the few institutions in the United States where it is still permissible to segregate on the basis of race and where race organizes all facets of institutional life. In Texas, prisons only desegregated under court order in the 1980s, and in California, in 2005, the state supreme court ruled it unconstitutional to lock-down individuals based on their ethnicity or racial group (Savage & Warren, 2005). The portrayal of those in prisons constantly fighting each other reinforces perceptions of those in prison as inherently dangerous, while research consistently documents that the escalating incarceration rates are due to drug-sentencing laws, not to a rise in violent crime rates (Mauer, 1999). On *OZ* most inmates, except for the *few* white everymen, are violent and uncontrollable, and require containment, not wishy-washy liberal rehabilitation.

OZ continues the Hollywood tradition of representing only male prisoners/prisons, despite the fact that women, specifically women of color, are the fastest growing prison population (Sudbury, 2005). In Illinois, between 1983 and 2002 the number of women in prison for drug-related crimes skyrocketed from 32 to 1,325, a 4,041% leap (Kane-Willis et al., 2006, Sec. 1:4). Overwhelmingly arrested for nonviolent drug-related offenses, Ritchie sketches this portrait of women in U.S. prisons and jails.

> Typically, prior to being arrested they live in neighborhoods where they experience many of the difficulties that have come to be associated with contemporary urban poverty. Less than 40% of women in state prisons report that they have been employed prior to arrest, and about 35% had incomes less than 600$ each month. Only 39% had a high school diploma or a GED. They come from communities where rates of homelessness have increased substantially, reaching 40% in some studies of women detained in U.S. jails. (Ritchie, in Mauer & Chesney-Lind, 2002, 138)

A 2001 survey conducted on October 31 by the Chicago Coalition for the Homeless at Cook County Jail (CCJ) offered the following data about women in jail: 54% were homeless in the 30 days preceding entering CCJ, 82% reported being mothers, 54% reported being unemployed in the 30 days preceding entering CCJ, 60% of those unemployed reported substance abuse as a barrier to employment, 29% reported being denied assistance from government programs in the 12 months prior to entering CCJ, and 34% were regularly involved in some sort of prostitution. In addition, 82% of the over 1,117 women in CCJ in October of 2001 *were charged with nonviolent offenses* (Goswani & Schervish, 2002, 2). A 1997 General Accounting Office report identifies that women in prisons and jails have a significantly higher rate of experiences with sexual or physical violence at 2 to 3 times the national average.

> Approximately forty percent of female inmates in federal prisons and approximately fifty-seven percent of female inmates in state institutions had histories of physical or sexual abuse prior to their incarceration. Sixty-nine percent of women under correctional-system authority reported that physical or sexual abuse occurred before they reached the age of eighteen. (Johnson, 2004, 7, see also Diaz-Cotto, 2006)

Most of my experiences with women in or exiting prisons suggest that these numbers are too low. These women are first and most significantly poor. They are mothers and they are in prisons and jails for nonviolent crimes that are intimately related to their status as poor mothers. They frequently have drug and alcohol problems that cannot be isolated from their histories of abuse and violence. They are "shut out" of access to higher education through punitive welfare laws, and therefore often consigned to low-wage employment (Bloom, 2006; Polakow et al., 2004).

By mid-2002 there were 657 prison films and 91 of them focused on women's prisons (Britton, 2003, 12). Between 1980 and 1990 prison films that addressed women were pseudopornographic films, sensationalizing sexual acts between women behind bars, that do little to educate audiences about the realities of the lives of women behind bars, notably the *Caged Heat* series (Britton, 2003, 12). While poor, homeless, and undereducated women are rarely stars on TV, and erasure of women in prison on *OZ* is hardly news, *OZ*'s myopic focus on the life of men behind bars is compounded by the extreme misogyny exhibited by most that are imprisoned.

Clearly, *OZ* does not accurately reflect the demographics of the U.S. prison population, nor does it offer a useful representation of daily life in a supermax prison. Far from the unbridled violence depicted, Rhodes's 2004 study of maximum security institutions' control units offers a picture that deviates markedly from *OZ*. Isolation in these facilities is a permanent condition. Rhodes describes a new technologized form of incarceration at control units overcrowded with folks that need major psychiatric care—not a prison. The main sentiment expressed by those locked up in a control unit in an almost permanent state of solitary confinement is boredom. Rhodes cites an individual's description of incarcerated life in Stateville, Illinois:

> If you expect the usual tale of constant violence, brutal guards, gang rapes daily, escape efforts, turmoil . . . you will be deeply disappointed. Prison life . . . is not a daily round of threats, fights, plots and "shanks" (prison-made knives)—though you have to be constantly careful to avoid situations or behavior that might lead to violence. . . . For me, and many like me in prison, violence is not the major problem: the major problem is monotony . . . boredom, time-slowing boredom, interrupted by occasional bursts of fear and anger, is the governing reality of life in prison. (Rhodes, 2004, 13)

On July 13 2006, also at Stateville Prison, I observed the 3 educational classes available in both Adult Basic Education (ABE), and General Equivalency Diploma (GED). Each class had approximately 20 students. The institution houses approximately 2,700 men with about 1,500 men in the permanent population. When talking with men on the tiers at Stateville and in the educational classes, some stated that they had been waiting 4 to

5 years to get into one of these educational slots in the three classes There are no college programs available in this prison.

Or Judge Barbara Crabb describing conditions in the 500-bed Super Maximum Correctional Institution in Boscobel, Wisconsin, in 2001:

> [Inmates] . . . spend all but four hours a week confined to a cell. The "boxcar" style door on the cell is solid except for a shutter and a trap door that opens into the deal space for the vestibule through which a guard may transfer items to an inmate without interacting with him. The cells are illuminated 24 hours a day. Inmates receive no outdoor exercise. Their personal belongings are severely restricted; one religious text, one box of legal materials, and 25 personal letters. They are permitted no clocks, radios, watches, cassette players, or televisions. The temperature fluctuates wildly, reaching extremely high and low temperatures depending on the season. (as cited in Elsner, 2004, 142)

Boredom within an institution populated by people suffering from mental illness and the impact of a lifetime of extreme poverty and extreme under-education would not sell advertising on HBO. Deranged and hyped sexualized criminals confined within a spectacle of the explicit public failure of the philosophy of rehabilitation sells. Yet *OZ* does more than sell advertising; this representation provides important scaffolding for the expansion of the prison industrial complex in the United States.

Tom Fontana, executive producer, creator, and author of *OZ*, challenges this vision of the show as just a package to exploit stereotypes about prison, racial strife, and taboo breaking. In a 2003 interview for Chicago's gay paper which had several double-page spreads on the series, Fontana explicitly stated that he wanted viewers to be educated by the show. "So that when you read in the paper, oh there was a riot in the prison, it isn't just, 'Those prisoners, they're always rioting or whatever . . . ' You will hopefully stop and think, 'Wait a minute. I wonder what the real reasons were.'" When asked about the "message" of OZ, Fontana responds:

> Well I think the ultimate message of the series is that it's easy to dismiss people; to put them in categories and negate their humanity. And I think what we've been trying to do over the last six years is to put a human face on the prison population in this country. Now, when I say a human face, I don't mean an idealistic face. I mean a face in all its humanity, good and bad. . . . And I also think that in my head the prison is a microcosm of society in general. So that even though things are played out to an extreme on the show because these are men of extreme action, it still relates to very basic things that con-

front all of us on a day-to-day basis. Whether it's racism or ageism or greed or whatever. There's an equal amount of all of those things outside of a prison as well as inside of a prison. (Guarino, 2003)

Fontana's desire to spin a decidedly nonuniversal issue (the crisis of mass incarceration and the experiences of life in prison) into a universal message about humanity, and Fontana's good intentions to offer a representation of an erased and marginalized community, is not an anomaly. From *Will & Grace* to the *George Lopez Show*, producers and writers frequently claim to work to present a subgroup with humanity in order to change the perceptions of the dominant class. Putting aside the error that incarceration is not a universal, or that the reality of the capitalist media market is that a TV show's life span depends upon its audience size and marketability, while Fontana may indeed have the best of intentions, the representation he offers is not able to transcend the political and social context. Film theorists suggest that for images to be politically effective, the representation needs to align with the prior knowledge an audience possesses about the subject. Ethnographic film theorist Cowrie writes that unless the representation conforms to the expectations of the audience, it will be judged to be unrealistic.

> But the mise-en-scene and its social actors will appear to be unrealistic if they do not confirm or conform to the expectations of the viewers. The poor, for example, must appear property poor in whatever way an audience may currently recognize poverty. Reality—such is the reality of poverty—is coded, it is read through conventionally understood signs. . . . The documentary film therefore presents the knowable world not only or necessarily in order to enable us to know the world as the new, but also—and perhaps more often—to know the world as familiar, to find again our known objects. (Cowrie, 1999, 30)

Her analysis is contrary to popular public beliefs that link education or information to awareness. Representations, she argues, generally simply conform to preexisting ideas or concepts. Even if the representation challenges these constructs, audiences resist and look for the familiar. Good intentions are not good enough.

Ignorances, Absences, and Mass Media

From the post–Civil War Black Codes that essentially reworded the Slave Codes to criminalize actions such as vagrancy and possession of a firearm only when the person charged was black, to the 1994 darkening of OJ's mugshot for the cover of *Time* magazine by an all-white staff at *Time*,

U.S. policy and media (and language) criminalize race, specifically blackness (Wolff, 1994; Mann & Zatz, 1998). Stereotypes about prisons and those in prison overlap the general history of the grotesque distortions about "crime" provided by mass media, but prisons and incarceration also occupy a separate place. Despite the enormous numbers of people required to work in the prison-nation and in supporting industries, prisons are oddly erased from a national landscape. As most U.S. citizens have not been arrested, their experience with prison, or the criminal justice system, is limited. Correctional facilities are isolated from the public by their physical location, as prisons are in rural, usually predominantly white, locations—far from urban centers. Prisons, jails, and other detention centers are extremely difficult or impossible to enter, and communication to and from prisons is regulated or controlled. Whereas other public institutions such as government or schools permit access, thereby permitting the possibility of more transparency and more accountability, as many of my allies who work in prisons often joke, prisons are much easier to exit than to enter. Mass media reproduces stereotypes, as evidenced on *OZ*, in part because prisons are a public social institution that is deeply protected from public scrutiny.

This practice of active censorship and erasure is also evident in research on the people who work inside prisons. Often prison staff describe their employment in ways that attempt to rewrite the context as similar to other kinds of routine factory or business labor, or they negate the material intimacy involved in the labor. Assistant Warden Gerald Clay (as cited in Johnson, 2004) states that he organizes his entire work life, within prisons, to erase the reality that it is a prison.

> I've never really talked to anyone about how they feel when they come in the fence and in the gate and come to work and punch in. For myself, it has no effect. It has no effect at all. It is almost as though I am going into a factory. You go in and do what you've got to do, and clock out and you go home. . . . If I would allow myself to think about the sentences people were serving, then I'd be entangling myself way too much into the atmosphere; that is, the obvious atmosphere; behind the wall, or behind the fence, or behind the gate. I don't like to think of it as that; I like to think that I am walking into an executive building downtown and I'm coming in to perform a job for a company, and to perform it to the best of my ability. (Clay, in Johnson, 2004, 224–225)[2]

---

[2] Also see Conover's *Newjack* (2001), and Britton's *At Work in the Iron Cage* (2003), for similar discussions about labor in prisons.

Perhaps this is a self-defense mechanism. Clay needs to not recognize the extreme intimacy of his work with those incarcerated because naming it might make it untenable for him to continue being employed in a prison. To work inside an institution that houses so much trauma and to see and recognize the people inside as individuals with histories and families and feelings might be too much for a body to bear. Clay's response to this overwhelmingly intimate daily contact is to simply actively erase the reality of a prison and to recast what he does as a factory or a business, but this process of ignoring or stating that it has no effect reads almost like willful conjecture, especially when we know that men who work in penal institutions have higher rates of domestic violence and depression than those who work in a factory or are businessmen (Conover, 2001; Elsner, 2004). In addition, Clay's comments invite larger questions about the field of corrections. How does job proficiency for a warden get defined so that knowledge of those incarcerated is viewed as a liability?

This removal of prisons from the everyday U.S. experience means that mainstream audiences depend heavily on popular media to offer meanings and representations of prisons. Mainstream audiences require mass media to interpret these spaces and the bodies housed within. The representations offered by mass media about crime and criminals, and prisoners and prisons, are wildly inaccurate, fostering stereotypes about race and violence.

> As I walked up to the [prison gatehouse] my heart was pounding. I was anxious because I had stereotypical views of what prison was like. I have to admit that I had never been inside a prison until this trip. Many of my views came from the movies. I thought the inmates would be behaving like wild animals. I thought they would be screaming at people and that they would be banging on the bars. I also had the impression that prison would be a dangerous place for anybody to enter because all of the prisoners would be armed. I was scared to be near anyone who was convicted of a crime since so many inmates on television are portrayed as very violent. *College Student reflecting on a prison tour.* (Britton, 2003, 13)

The college student's fears about prisons and prisoners come directly from TV and movies. Those inside prisons are perceived to be "wild animals" "banging on the bars." Above all, prison would be a dangerous place. If the people inside are not dangerous, why would we need to cage them? As prisons are an institution where access is deeply regulated, few alternative media sources, or representations that challenge the dominant stereotypes about violent and crazed "felons," get to emerge.

Prisons are an "absent site," a social institution that anthropologist Rhodes argues is represented only through fetishized details or metonymy. When addressing crime, criminals, or prisons, mass media does not offer audiences an entire portrait but instead circulates similar themes and images intended to trigger feelings and beliefs: prison bars, uniforms, and violence. Stereotypical fragments of prison life are used in everyday popular culture to invoke racialized fears, and to sensationalize.

For example, in 2002 the soft drink company 7 UP ran a commercial on mainstream TV channels that suggested male prison rape that was intended to be humorous. The commercial, where the 7 UP marketers go to prison to find a captive audience for the soft drink, was pulled after two months due to protests (Elsner, 2004, 64). The commercial traded on fear of male rape, and even though this is not precisely homophobia, the use of prison rape in popular culture is a persistent "joke" intended to titillate. Sexual violence is prevalent in prisons, and is hardly a joke, but it is the prison system that shapes this violence. The 7 UP commercial not only trivializes a significant issue that has been the subject of congressional inquiry and lawsuits, but also negates the larger contexts of systemic gendered violence built into the prison system (Bell, 2006; Human Rights Watch, 2001). Sexual violence is a problem in prisons because of how prisons are constructed, not simply because of deranged and hypersexualized prisoners. In addition, numerous studies document that male officers do sexually assault women in prison, and that sexual violence from guards to incarcerated females is persistent (Amnesty International, 1999; Human Rights Watch, 1996). OZ problematically skewers this reality. For example, in one episode a sadistic female guard Claire (actor Kristin Rohde) coerces sex with incarcerated men and gets pregnant. This is hardly representative of the real issues surrounding sexual violence in prisons.

The saturation of representations of violence in mainstream media, coupled with this "absence" of representations of the realities of life for those in prison—save the metonymic—may function to also create prisons as a kind of "abstract" site.

> Looming cellblocks, stone faced guards, dangerous and deranged felons: these tropes tell us in advance what to expect of prison. Allen Feldman writes of what he calls "cultural anesthesia": the fact that we are bombarded with images representing all kinds of violence but are also able, by means of these same images, to evade the disturbing physicality and immediacy of violence itself. Many aspects of the contemporary representation of crime and punishment carry the danger of this kind of anesthesia. One consequence is that prison becomes an "abstract site" in the public imagination precisely through the fetishization of its concrete details. (Rhodes, 2004, 8)

This absence and abstraction means that the public depends on mainstream media to supply information about prisons, and those within prisons, yet simultaneously the media offers audiences very particular images and tools to interpret these events. Abstract images frequently circulated on TV news shows during stories that refer to crime, such as the cell block, handcuffs, the "perp" walk, or the high fence or the fortress-like walls, are intended to signify for audiences the prison and the state of incarceration yet they convey little of value. Rhodes uses the word tropes, or words that are simply weighted signifiers, to describe how the prison is signified for the mainstream, and I argue that mass media reproduces these tropes shaping "commonsense" understandings about crime and prisons.

From *COPS* to *Law & Order, CSI,* and *Court TV,* popular culture participates in the construction of public consciousness. Rapping, in *Law and Justice as Seen on TV,* writes that mass media has "chosen crime as the issue and criminals as the enemy against whom we as Americans can most readily and passionately unite against" (Rapping, 2003, 264). By manipulating audiences, mainstream media works to create and define "crime" and to represent the "common sense" about who we should fear. The techniques used are obvious and effective:

> Among these are the construction of criminal stereotypes; presentation of opinion as fact; masking of opinion by seeking out expert sources who will agree with their preformed opinions; use of value loaded terminology; selective presentation of fact; management of information through framing and editing techniques; and vague references to an unnamed official or "those close to criminal justice theories and policies." As a result, many Americans support the "War on Crime" with passion. They are determined to keep themselves safe in what they perceived as a social landscape filled with mass murderers run amok, with teenage "superpredators," and with murder and mayhem around every corner. In reality, statistics show a dramatically declining crime rate. (Rapping, 2003, 72–73)

Mass media plays a significant role in supporting a public culture of racialized fear. This fear is central, as Rapping notes, because it is used to support public policies, or more conservatively, this fear is needed to maintain an active public indifference or ignorance around the establishment of regressive and punitive policies and laws. These representations also have wider consequences as they shape mainstream understandings about our justice system and its role in society. Typically, mainstream shows advance discourses around victim's rights that naturalize the role of prisons and incarceration, and solidify frameworks about innocence and evil, victim and perpetrator, that do nothing to address the violence of the crime, or the realities of those impacted.

In particular, the use of "victim" and "perpetrator" with seemingly conflicting interests has bled into our legal (and popular) conceptions of justice. Mainstream U.S. culture is unable to see these two categories "victim" and "perpetrator" as anything other than in direct opposition, and these terms function to cloak histories, conditions, and contexts. "Victim" and "perpetrator" categories function to erase or significantly limit important possibilities for other ways for those impacted by violence to heal or address their trauma, and also limit the ways that those who perpetrate crime can change. Often the entrenchment of these categories, and the associations built up around them, makes it extremely difficult for those impacted by violence to enact other forms of justice and healing. The opposition inherent in these categories of perpetrator and victim also mitigates against more complex, and possibly more effective, modes of restorative justice. "We have evolved a public discourse where paying attention to these situations [incarceration] is taken as a sign of indifference to the suffering of those who have been harmed by others and of lack of common sense in the face of obvious social dangers" (Rhodes, 2004, 6). Mass media shapes what the public considers to be commonsense ideas: victims need closure, and a trial (or sentencing or an execution) is an important form of healing, foreclosing on other options. As an advocate for those in prisons, Michael Marcum, one of the starters of the Bay Area restorative justice program, *Resolve to Stop the Violence Program* (RSVP), notes, it is imperative for those interested in progressive and radical changes in the PIC to engage with these discourses of victim's rights. Marcus observes that "victims" can be important allies in struggles for change (Marcum as cited in Chevigny, 2000). It is important to investigate how the mass media solidifies these constructs, victim and perpetrator, and to work to supply and communicate alternative models of reconciliation.

Yet, it is too simplistic to blame mass media. I argue that the expansion of the PIC requires not just a mass media that reproduces commonsense ideas about crime but a corresponding persistent, willful, public ignorance; a public that asks few questions about incarceration.

Systems reproduce specific ways of knowing. For example, Omi and Winant illustrate how "racial rule" in the United States is reproduced through the maintenance of stereotypes and Rapping's media analysis illustrates how the representation of categories of crime is initially connected to white supremacy, I argue that we also need to investigate how ignorance is maintained. In an earlier chapter that examined the role of the profession of teacher education to participate in the school to jail pipeline, I used the concepts of the *Racial Contract* and the *epistemology of ignorance* to argue that white supremacy is the foundation of Western culture and that perhaps using "the vocabulary and apparatus already developed for contractarianism to map this unacknowledged system" (Mills, 1997, 3). The racial contract is both "obvious" because there is irrefutable historic evidence (i.e., racist tracts debating the humanity of nonwhites, miscegenation laws) and "nonobvious" because, as Mills writes, the racial contract constructs what he terms an *epistemology of ignorance*, or deliberate scaffolding to protect white folks from a material awareness of the flawed institutions, discourses, and laws created by white supremacy.

> [T]he Racial Contract prescribes for its signatories an inverted epistemology, *an epistemology of ignorance*, a particular pattern of localized and global dysfunctions (which are psychologically and socially functional), producing the ironic outcome that whites will in general be unable to understand the world they themselves have made. (Mills, 1997, 18; emphasis mine)

The epistemology of ignorance shapes whites to be "cognitively impaired," that is, kept from knowing the effects of the white supremacy they themselves have constructed.

A fundamental tenet of the Racial Contract is a kind of *collusion, naturalization,* a taking for granted by those who benefit that the current misallocation of resources, education, status, power, is natural or normal. The acceptance that prisons are a natural by-product of a democratic social order, that victims need the closure that only a trial or sentencing can offer, and that at least 1 in 4 black men will be housed within prisons and jails; this is *common sense* and a kind of willful persistent ignorance that certain communities and individuals can afford to possess. How prisons are portrayed in popular media and, sometimes, in activist or academic spaces, myself included, frequently erases not just the centrality of race, but any recognition of the state's ongoing commitment to white supremacy. Language is of course a limitation, and terms such as deindustrialization, and policies such as Temporary Aid to Needy Families, both function adequately and often to deracialize what are highly racialized systems and practices. "Death penalty" does not conjure up genealogies of lynching. Mills argues that this story of *white* ignorance is an old one in the United States.

In *The Epistemology of the Closet*, Sedgewick also highlights that ignorance is the result of a particular education, and that active schooling in ignorance is central to modern Western cultures. For example, a man who rapes a woman can claim that he did not know that she did not want to have sex, and that the US Justice Department ruled that ignorance of the facts related to HIV transmission is an adequate defense for employers who fired employees because of their HIV status (Sedgewick, 7, 1990). Many mechanisms are required to manage, activate and maintain particular ignorances. Sedgewick also warns against invoking simply ignorance, "from which the heroics of human cognition can occasionally wrestle facts, insights, progress" as ignorance too frequently makes it appear that simple education can be a remedy (1990, 7).

My emphasis on these concepts of the Racial Contract and ignorance is that it was not merely profit or the state that pushed the expansion of prisons, or deindustrialization, or larger shifts in the health and welfare state, or the persistent erasure of prisons from our mass media and our public landscape outlined in earlier Chapters. Rather, white supremacy, and a corresponding willful public ignorance, has been and continues to be inextricably connected to each of these shifts. Changes in welfare from a human right to a perk required the image of the "lazy black mother," even though rates of welfare use at every socioeconomic level are relatively consistent across racial categories (Quadagno, 1994; Zuchino, 1999), and the expansion of the punitive arm "tough on crime" of the state requires a racialized fear. Or, to rephrase Mills's ideas for this context, who talks about prisons, the exponential growth in prison expansion, and how do they talk about it?

> One could say then, as a general rule, that *white misunderstanding, misrepresentation, evasion, and self deception on matters related to race* are among the most pervasive mental phenomena of the past few hundred years, a cognitive and moral economy psychically required for conquest, colonization, and enslavement. And these phenomena are in no way *accidental*, but *prescribed* by the terms of the Racial Contract, which requires a certain schedule of structured blindnesses and opacities in order to establish and maintain the white polity. (Mills, 1997, 19; emphasis original)

The Contract is maintained through ignorance, a *persistent willful ignorance* about white supremacy; an ignorance that permitted the media's deeply racialized characterization of those attempting to survive after the 2005 hurricane Katrina. When the body was black and taking life necessities from a store they were named criminal looters and when the body was white they were named brave survivors. Backlash against this depiction was swift, yet media did not catch this "error" because it was not viewed as a problem. Ignorance about the structural nature of white supremacy is not arbitrary or coincidental. It is a systemic practice, exemplified in patterns of "structured white ignorance, motivated inattention, self-deception, historical amnesia, and moral rationalization" (Mills, 2003, 190).

White supremacy is reproduced as these interlocking trends that facilitated prison expansion continue to marginalize people of color, and, simultaneously, race and gender are central to the development and rationalization of these very policy initiatives.

The Racial Contract is not static. Just as whiteness "changes over time and space and is in no way a transhistorical essence" (Frankenberg, 1993, 236), the contract is constantly being rewritten and recast for shifting economic, political, and social contexts. With this analysis, *OZ* is then the commonsense successor of news media and tabloid shows that fixate on superpredators. *OZ* is simply the continued manifestation of the circulation of the same ideas of race and crime in mass media. *OZ* ushers in a new mask for these old ideas about race and crime. Perhaps *OZ* is more dangerous because of its verisimilitude, the simultaneous racialization of "whiteness" that *OZ* performs, the emasculation of rehabilitation models, and the absence of other accurate representation of incarceration. This spectacle of punishment played out on screens in living rooms and theatres across the United States has consequences that persist. Davis, in a discussion about the pleasure people still feel when watching westerns, suggests that these kinds of mass media representations permit viewers to regress.

> This racism is very much a part of the collective fantasy, the collective psyche. It invites people to slip into a certain kind of regression, a kind of infantilization, so that political positions are based more on the passive entertainment people experience rather than on informed engagement and active involvement with issues. (Davis, 2005, 127)

The white supremacist constructs, in active and legal existence in the United States for centuries, shape our nation's collective imaginations. Whether it is the old stories of "cowboys and Indians" or the new stories of, as Davis notes, "deranged criminals and weary working stiff cops and prison guards," the core racialized tropes and contexts about the legitimacy of the prison-nation go unchallenged. Whereas the previous half-century of active work to dismantle these constructs in the public sphere has resulted in limited success, the underlying fictions, stories, persist in our collective psyche. TV shows such as *OZ* resonate because, not unlike the westerns, they circulate the familiar same old stories of good, bad, and evil, where the everyday white people are flawed but inherently good, and the women are attractive backdrops or they are actively erased. These representations do not just reside in fantasies or on TV; they circulate in policies.

Rising Incarceration Rates, and Unjust Policies

With the highest incarceration rate for a western industrialized country, over two million and counting, the PIC devastates communities of color, and as the popular writer John Conover, in *New Jack*, his account of a year as a guard at Sing Sing, writes, "Incarceration, the best punishment we have been able to think up, has itself become a social problem" (2001, 18). Why such a dramatic increase in incarceration rates (and the corresponding need for prisons and extra-penal function of schools?). Crime rates have not risen significantly rather the most central factor that has influenced the phenomenal growth in the prison population in the US are public policies regarding crime. Most research on crime rates, including violent crimes, indicates, "in the 45 year period leading up to the 1970's, what is most notable is the remarkable stability of the rate of incarceration, averaging about 110 per 100,000 (excluding the jail population)" (Mauer, 1999, 16). In 2005, "there were an estimated 488 prison inmates per 100,000 U.S. residents" (Bureau of Justice Statistics, 2005). This growth in the prison (and jail) population cannot be explained by crime and victimization rates, as between 1970 and 2005, "the murder rate in 1995 was essentially the same as the rate of 8.3 per 100,000 in 1970" (Mauer, 1999, 84). Most research suggests that while there have been some fluctuations in crime rates in the last thirty-five years, the rise in the number of those incarcerated cannot be attributed to rising waves of violence, or even growth in any specific category of crime. For example, the 4,041%, leap in the number of women in Illinois's prisons for drug related crimes between 1983 and 2002 (Kane-Willis, Janichek, and Daniel, 2006, Sec 1:4), signifies not the equity theory that we *were* uncomfortable as a nation with incarcerating women and really we have caught up and applied the law equally to men and women, or that more women are committing crimes or using drugs, but changes in policy:

> Examples of drug-related and mandatory sentencing laws include New York's Rockefeller Drug Laws, Second Felony Offender Laws, Violent Felony Offender Laws, changes in Consecutive Sentence Provisions, California's Three Strikes Law, and Truth-in-Sentencing Laws. These laws were complemented by the 1994 Federal Crime Control Act. In 1991 there were over 100 federal crimes regulated by mandatory sentencing laws. By 1994 all fifty states had passed at least one such law. (Diaz-Cotto, in Sudbury, 2005, 150, fn. 18)

Rising incarceration rates are directly related to these changes in sentencing policy and laws that require stiffer penalties for those convicted of nonviolent offenses, specifically drug-related offenses, and for longer sentences for recidivism.

This is an important distinction between crime and victimization rates and incarceration as the declining crime statistics, coupled with the high numbers of those incarcerated, is also used to demonstrate the "success" of these punitive policies. Crime rates are down, or stagnant, becuase of the high numbers of those locked up. There is little research that supports these linkages that incarceration either functions as a deterrent to crime, or that punitive laws significantly decrease crime rates, or victimization rates. The majority of research concludes that the high numbers of those locked up correlates most strongly with stricter, determinate, sentencing guidelines.

> A regression analysis of the rise in the number of inmates from 1980 to 1996 concluded that one half (51.4 percent) of the increase was explained by a greater likelihood of a prison sentence upon arrest, one third (36.6 percent) by an increase in time served in prison, and just one ninth (11.5 percent) by higher offense rates (Mauer, 1999, 34).

The epidemic of incarceration does not make us safer, and it does not function as a deterrent. It is, however, expensive, and in 2002 Illinois spent $280 million just to incarcerate the 12,985 people convicted of drug offenses (Kane-Willis, Janichek, and Daniel, 2006, Sec 1:41). At approximately $21, 563 per person, that significantly more than the state allocates for higher education and K-12 education combined.

In particular, the 1986 Anti–Drug Abuse Act has dramatically impacted incarceration rates. The act introduced stiffer penalties for those convicted of drug offenses through new sentencing guidelines that included mandatory minimums, and states passed *three strikes and you are out* laws that extended sentencing for those with multiple convictions, regardless of the significance of the convictions. These policies enacted in the 1980s and 1990s translated into escalating prison populations. On October 27, 1986, President Ronald Reagan gave the following speech as he signed into law the Anti–Drug Abuse Act (ADDA):

> Well, today it gives me great pleasure to sign legislation that reflects the total commitment of the American people and their government to fight the evil of drugs. Drug use extracts a high cost on America: the cost of suffering and unhappiness, particularly among the young; the cost of lost productivity at the workplace; and the cost of drug-related crime. Drug use is too costly for us not to do everything in our power, not just to fight it but to subdue it and conquer it.

> The magnitude of today's drug problem can be traced to past unwillingness to recognize and confront this problem. And the vaccine that's going to end the epidemic is a combination of tough laws—like the one we sign today—and a dramatic change in public attitude.

We must be intolerant of drug use and drug sellers. We must be intolerant of drug use on the campus and at the workplace. We must be intolerant of drugs not because we want to punish drug users, but because we care about them and want to help them. This legislation is not intended as a means of filling our jails with drug users. What we must do as a society is identify those who use drugs, reach out to them, help them quit, and give them the support they need to live right. (Reagan, 1986)

Despite Reagan's statement, the 1986 Anti–Drug Abuse Act heralded draconian changes in policy for those with drug convictions. The consequences of the war on drugs is one of the central mechanisms propping up this incarceration-nation, and it is not simply the mandatory minimum sentences required by this law, but the postincarceration consequences that actually create intolerable living conditions for those convicted of these crimes, even after release: the civil death. Although Reagan professed to help those who use drugs and to give them the support they need to "live right," the 1986 ADAA ushered in regressive, "hateful" laws that functioned to stigmatize and to deprive those convicted of drug offenses, from personal use to trafficking, of their basic civil rights.[3] In the United States a number of restrictions were placed upon those with drug convictions that related to accessing public benefits and accessing public institutions and resources. These postincarceration policies, specifically concerning housing and social assistance benefits, actively targeted those with drug-related convictions and restricted their economic, civic, and educational possibilities.

Section 9 of the Housing Opportunity Program Extension Act of 1996 permits local public housing authorities to discriminate on the basis of drug convictions. Specifically, public housing authorities are able to evict or to deny housing to individuals because of drug use or drug convictions. Illinois applies this act to prohibit those with drug-related felonies from participating in public housing for five years. The prohibitions in most states extend beyond the use of drugs or drug-related convictions for those residing in public housing, as the law makes the occupants culpable for the drug use or convictions of all guests or visitors and ignorance is not an adequate defense (Allard, 2002; O'Brien, 2002). A 2003 Report from the General Accounting Office documents that in 13 of the largest public housing agencies in the nation, approximately 6% of 9,249 lease terminations were because of drug-related criminal activities; and 15 large public housing agencies reported that about 5% of 29,459 applications for housing were denied admission for these reasons (General Accounting

[3] I am indebted to my conversations with Leslie Bloom, and to reading her work on the consequences of federal poverty policies, for reminding me to name these laws as *hateful*.

Office, 2005). This knowledge also keeps people away from needed housing resources.

Focusing only on drug convictions and not other felonies, the federal government denies social assistance benefits to those with drug-related convictions. Section 115 of the 1996 Temporary Aid to Needy Families (TANF), a federal grant program, enacts a lifetime ban on women (and men) who have been convicted of a state or federal felony involving the use or sale of drugs (Allard, 2002, 1). States choose to "opt out" or alter this prohibition. As of March 2002, 21 states have the full ban in place. California, the state with the largest number of persons incarcerated for drug offenses, has maintained a full ban on TANF and food stamp benefits. Over 10,000 women in Illinois have been denied welfare benefits because they have a drug conviction (Allard, 2002, 1). In Illinois the Chicago Coalition for the Homeless found that 29% of the women at Cook County Jail had been denied governmental benefits (Goswani & Schervish, 2002).

In addition to these consequences, employment and licensure prohibitions, and the passage of *Termination of Parental Rights Laws*, target, directly or indirectly, those convicted of drug-related offenses. These punitive postincarceration policies and laws that specifically target those convicted of drug-related crimes, upheld in state and federal supreme courts, also exist in conjunction with multiple "informal" prohibitions. Those with a record have a difficult time securing housing or employment, outside of these formal prohibitions. Informal barriers are clearly supported by the abject legal disqualifications that are built into policies. Ritchie argues that women are "compelled to crime" because of economic and social situations, and it is no stretch to see how these policies, including the denial of postsecondary educational access, formally in place until 2006 with the refusal of benefits to those with drug-related convictions, limit women's abilities to secure respectful living wage employment. Denial of access to federal benefits ensures that those with the least amount of power will not have a safety net. It doesn't seem a stretch to see that denying benefits to someone, who is probably poor, perhaps a parent or mother, unemployed, and with a drug problem, might create an untenable environment. As Chicago-based poet and antiprison activist Pamela Thomas states, those formerly incarcerated spent the rest of their life with an X on their back, and "*What is the procedure* when you are asked to reenter a society that you were never a part of? You tell me" (Thomas, n.d.).

As identified, each of these policies plays a role in increasing jail and prison rates for women. The explicit racialization of many of the laws is well documented. For example, the 1986 Anti–Drug Abuse Act stipulates that 5 grams of crack cocaine results in a mandatory five-year sentence whereas 500 grams of powdered cocaine results in a mandatory minimum five-year sentence.

The critical difference is that crack cocaine is predominant in Black and Hispanic communities and powdered cocaine in White. Beyond this, nothing rationally justifies the great disparity in sentencing for the two variations of this substance. (Johnson, 2004, 46)

As Johnson further documents, although there is ample evidence that this law has discriminatory consequences and there is also debated evidence that this law was racially motivated, the courts have not moved to strike this law.

In addition to the regressive drug laws and policies, escalating incarceration rates are also connected to changes in other social policies. The rise of the incarceration-nation also coincides with the deinstitutionalization of mental health patients (and the reorganization of the welfare system). In 1963 the passage of the Community Mental Health Center Act (CMHCA) signified a shift in mental care policy, from the institutionalization or warehousing of the mentally ill to the use of community clinics, group homes, and pharmaceuticals. According to critics, the CMHCA was never fully funded, yet the major mental health institutions were shut down, placing most mentally ill in the streets and in poverty. In the 1990s more than 40 mental institutions were permanently closed, whereas more than 400 new prisons opened (Sentencing Project, 2002, 3). Today, the Bureau of Justice Statistics acknowledges that *the three largest de facto mental institutions in the world are Riker's Island (New York), Cook County Jail (Illinois), and Los Angeles County Jail (California)* (Elsner, 2004, 85; Sentencing Project, 2002). In Florida, the mentally ill in prisons and jails outnumber patients in state mental institutions five to one (Sentencing Project, 2002, 3). With no access to housing, the poor and mentally ill fill U.S. prisons and jails. Whereas policies and laws contribute to the escalating incarceration rates, shifts in health and welfare policies also function to criminalize those without access to housing or adequate mental healthcare services.

Our "tough on crime" framework emerged in tandem with shifts in health and welfare policies. There are several rationales for the development of the "tough on crime" or the "war on crime" rhetoric and policies that emerged in the 1960s. Nixon's "war on crime" was simply an attempt to interrupt Johnson's "war on poverty" and the civil rights agenda of the 1960s, and forefronting crime in the 1960s at a time of struggle for civil rights was a political strategy designed to mobilize white southerners to vote Republican by mobilizing their barely submerged race-based fears (Mauer & Chesney-Lind, 2002, 10). This *tough on crime* stance, a significant theme in the campaigns of Reagan and Bush I, was a prevailing bipartisan theme by the mid-1990s as many political leaders sought to persuade the public of the need for stiffer legislation to increase prison sentences for newly convicted criminals and repeat offenders. Mass media aided and abetted the "war on crime" because it made good copy.

In September 1986 alone, the *New York Times* ran 169 articles about drugs. Not surprisingly the proportion of Americans who identified drugs as the nation's number one problem climbed from 3 percent to 13 percent in 1986 and hit 65 percent by late 1989. (Elsner, 2004, 18)

Clearly correlation does not (always) mean causation, but mass media's representations of crime in the 1980s cocreated the war on drugs and legitimated drugs as a public enemy (Page, 2004; Rapping, 2003). Even though mass media and politicians circulated the fear of rising crime, public opinion polls from the mid-1980s into the 1990s suggested that the general public was in favor of academic, vocational, and substance abuse programs for those in prison and supported alternatives to incarceration. In poll after poll, even if respondents identified crime as the number one social problem in the United States, "when given policy choices the American public favors prevention over enforcement" (Mauer & Chesney-Lind, 2002, 28).

This political philosophy of being tough on crime increased costs (and demand) for prisons and jails subsequently requiring higher budgetary allocations for corrections. The 1994 Violent Crime Control and Law Enforcement Act (VCCLEA), a 6-year bipartisan initiative, represented the largest crime bill in the history of the country and provided resources for new police officers, prevention programs, and $9.7 billion in funding for prisons, *despite the reality that crime rates were dropping.* The Crime Bill provided $2.6 billion in additional funding for the Federal Bureau of Investigation, Drug Enforcement Agency, Immigration and Naturalization Services, United States Attorneys, and other Justice Department components, as well as the federal courts and the Treasury Department (U.S. Department of Justice, 1994). The VCCLEA also terminated an inmate's right to apply for Pell grants (started in 1965) to support college tuition and book fees. Politicians supported this ban by suggesting that the general public did not want their tax dollars going to support college programs for inmates, yet this finding was not supported by polling data.

Senator Kay Bailey Hutchison, a Texas Republican, introduced the ban on Pell grants for inmates into the VCCLEA. Hutchison stated: "It is not fair to the millions of parents who work and pay taxes and then must scrape and save and often borrow to finance their children's education" (Zook, 1994, A24). Even if polls were inaccurate and public sentiment regarding education programs for inmates had really shifted, which is unlikely, it is still important to note that only 1.2% of the total number of Pell grants were ever awarded to inmates (Taylor, 1993) and that Pell grants are essentially allocated on the basis of entitlement—all who are eligible are entitled. The conflict that Senator Hutchison constructs between working poor families' access to Pell grants and those in prison is not accurate. Furthermore, the subsequent erasure of Pell grants for those in prisons did not result in new nonincarcerated undergraduate students receiving any additional financial aid which is difficult to accurately track. While difficult to precisely track, the VCCLEA directly contributed to the reduction of the numbers of education programs in prison from over 200 in 1993 to 8 in 2003 (Fine et al., 2001), and by 1995 342 of the nations' 350 college programs were shut down (Eggers et al., 2005, 132).

Public Enemies

Clearly public policy regarding prisons in the 1990s does not correlate with research findings. For example, how does the elimination of education programs from prisons control violent crime? Research consistently documents that education reduces re-incarceration, as the more education those in prison receive, the lower the recidivism rates. Postsecondary education, in particular, has the highest rate of reducing recidivism (Batiuk, 1997; Fine et al., 2001; Taylor, 1992). Research also documents that those in prison clearly need education. Of those in prison 40% are functionally illiterate, meaning they would be unable to write a letter explaining a billing error, compared to 21% of the adult population in the United States that is functionally illiterate. Postsecondary correctional education alone would produce net national savings of hundreds of millions of dollars per year (Cypser, 1997; Lochner & Moreti, 2004; Kane-Willis, Janichek, and Daniel, 2006). In 2002, if postsecondary programs were offered to those incarcerated, Illinois would have saved "between $11.8 million and $47.3 million" from the reduced recidivism rates (Kane-Willis et al., 2006, Sec. 1:4). Research also indicates that educational programs in prisons facilitate stability inside the prison (Fine et al., 2001). Betty Tyson, falsely convicted of murder by an all-white jury in the 1970s, who is now released, describes the need for meaningful programs in prisons and the shifts in these programs over time. Before her release, Tyson was the longest serving female in prison in the state of New York.

> Things change in there over time. The program offerings were depleted from twenty vocational programs to about five. Vocational programs help people learn skills that they need once they leave prison; they help rehabilitate prisoners. The programs just kept getting cut. We would learn a skill and then work for a quarter a day. Taxpayers want to punish us, but what we really need are prisons that rehabilitate prisoners, teach them a skill and help them deal with their problems. (Tyson, in Johnson, 2004, 166)

The elimination of meaningful education programs does not contribute to the reduction of public fear of violence or make society safer or better. As Tyson suggests, it probably has inverse impacts, and actually increases the probability that those released will resort to crime to survive. I am careful here not to suggest that education is an inherent good, because as documented in earlier chapters, and as the youth who started this movement accurately named, formal state-organized education also functions to prepare bodies for prison (Acey, 2000). Yet, without any access to education, little change is possible.

Hutchison's argument utilizes familiar tropes. If, as previously discussed, the equivocation of race and crime is a too-familiar U.S. story, an equally popular public myth is the lazy and undeserving man and woman who siphon resources as "welfare queens" to continually thwart the working class man's economic mobility. In his persuasive article "Eliminating the Enemy" Page argues that this trope is simply being extended, for new audiences, in discourses that circulate about the eradication of the Pell grants for those in prison. Page argues that the tough on crime rhetoric, including the elimination of the Pell grant, functions as a way for politicians to indicate solidarity with white working class families without actually doing anything to improve their economic or social problems.

> The legislators framed the Pell grant issue in a way that allowed them to show politically valuable audiences that they felt their pain, worked to improve their plights and struggled to ward off their enemies (in this case prisoners). In other words, the politicians took the opportunity to accumulate political capital by speaking to (at times in coded language) voters' fears, prejudices, desires, and anxieties. (Page, 2004, 374)

Politicians such as Senator Hutchison (and former presidents Reagan and Bush) utilize the absence of media representations about prison, and the metonymic images of prison with their coded racialized fears, to exploit already existing tropes about crime (and race). When we consider that fears and beliefs about crime are represented in a mass media that disproportionately represents crime as "street" crime, not the "white collar crime" that has a deeper financial impact on our lives, and circulates images of violent criminals when we are most likely to be assaulted by someone *in our life* and of our own race, the relative public indifference to the "tough on crime" policies is easier to understand.

Scapegoating, as discussed in the previous chapter, is an old story, and mass media makes the process simpler as it ideologically trafficks racialized images and beliefs about career criminals, welfare queens, and illegal aliens to deflect attention away from economic shifts.

> To hear Reagan tell it, the problems faced by white workers did not derive from corporate greed for even greater profits, from deindustrialization and the "down-sizing" of workforces; rather their troubles emanated from the welfare state, which expropriated the taxes of the productive citizens who "played by the rules" and "went to work each

day" in order to subsidize unproductive and parasitic welfare queens and career criminals "who didn't want to work." (Winant, 2004, 181)

Hutchison utilizes the tropes, as did Reagan in the 1980s, that position people of color both as scapegoats for larger economic tensions and as signifiers for a deeply held and persistent fears. In particular, by emphasizing the dangerous criminals, the sociopaths, who will never benefit from rehabilitation, the TV show *OZ* functions to justify the necessity of the expansion of supermax institutions. Through the depiction of the deranged sociopathic felon, *OZ* supports the need for containment. *OZ* functions, then, to erase the reality; those in prison are poor, deeply undereducated, and frequently victims of violence themselves. Supermax institutions do not make "us" any safer.

Ironically, new TV shows such as *Prison Break,* which premiered in 2005 on the FOX TV station, representing the struggles of two "innocent" brothers to break out of a maximum security prison, also reinforces mainstream beliefs that prisons are required social institutions to house the dangerous.[4] By emphasizing that there really are "innocent" (white) men behind bars, *Prison Break* again negates reality that the general conditions in prison are unjust, in order to characterize the innocence of the two brothers, a context of guilt is required.[5] *Prison Break* does little to educate viewers about the reality of life in prison. The central white and sympathetic male characters are really innocent, meriting our support and affect, yet they are surrounded by the hapless, the deranged, and the really guilty.[6] These mass media products reflect the popular sentiment that the justice system is flawed and catches "innocent" people unjustly in its net, but not that the justice system is *too flawed*, or too racist or sexist. These inaccurate representations of prison life found in *OZ* and *Prison Break,* which trade on historic tropes about race and crime, coupled with the

---

[4] Also the short-lived 2006 ABC TV drama *InJustice*, where a team of lawyers from the National Justice Project take on the case of a wrongly convicted man.

[5] Chapter 5 (and more specifically chapter 6) take up this discussion about innocence.

[6] As the *Prison Break* show was filmed in Joliet, Illinois, there was significant press coverage about this series. Shaena Fazal, colleague, staff member of the John Howard Association, and Soros Fellow, and I wrote a letter to the *Chicago Tribune* in an attempt to challenge the way the show was being interpreted in the press and to highlight just some of the factual inaccuracies in the premier episode: "On Monday night the new FOX TV show *Prison Break* debuted. While it is receiving rave reviews across the nation, critics have commented that it is somewhat implausible. For example, in Illinois two brothers would never live together in the same prison, it is prohibited, and it would be highly unlikely that a judge would grant a convicted defendant's request to be incarcerated in the institution he selects. And, unlike *Prison Break*, death row inmates (and lifers) in Illinois are ineligible to work in correctional industries, and are not allowed conjugal visits. There is nothing wrong with entertaining fiction about prisons, but we shouldn't ignore the reality of our penal system" (Fazal & Meiners, 2005).

absence of real stories of life in prison, make it easier for politicians such as Hutchison as for Reagan to politically benefit by trading on public beliefs about the righteousness of law (and that law is order), and that criminals deserve their just desserts.

Ironically, a real story might economically benefit the somewhat mythic audience that Hutchison is pitching to, as their "enemy" is not the criminal, mothers in workfare, not welfare, programs, or those working without documentation in the United States. As previously discussed, this production of the criminalization of the urban poor youth shifts focus and resources away from state institutions, such as public education. The construction of supermax institutions in the 1990s translates into fewer resources and less of a state focus on other public institutions. Winant argues that these policies and practices deeply impact all communities:

> Neoconservative scapegoating thus has perverse consequences for many whites as well as for racially defined minorities. It holds down white income level and props up unemployment. It stigmatizes women and gays, white as well as non-white. And despite its "color-blind" façade, it depends on rigid concepts of racial, gender and sexual identities that accord less and less with the authoritarian and repressive morality (Republican "family values") it seeks to enforce. (Winant, 2004, 185)

While I do not disagree that white supremacy negatively impacts white people, this message is not proliferating. Going to all-white schools, living in predominantly white communities, practicing faith in predominantly all-white religious organizations, socializing in predominantly all-white friendship networks, is not flagged as problematic or a deficiency for the majority of white people. "We do not question the fact—it does not strike us as a *political* fact—that race is the most important shaper of white's lifeworlds" (Mills, 2003, 170). Consider, for example, the eerily and persistently white world of the smash TV show *Friends* that epitomized the 1990s. *Friends* was remarkable for its all-white cast including almost all of the guests on the TV show. Particularly, *Friends* was stunning for its studied erasure of blackness, despite being set in a nonwhite city, New York. The whiteness of *Friends* received some note, but it still remained a wildly popular series. This artificially white world went largely unremarked in mainstream media, in part, I argue, because the vast majority of white viewers also live and go to school in predominantly all-white environments that are not seen as *de jure* segregation, or as a political fact, or as an earlier chapter discussed, a kind of "cognitive handicap." These all-white environments are not seen as negative, or even as artificial. Winant's point is well taken; however, whites clearly are negatively impacted by these scapegoating strategies, and there is little uptake on the message that whites are cognitively arrested by the practices of white supremacy.

Even the obvious strategy of the spiraling economic cost does not motivate a widespread investigation of this production of enemies. How do whites, working poor and otherwise, benefit from the seeming withdrawal from one institutional structure that they benefit from, public education, and the augmentation of another institution that they do not, prisons? Even the promise of prisons as economic development for rural communities, decimated by the demise of family farms through agribusiness, the eradication of small-town business and retail districts through the saturation of big-box stores, and more, is false, as discussed in the previous chapter. Fine writes in her meaningful study of white working class men's self-understanding that this construct of the public enemy becomes crucial to how they understand their own white identity:

> African-American men . . . are discursively imported to buffer the pain, protest the loss, and still secure the artificial privilege of whiteness. Occluded are the macrostructures that have forced white working class men out of the labor market and into an obsession with Black men, affirmative action, and welfare. (Fine et al., 1997, 62–63)

Regressive prison policies that enhance the incarceration-nation and the school to jail pipeline are made possible through the persistence of the ignorance that is, ironically, central to maintaining white supremacy. The persistence of white working class communities electing not to align themselves with communities of color, but instead with actions and decisions that actually harm or decrease their social or economic options in order to preserve white supremacy, is another all too familiar story in the United States. "[W]hite workers, preferring incorporation into white domination, even as junior partners, to joining a transracial struggle that might endanger their privileged status" (Mills, 2003, 169).

Through mainstream representations that erase class solidarity or histories of working class and labor movements, or that fetishize socioeconomic status, popular culture does not equip viewers to understand the historic and complex intersections between race and class (and gender). By simplistically offering one-dimensional portrayals of either race or class (*The Cosby Show, Roseanne*), popular culture does not represent the *slim* history of solidarity across race that has been enacted (Alper & Leistyna, 2005). With these representations that associate blackness and otherness with crime and degeneracy, except in exceptional situations that are decontexualized from everyday life, and through the naturalization of predominantly white lifeworlds, mass media works to solidify ideas that cross-racial alliances are unthinkable, undoable, and distasteful. When audiences are not equipped to analyze and deconstruct the representations available, and mass media consolidation means that few messages are available, save those that support consumption or dominate values, conforming representations can translate into conforming ideologies. The public are not all cultural dupes, it's just that media matters.

I am mindful that the frame of ignorance has its limitations. Clearly, one of the unintended by-products of such a relentless focus on the management of ignorance is the possible reification of the construct of knowledge, and the unwitting assumption that simply more education would alleviate the problem of ignorance.

> Inarguably, there is a satisfaction in dwelling on the degree to which the power of enemies over us is implicated, not in their command of knowledge, but precisely in their ignorance. The effect is a real one, but it carries dangers with it as well. The chief of these dangers is the scornful, the fearful, or patheticizing reification of "ignorance"; it goes with the unexamined Enlightenment assumptions by which the labeling of particular force as "ignorance" seems to place it unappealingly in a demonized space on never quite explicit ethical schema. (Sedgwick, 1990, 7)

This discussion of ignorance is not intended to generate this monolithic construct of ignorance that will or can be cured with a good dose of reliable knowledge exercised by intrepid humans, but is rather intended to focus on how these very particular ignorances, surrounding race and crime, or related to whiteness, heteronormativity, and education, shift and are recast in new socioeconomic contexts, and actively "correspond to particular knowledges and circulate as part of particular regimes of truth" (Sedgwick, 1990, 8).

Conclusion

Using the HBO TV series *OZ* as an example, this chapter shows how mass media consolidates and frames readings of crime and incarceration and advances an epistemology of (racialized) ignorance. For those interested in radical prison abolition initiatives and material reforms to the schooling and prison system, change may require strategically capturing the imagination and the affect of mainstream U.S. audiences. Good intentions are not enough. Structured intimate experiences seem to be key to understanding and becoming less "cognitively impaired." As Roland, incarcerated in a supermax institution, writes about the inhumanity of these facilities, "I don't know if you can get your point across except by bringing the public in and sticking them in one of those little cages for a week or two" (Roland, in Rhodes, 2004, 1).

Educators must decipher with and for themselves and students the representations that mass media offers, but also continuously pay attention to how, precisely, mass media works to scaffold regressive agendas of the state. Teacher education programs must do more than enable educators to acquire technological proficiency or to create learning environments for K–12 students to be equally proficient. Media literacy means the ability to deconstruct the meanings and histories behind representations, and the consequences of these images and recycled tropes in particular economic contexts. Youth, a shifting and invented category, is also a lucrative demographic, which cannot afford to not possess an analysis of how mass media is used to facilitate the movement between schools and jails.

> While youth continue to represent "fun" and pleasure in the advertisement text, and while self- and group identity are increasingly tied up in those interpellations of "youth" in a changing global economy, North American youth straddle a contradictory space. They are contingent consumers, in general one of the most materially blessed generations in human history, but for whose economic decline looms as a real threat as they prepare to enter a shrinking job market. (Hoechsmann, 2004, 112)

Whereas I may disagree that this is really the most materially beneficial generation, I concur that economic shifts in Canada and the United States mean that youth are, as always, also being prepared through public institutions such as school to participate unequally in the economic sphere. Equipping youth to make media and to deconstruct media offers not only tangible skills but also needed media literacy. These sites of media production by and for youth are hard to sustain in institutions, as Hoechsmann's work documents.

Mass media functions to smooth the movement of youth from schools to jails by offering persuasive representations of those incarcerated as biologically determined to be violent. These compelling fictions exist in collusion with skewed data that suggest an increase in youth violence, and with representations that erase the economic and schooling contexts of undereducation, underemployment, and punitive surveillance structures. This mass media landscape combines in an attempt to produce the outcome that some of us just need to be contained. OZ shepherds in new versions of an old story about race, crime, and media. In a decade of rampant supermax construction, an entertaining mass media product that justifies this institution is no surprise.

Beyond naturalizing the inevitability of prisons and jails, or reflecting the values embedded in mass media, schools explicitly traffic in central concepts that legitimate the expansion of the PIC. Schools works to naturalize practices outside of everyday life inside the classroom. Anyon, in her work studying classrooms in different socioeconomic communities, documented differences in teaching styles and strategies, evaluation methods, curriculum, disciplinary mechanisms, and more. Each of these cognitive and behavior practices prepares students in different socioeconomic schools to possess unequal possible relationships to physical and symbolic capital, to leadership and to authority, and to the labor market (Anyon, 1980). Whereas Anyon suggests that, "hidden" inside schools, curriculum and pedagogy are mechanisms of economic and social reproduction, the inverse is also the case. Schools hide how their very foundational concepts, "the child" or "knowledge," are deeply interconnected to wider systems, notably capitalism, patriarchy, and white supremacy. Anyon documents that the "hidden curriculum" is the cognitive and behavioral skills that schools distribute and that are deeply stratified by race and class and gender; nevertheless, as I argue, school- and schooling-based discourses also cloak precisely how the artifacts central to schooling are intimately linked to larger political forces. Schools, daily, deal in ideologies to support the creation of public enemies.

In the previous chapters I outlined forces that shape the relationships between the prisons and education, emphasizing both the deconstruction of in-school policies and practices, such as school discipline, and linking mass media and prison policy to progressive educational change. The subsequent two chapters use the analysis provided by these first three chapters, an overview of the school to jail nexus, a discussion of shifting economic landscapes, and the role of mass media to support these shifts, to investigate the PIC's relationship to education from other vantage points. Chapter 4 illustrates how schools naturalize the construction of select children as vulnerable and in need of protection, and therefore requiring to increase in the PIC, and how schools minimize or erase more statistically "real" dangers to reproduce other fears that legitimate the expansion of the PIC. Chapter 5 outlines how schools participate in the privatization of public issues through naming and shaping experience.

CHAPTER 4

Awful Acts and the Trouble With Normal

I arrive at school on the evening of November 8, 2005, at 7 p.m. and Michael is pacing madly. A white guy with colorful arm tattoos and a speech impediment and a slight southern accent, Michael is the janitor in the building that houses the high school where I teach. For the last year, I have talked to him for a few minutes every night—the weather, the traffic, the photocopier—or I admonish him not to listen to the homophobic radio call-in show that is always on in the background. He says he likes the music. I have taken to random, firm, and polite weekly counterresponses to try to move him from the "god hates fags" spot on the radio dial.

Today, he is pacing. He is having serious housing problems. He blurts out to me that he moved over the weekend and can't get registered as an SO and his 10 days are up. He talks a mile a minute and trips over his words and repeats himself. I am barely tracking the conversation, but I can see it is important to him so I stop and ask him to slow down for me. He tells me that he had to move from his apartment as there were too many registered sex offenders in the neighborhood and he has not been able to get in contact with his parole officer so he is not compliant with the regulations that require him to register within 10 days.

I know too many women in my life who have been assaulted by men. I resent that he shows no shame or hesitation in telling me this and my first response is to tell him to fuck off and good riddance, and to walk away. I mumble something neutral—and walk up the three flights to the classroom.

This conversation changes how I act and think about Michael. This conversation moves through my head for weeks. Even though I have worked with men who are sex offenders through a number of programs, I work to never recognize this fact. I avoid Michael—no chitchat about the antigay radio station—but he continues to be present, mumbling about his housing issues.

I know that the state actively produces criminal justice policies that have little to do with safety, and as a nascent prison abolitionist, I am suspicious of any response to violence that is simply punitive. Interrogating how fear is produced and exploring the sites that augment and cement this fear is imperative. Michael moves me to examine awful acts or "real bad people" and the limits of my compassion.

In 1996, a national sex offender registry was established to coordinate all the state registry systems that emerged in the 1990s. The national registry system of sex offenders, easily accessible online, resulted in the circulation of information about known sexual offenders in neighborhoods across the United States. Even though the majority of all assaults on children are perpetrated by acquaintances or family, not strangers, the popularity of these registries grew during the 1990s. Civil commitment laws upheld by the Supreme Court in a 2005 and passed in as dozen states by 2006, aim to geographically detain and segregate certain categories of sex offenders, *indefinitely*, after release (Feuer, 2005; Ferak, 2006; Medina, 2006). Although the violence enacted by those convicted (or not) of assaults is horrific, I am deeply suspicious of the state's moves to sequester and stigmatize *any* population in the name of the safety and the innocence of specific groups of children, and by default some women who benefit from the protection of the state if they possess the central characteristic of the child, innocence.

This chapter offers a preliminary discussion on registries for those convicted of sexual offenses and how these policies emerged in an era characterized by a moral panic surrounding (white) children and youth and (hetero)sexuality. In addition, these registries require and subsequently produce specific meanings of the child. Organized into four sections, this chapter examines the efficacy of the policies that have been implemented and how schools contribute to this naturalization of public enemies through a reification of the category "child", which requires surveillance and protection, and through explicitly legitimating particular discourses about risk and fear. The first part is a summary of the current laws, a brief discussion of sex offender classifications and registries and an overview of statistics that outline victim/perpetrator profiles, and place these discussions in the public sphere. Part two shifts to discuss the concept of childhood, specifically, to look at our anxieties about the racialized constructs of gender and innocence within the construct of the child. Part three examines the histories of these registries, and schooling's commitment to heteropatriarchy, and looks at the relationship between sexual deviance, the law, and constructions of normalcy. With part four, I conclude by returning to the theme of this book, the production of public enemies. How might mainstream educational discourse be complicit in the reproduction of discourses, a kind of soft extension of the prison-nation, that reify these constructs and assist in the production of public enemies?

I write this chapter with much trepidation. I know many girls and women who have been physically and emotionally assaulted by men—fathers, uncles, acquaintances, boyfriends, coaches, husbands, and a few by strangers. I have worked with more women (in bars, universities, fast-food restaurants) than I can count who have disclosed histories of male violence. These disclosures happen in student writings, in classroom discussions, in hallway conversations, during smoke and lunch breaks, and more. These disclosures are calculated and casual and disjointed and sometimes surprise the speaker. I have no doubt that male violence is an everyday reality in the lives of women and girls.

Through problematizing sex offender registries in this chapter it is not my intent to minimize this persistent, pervasive violence either through valorizing or creating sympathy for the perpetrators, or by challenging the limited efforts of the state to actually care or to do something about violence against children and women in our communities. Rather, I note that through laws, allocation of rights, and more, the state has valued the lives and the innocence of specific children and women more highly. For example, I lived in the Strathcona neighborhood on the East Side of Vancouver during the late 1990s where more than two dozen female sex-trade workers, many under 21 years old and First-Nations, disappeared. The police's nonresponse during this time period indicated that the state perceived these individuals not to be girls or children, but disposable women who did not merit the full protection, *or* interest of the state. If any violence occurred to these women, they were partially culpable. They were not innocent. They were certainly not presented by mass media or the police as *children* (Travis, 2006).

It is hardly news that the state has typically enacted or interpreted laws and policies to protect the purity of white women because white women's bodies are central to the very idea of a nation-state. From access to reproductive rights for white women that depends on the sterilization of women of color and on the premise of their sexual unfitness and immorality, to miscegenation laws that protect the constructed category of whiteness through the criminalization of "interracial" marriage and sexual acts, to the lynching of black men to preserve the safety and the racial purity of white women, the innocence of white women is enshrined in policies and into the very conception of the nation-state itself (Frankenberg, 1993; Silliman & Bhattacharjee, 2002; A. Smith, 2005). Reproduction and sexual identity is closely tied to the nation-state, and perhaps when empires are in decline, female sexuality and reproduction need to be regulated. As social demographers Castles and Davidson write, "The control of female sexuality and reproduction is crucial to nationalism. If women are signifiers of community, access to their bodies is a key aspect of ethnic closure" (2000, 122).[1] Smith argues that in this framework "women of color become particularly dangerous to the world order as they have the ability to reproduce the next generation of communities of color" (A. Smith, in Silliman & Bhattacharjee, 2002, 123). Because of this ongoing history, I am perennially suspicious of what the state establishes to protect the innocence and the safety of (white) children and women.

By exploring the establishment of these sex offender registries I aim to consider the following questions: Whose interests does the state protect through these laws? What kinds of violence against women and girls is prioritized and targeted stranger assaults, and what kinds of violence against women and girls are negated and obfuscated violence in the family and home? What constructions of women and children are created? What meanings about childhood and families are reproduced through these policies? Who becomes a public enemy or who is safe? In addition, although these registries are not constructed to target queers, any discussion of "sexual offenses" in the United States cannot be examined in isolation of larger discussions about deviance and purity, and natural and unnatural sexual practices and families, artificial categories that schools and curriculum have attempted to render natural.

Perhaps for some, this discussion may appear out of the realm of a book project geared toward educators. What do sex offender registries have to do with schools? And what is the connection to the expanding prison-nation? Clearly there are surface responses to this question that should be clear motivators: schools are physical spaces that feature prominently in sex offender registries, school-based personnel must screen and do back-

---

[1] "Women are not only the biological reproducers of an ethnic group, but also the 'cultural carriers' who have a key role in passing on the language and cultural symbols to the young. In nationalist discourses, women often serve as the symbolic embodiment of national unity and distinctiveness. They nurture and support the warrior citizens (invariably seen as male). In defeat and suffering, the nation is portrayed as a woman in danger (implicitly of penetration or rape by the Other), or as a mother who has lost her sons in battle. Women embody the nation, while men represent it politically and militarily. (Castles & Davidson, 2000, 121).

ground checks on all employees, and so on. But beyond these pragmatic responses, there are two additional compelling reasons to investigate sex offender registries. First, school-based discourses participate in the naturalization and the construction of particular meanings about children, and these constructs of the natural child (and the family) are used to justify and require the expansion of the PIC. Tougher sex offender laws and more punitive policies are required because select children are vulnerable and "at risk." The very definition of the "child" that schools advance requires increasing surveillance and protection, hence justifying the expansion of the PIC.

Furthermore, schools legitimate constructions of risk. Schools reproduce the fear of strangers ("stranger danger"), and minimize or even erase the reality that the garden-variety everyday heteropatriarchy is just about the most violent, risky context for children. In this book project that is examining the production of public enemies and how education is interconnected to the PIC, arguably a significant danger for youth is sex offenders. This is a legitimate fear, but a quick look at the statistics surrounding violence against children or youth indicates that it is not the largest risk. By deconstructing categories of both sex offender and the child in this chapter I explore not just the facts behind these categories but what these fears shield. These registries offer a moment to examine the PIC's relationship to education from a new vantage point and to document how schools function to normalize categories. Registries are used to create new tentacles of punitive state surveillance for the PIC, and show how schools actively collude with the state to manufacture fears that cloak "real" dangers. This exploration might enable different conversations about how to respond to violence against children and might even move "us," in schools, to examine our complicity in reproducing discourses about the child or the family that actually contribute to violence.

Registries and Public Discourses of Safety

The move in the 1990s to create a national system of tracking sex offenders and to provide the public with data about those convicted of sex offenses was a direct response to two violent and high profile child abductions and assaults of young white girls—the 1993 murder of 12-year-old Polly Klaas, and the 1994 murder of 7-year-old Megan Kanka. Repeat offenders, men who had a history of convictions for violent sexual crimes, killed both girls. Parents, specifically the mothers of both girls, organized to establish a national system of tracking those who have been convicted of sexual crimes, which was readily accessible to any community.

Prior to 1996, most states did have their own registries in place, but states could not easily communicate this information to each other because there was not a national registry. In an order dated June 25, 1996, President Clinton directed Attorney General Janet Reno to develop a plan for a national sex offender registry by August 1996; this was called *The Pam Lychner Sexual Offender Tracking and Identification Act*. The attorney general insisted that the Department of Justice would work together with the Federal Bureau of Investigation, which would maintain and operate the registry (Federal Bureau of Investigation, 2006). The National Sex Offender Registry (NSOR) is public and contains the following information about those convicted: Name, Date of Birth, Height, Weight, Race, Sex, Address, City, Zip Code, State, Victim Age(s), Crimes Committed, and a Photo (U.S. Department of Justice, 2006). In Illinois, the Illinois State Police Web site describes the intent of the registry as follows:

> The Sex Offender was created in response to the Illinois Legislature's determination to facilitate access to publicly available information about persons convicted of sex offenses. ISP has not considered or assessed the specific risk of re-offense with regard to any individual prior to his or her inclusion on this Registry and has made no determination that any individual included in the Registry is currently dangerous. Individuals included on the Regisry are included solely by virtue of their conviction record and Illinois state law. The primary purpose of providing this information is to make the information easily available and accessible, not to warn about any specific individuals. . . . ISP updates this information regularly in an effort to assure that the information on the Registry is complete and accurate; however, ISP makes no representation, express or implied, that the information contained on the Registry is accurate. . . . The information contained on this site does not imply listed individuals will commit a specific type of crime in the future, nor does it imply that if a future crime is committed by a listed individual what the nature of that crime may be. ISP makes no representation as to any offender's likelihood of re-offending. (Illinois State Police, Sex Offender Registry, 2006)

As of 2006, registration is required for those designated sex offender, sexual predator, and sexually dangerous. These are escalating categories and the frequency of convictions and severity (under the criminal code) of the acts impacts the designations. The classification of sex offender encompasses felony and misdemeanor convictions that range from public indecency to aggravated criminal sexual assault (Illinois State Police, 2004).

For 10 years following release (or parole or probation) the person convicted of a sex offense must register once a year at their local law enforcement agency and have his photo taken by the law enforcement agency. If the person moves, he has 10 days to inform the local law enforcement agency. If a person travels to another state and remains for more than 10 days, he must register with local law enforcement agencies. Law enforcement agencies must verify, in person, the residence of those on the registry. When the 10 years are up, their information will be removed from the Web site. Those designated "Sexually Dangerous" or "Sexually Violent" (classifications of offenses that the criminal code designate as more severe than sex offender) must register every 90 days for the remainder of their lives. Failure to register, to provide notification of a change of address or employment, is a Class 3 Felony the first time and mandatory confinement. The offender is required to serve a minimum of seven days in the local county jail. Violation of the registry also implies a host of other consequences, for example, a monetary fine, a 10-year extension of the registration period, and revocation of parole (Federal Bureau of Investigation, 2006).

SORs specifically restrict mobility in particular public spaces where children congregate. Parks and schools feature prominently. States create their own laws pertaining to mobility, and in Illinois the restrictions are as follows:

> It is unlawful for a child sex offender to be present in any school building or property, or loiter within 500 feet of school property without the permission of the superintendent or school board, or in the case of a private school the principal unless the child sex offender is a parent of children at that school, and the parent is on school grounds for one of the following reasons: to attend a conference at the school with school personnel to discuss the progress of his or her child academically or socially; to participate in child review conferences in which evaluation and placement decisions may be made with respect to his or her child regarding special education services; to attend conferences to discuss other student issues concerning his or her child such as retention and promotion; or the offender's voting place is the school. . . . It is unlawful for a child sex offender to reside within 500 feet of a school, playground, or any facility providing programs or services exclusively directed toward people under age 18, unless they owned the property prior to July 7, 2000 (Illinois State Police, Sex Offender Frequently Asked Questions 2006).

In Iowa, the requirement is that convicted sex offenders cannot reside within 2,000 feet of schools or places where children congregate, thus

effectively prohibiting anyone from living in any urban center (Eby, 2005).[2]
Iowa foreshadows a national trend toward heightened regulations that
highlight public spaces typically associated with children, and increased
surveillance toward those convicted of sexual offenses. Through these
mobility and public space restrictions, SORs construct meanings about
what kinds of public space are dangerous for children, where children are
most at risk or vulnerable, and, by default, what kinds of spaces are safe or
risk-free public and private spaces. With 70% of all reported sexual assaults
on children occurring in the residence, usually that of the victim (Bureau
of Justice Statistics, 2000, 6), this emphasis on schools is misplaced.

Almost every state has also adopted "drug-free zones" around schools,
and as a 2006 Justice Policy Institute Report identified, these zones overwhelming "blanket" neighborhoods in urban areas; for example, "76 percent of Newark, and over half of Camden and Jersey City" (Greene et al.,
2006, 26), where predominantly people of color reside. These zones also
result in the express targeting of these communities of color by police,
and, moreover, they fail "entirely" in their function, that is, to keep drugs
away from schools (Greene et al., 2006). In addition, I would add that, by
highlighting schools, these policies, not unlike the mobility restrictions in
sex offender registries, create false perceptions of what space is "safe," or
how spaces can be made "safer."

The U.S. government endorsed the creation of sexual offender registries
because of violence against white, female children, not because of violence
against women. Registries specifically highlight activities that involve
children, for example, juvenile prostitution and child pornography, and
they do not include convictions for domestic violence, work site sexual
harassment, or racially motivated crimes against adults. The criminal code
invents and shapes what counts as crime, and values these assessments
through the classification of these offenses. Examining the kinds of convictions that require registration illustrates that these registries were created not to protect women against men, but children against predators.
Women (and even men) are occasionally included under the broad category of child.

The development of a national SOR was also a maternal movement, as
the mothers of Polly Klaas and Megan Kanka played visible and powerful
roles to establish national systems to register sex offenders for children.
This system was established as a direct result of the death of their two
daughters. Race, gender, class, age, sexual orientation, and more play a sig-

---

[2] The high profile murder and sexual assault of a 10-year-old white girl, Jetseta Gage, by
a family friend, Roger Bentley, was the impetus for these new restrictions (Gravelle,
2005).

nificant role in which stories can be used to mobilize public sentiment and policy and law changes [further discussed in the subsequent section of this chapter]. The violent murders of a range of other people, older African American women, white female sex-trade workers, transsexuals, and Latinos, also by men who had been previously convicted of sexual offenses or other crimes, rarely warrant policy changes.

As the national SOR was implemented relatively recently there is not sufficient data to track how this registry impacts recidivism. However, the Bureau of Justice Statistics (BJS) has data from a longitudinal study early in the 1990s, prior to a national registry system, that tracked those convicted of sex offenses, which offers a general portrait of recidivism rates. The Bureau of Justice reports that although convicted sex offenders are less likely than convicted non-sex offenders to be rearrested for any offense ("43 percent of sex offenders versus 68 percent of non-sex offenders"), if sex offenders reoffend, they are about "four times more likely than non-sex offenders to be arrested for another sex crime after their discharge from prison—5.3 percent of sex offenders versus 1.3 percent of non-sex offenders." The BJS further notes:

- An estimated 24% of those serving time for rape and 19% of those serving time for sexual assault had been on probation or parole at the time of the offense for which they were in a state prison in 1991.
- Of the 9,691 male sex offenders released from prisons in 15 states in 1994, 5.3% were rearrested for a new sex crime within three years of release.
- Of released sex offenders who allegedly committed another sex crime, 40% perpetrated the new offense within a year or less from their prison discharge (BJS, 2003a).

There is little conclusive data that illustrate that SORs reduce the likelihood of reoffending, but there is data about who is most likely to be a perpetrator. When examining the data, stranger abduction is the least prevalent.

The 2000 Bureau of Justice Statistics report, *Sexual assault of young children as reported to law enforcement: Victim, incident, and offender characteristics* (BJS, 2000), clearly identifies that for all female victims, acquaintances are the highest risk category to assault children: 25.7% of the offenders are family members, 59.5% are acquaintances, and 14.7% are strangers. The stranger category is lowest for younger children, with only 4.8% of perpetrators in assaults of girls between the ages of 6 and 11 identified as strangers, whereas 51.4% are acquaintances, and 43.8% are family members. For males, the numbers are similar, with an even lower prevalence of stranger assaults. The BJS documents that in sexual assaults against male children, the perpetrators are more likely to be family members, at 32.8%, and 59.8% are acquaintances, and 7.3% are strangers. Younger male children are also less likely than older male children to be assaulted by strangers. For boys 6–11, 37.7% are family members, 57.7% are acquaintances, and 4.6% are strangers. For children under 18, strangers are consistently the least likely, generally significantly less than 10%, to be the perpetrators of sexual assaults. The younger the child, the more likely the perpetrator is a family member. These are reported incidents to law enforcement, and the sanctions for children (or anyone economically or otherwise dependent) against naming relatives or family friends as the perpetrators of violence are high. Given this reality, I suggest that the incidents of sexual assaults in general are underreported, and in particular those perpetrated by family and acquaintances.

These registries operate on the premise that communities that are aware of who is a designated sexual predator will act to protect or monitor their children. Yet, the above statistics indicate that a child is more likely to be assaulted by someone in her sphere: family or an acquaintance. If there is an enemy, "the enemy is us," writes Levine in *Harmful to Minors* (2002). SORs are organized not to monitor family members or acquaintances, the most likely to assault or to abduct children, but to protect children from dangerous strangers. Although strangers do assault children, these registries contribute to a culture where the perceptions of violence and harm to children and youth is external to the life of the child. The circulation of photos and addresses of known sex offenders is perhaps useful to raise awareness of stranger assaults, but it fosters the assumption that strangers are the most risky or the most significant threat to the safety of the child.

Schools function as a central site to solidify these ideas of "risk" as external to the everyday, natural life of the child. In 2005 Illinois implemented the *Child Lures Prevention Program*, a national initiative, to prevent child abduction and exploitation through the use of the 3,200 elementary and middle schools in Illinois to "teach parents and children to recognize potential dangers and make smart decisions to avoid child predators." The press release further stated:

> At least 1 in 5 girls and 1 in 10 boys will be sexually abused before they turn 18, according to the National Center for Missing and Exploited Children. The Illinois Department of Children and Family Services estimates that more than 8,000 children are sexually abused every year in Illinois. (America's Missing, 2005)

Nowhere in this press release does it state that children are much more likely to be assaulted by family or friends. In fact, the framework of the *Child Lures* curriculum emphasizes how to recognize "predators" and "danger," negating the reality that those who do violence to children overwhelmingly do not appear in the child's life as a predator or a stranger, but as someone they already trust and care about. Schools function to legitimize these constructions of "risk" and who to fear, because educational discourses are imbued with authority and schools are frequently perceived as neutral, apolitical spaces.

Mass media, in recycling familiar and profitable storylines of "child-saving," disproportionately emphasizes stranger-assault cases and supports the construction of the fear of stranger assaults (Best, 1990). Just as mass media is used to scaffold the production of select youth as dangerous, or prisons as the natural containment sites of those inherently evil (as in the TV show *OZ*), mass media is also used to reproduce the fear of stranger danger and the requirement of child protection from external enemies. In the fall of 2005 Oprah Winfrey began what she termed a "sex offender round up." Her media outlets were used to feature a known sex offender and to publicize his (as of 2006, all male) image, crimes, and modus operandi, in order to assist in his capture. On her Web site, Oprah writes:

> Today I stand before you to say in no uncertain terms, as a matter of fact in terms I hope are very certain, that I have had enough. With every breath in my body, whatever it takes, and most importantly with your support, we are going to move heaven and earth to stop a sickness, a darkness, that I believe is the definition of evil that's been going on for far too long. The children of this nation, the United States of America, are being stolen, raped, tortured, and killed by sexual predators, who are walking right into your homes. How many times does it have to happen, and how many children have to be sacrificed? What price are we as a society willing to continue to pay before we rise up and take to the streets and say, "Enough. Enough! Enough . . . " (*Oprah's Child Predator Watch List, 2006*)

According to the Associated Press, the same week Winfrey began devoting her show's time to rounding up these offenders, William C. Davis, a convicted sex offender wanted in Indiana, was captured in Fargo, North Dakota (ABC News, 2005). Winfrey offers a $100,000 reward to viewers whose clues lead the FBI to the apprehension and arrest for the cases highlighted on her show. Oprah provides no statistics or comments concerning the largest predatory threat to children: family and acquaintances. In the section titled *Protecting Your Children*, the Web site does not directly address what to do if a family member, friend, or someone a child trusts is the danger.

Whereas Oprah does not specify *who* is walking into our homes to steal our children right out from under our noses, neither does she imply familiarity. Oprah's failure to make this clear perpetuates common myths that strangers commit crimes, not friends, families, and neighbors. By failing to discuss the largest percentage of cases and the perpetrators of those crimes, Oprah is not unique. When mass media represents violence against children, stranger assault cases are more frequently depicted and sensationalized and the media is much less likely to attempt to be unbiased in their reporting of this topic. (Best, 1990, 99).

I am unclear whether there is a vested interest in expanding the fear of the stranger, or whether this kind of representation is simply easier than addressing the complicated issues of child sexuality, or the sexualized violence built into patriarchal systems. Other factors also shape the focus on fear of the stranger. Kincaid, in *Erotic Innocence*, offers a list of reasons for the explosion of public panic in the 1980s in the United States surrounding stranger child abuse and child abductions. His list ranges from "it directs our attention away from more pressing ills," to "it attacks working mothers most viciously," and "it gives the police and policing agencies, god-like power" (1998, 21). Or, perhaps, as theorists such as Berlant suggest, the demonization of select vulnerable populations, such as sex offenders, functions as one way to signify participation in society.[3] Regardless, the consequences of this disproportionate representation are clear. The expansion of the fear of the stranger, through policies and mass media, functions to erase the reality of the much more prevalent threat of violence in the family, a space that is conceptualized as both natural and safe.

> More important still, if damage to children can be shown to stem from lone abusers, then the wider culture—with its responsibilities, trials and dangers in relation to children—can be absolved. Thus childhood returns to a pre-Freudian state of sexual innocence, and a family, that is families without abusers, revert to the ideal. (J. Rose, 1992, xi)

The perpetuation of stranger danger takes responsibility off the construct of the family *or patriarchy*. If violence to children is represented as the stranger, a nuclear family is preserved as a natural and a safe institution. The construct of the normal home life—a mother, a father, and one other biological sibling—is unaltered. This is the normal, the average, and the good. The danger is outside of this system. This template of the normal still persists, even though it is clearly not the norm demographically, and, as this discussion works to illustrate, it is a violent space and institution for children and

---

[3] Compassion for children, old people, or a fetus is socially acceptable. By recycling dominant discourses about who is worthy of our compassion and who is not worthy, those marginalized seek to maintain some inclusion by demonstrating compassion toward these universals (Rhodes, 2005; Berlant, 2004).

women. The Bureau of Justice Statistics consistently documents that the home is one of the most dangerous places for women, and children:

- On average, more than three women are murdered by their husbands or boyfriends in this country every day. In 2000, 1,247 women were killed by an intimate partner. The same year, 440 men were killed by an intimate partner (U.S. Department of Justice, 1998a).
- [Child abuse] perpetrators are, by definition, individuals responsible for the care and the supervision of their victim. In 2002, one or both parents were involved in 79 percent of child abuse or neglect fatalities. Of the other 21 percent of fatalities, 16 percent were the results of maltreatment by nonparent caretakers, and 5 percent were unknown or missing (National Clearinghouse on Child Abuse and Neglect Information, 2004).
- Three in four women (76 percent) who reported they had been raped and/or physically assaulted since age 18 said that a current or former husband, cohabiting partner, or date committed the assault (U.S. Department of Justice, 1998b).

These are just a fraction of the statistics that illustrate that the leading cause of violence to women and children is the intimate men in their lives. Generally, this violence occurs in the home, and the fear for women and children is not the stranger, but the men who are known to women and children. Mass media and schools, through highlighting stories of children being lured by strangers where danger and fear is outside of the home, contribute to this process. Schools are invested in maintaining heteropatriarchy, despite the documentation that it is dangerous to women and children.

Investments extend beyond patriarchy or even the hegemony of the nuclear family. Adults construct the child in particular, peculiar ways. Adults read narratives of child survivors or victims with the eyes and reasoning abilities of ourselves at that age (Hirsch, 1999, 15). Representations of children, Hirsch states, "invite a particular kind of spectatorial look, a specific kind of investment" (12). The child is framed by adults' fears, fantasies, and memories of childhood experiences. In this sense our gaze at childhood/children is a palimpsest that is layered with our adult memories of ourselves as children, and we are deeply invested in our constructions.

Culturally, at the end of the twentieth century, the figure of the "child" is an adult construction, the site of adult fantasy, fear, and desire. As recent controversies suggest, our culture has a great deal invested in the children's innocence and vulnerability—and at the same time, in their eroticism and knowledge. Less individualized, less marked by the particularities of identity, moreover children invite multiple projections and identifications. . . . This could be the effect of the "it could have been me" created specifically by the image of the child. In the present political climate that constructs the child as an unexamined emblem of vulnerability and innocence, the image of the child lends itself too easily to trivialization and stereotype. (Hirsch, 1999, 13, 16)

Hirsch suggests that adults reserve a certain suspension of disbelief for the epistemic positioning of a child. This child-victim position, Hirsch suggests, is then deeply vulnerable for exploitation and trivialization precisely because we are invested so deeply in this connection.

Inventions of Childhood and the Trouble With Innocence

As discussed, SORs were established to protect children from harm. While laudable, as one who is perennially suspicious of the state's agenda, what makes this population special? Without appearing heartless or crass, what are the defining characteristics of this population, "children," that enable these protections or benefits? And, more centrally, do all children benefit from an affiliation with these characteristics or are some children excluded from possessing the central characteristics of childhood that afford significant benefits? In addition, if as the previous section outlined, the natural family, or patriarchy, is a site of violence, how does the very concept of the child contribute to the erasure or the naturalization of this violence? Do schools and child-centered educational discourses reproduce meanings of the child that contribute to the expansion of the PIC? And, do adults have too much invested in the meanings associated with the child? *Do we need them more than they need us?*

Responding to these questions requires an examination of the fundamental concept of the child. Childhood, like other categories such as adolescence, or old age, is a shifting and invented construct, not an a priori category (Aries, 1962; Lesko, 2000; Postman, 1994). Clearly developmental processes occur and these developments can be mapped chronologically, such as physical growth and the acquisition or the loss of motor skills or speech. I am not questioning that these developments occur, rather I am interested in the cultural meanings attached to these developments, and how communities, formally or informally, have organized and named these developments. I will not do justice to the significant and lengthy research on the construction of childhood, the debates within the field of childhood history, as this work is really outside the scope of this project, but I do want to illustrate the gendered and racialized constructs of a core characteristic of our modern construct of childhood: innocence.

Aries, in the influential and debated *Centuries of Childhood* (1962), argued that the perspective of understanding children as simply miniature adults, as evidenced in medieval portraiture, capable of sexual relations, culpable of crime and treated the same as adults for offenses, began to shift in the 16th century with religious and economic changes. Specifically, industrialization impacted the domestic arrangements, as more resources were available, and new meanings affiliated with childhood emerged "as a middle class idea, in part because the middle class could afford it. It took another century before the idea trickled down to the lower classes" (Postman, 1994, 45). Industrialization provided a new middle class with the wealth to purchase larger homes, to spend more on clothing and education and paid more attention to children's health, yet 18th-century industrialization was "a constant and formidable enemy of childhood" (53) as these changing economic practices required cheap and malleable labor, children. Children, marginalized economically or racially, were the least likely to be able to benefit from "new" constructs of the child. Even when child labor laws were implemented and became tougher throughout the 20th century in the United States and England, these laws were not uniformly applied to all. In white families, the consequences of new labor laws meant that children and adolescents lost hours at work and could no longer earn wages to help sustain the family. Shrinking incomes contributed to the decrease in family size even in some working-class families. With fewer bodies in the house, parents could pay more attention to the children they possessed. Changing economic forces shaped children's shrinking monetary value and growing emotional status (Postman, 1994; West, 1996).

The meanings that are attached to childhood are deeply interrelated with other social institutions. Kincaid offers a description of the modern-day child as a holdover from a Romantic construct that is malleable and largely characterized in contrast to an adult:

> [T]his Romantic child was largely figured as an inversion of Enlightenment virtues and was thus strangely hollow from the start: uncorrupted, unsophisticated, unenlightened. The child was a lot of things, things it was better off without, presumably, but still oddly dispossessed and eviscerated, without much substance. As we have slowly succumbed to the collective illusion that the child is a biological category, we have managed to hold that category open so that we can construe it any way we like. We have, according to the needs of history and to our own whim, made children savages and sinners, but

we have also maintained their innocence. A quality we seem to need much more than they do. (Kincaid, 1998, 53)

The modern construct of the child continues to be characterized by *innocence*. Beginning in the 1340s and lasting until the second half of the 119th century, children were frequently referred to as "innocents." Innocent means "pure, unpolluted" beings free from sin and guilt (*OED*, 1989) and today, although less common, children are still referred to as *innocent*, but this is used more often as an adjective instead of a noun.[4]

More concretely, the inventedness of these categories of childhood (and adolescence[5]) is evidenced, for example, in U.S. laws that offer conflicting ages of consent (AOC) to a range of practices usually connected to adulthood: drinking alcohol, sexual acts, marriage, voting, and so forth. As of 2006, the AOC to marry differs from state to state, and across states there are often exceptions to these ages of consent if parents support the marriage, or if the woman is pregnant.

For example, in Iowa, the AOC is listed as 14, or 16 if the partner is less than 5 years older, and 16 for all other partners. State law in Iowa further imposes mandatory life banishment from Iowa cities if a person violates the state's AOC law. Iowa's ban applies to conduct that occurred in other states even if it was legal in those states. In addition, federal law forbids adults from taking a person under 18 across state borders to escape a state's AOC law, unless the two have consent from the minor's parent(s) or legal guardian (AVERT, 2006).

I am not trying to make the argument that there should be no age of consent; rather, I am asking readers to consider the consequences of the meanings attached to childhood. A quick turn to the judicial system illustrates the concrete privileges affiliated with legitimate status as a "child," and the conflicts between our concern about consent and sexual practices,

---

[4] I will return to this question of innocence and who gets access to this category in the last chapter.

[5] If childhood is a modern construction, adolescence is more contemporary, arriving in the late 19th century, also shaped by economic and social forces. These new adolescent years were considered dangerous; there were opportunities everywhere for children to swerve off the path of morality (West, 1996). Adolescence is also a gendered and racialized construct. For example, whereas young men were more often found guilty of crimes like theft, vandalism, robbery, and assault, young women were convicted of "immoral conduct." According to New York's Wayward Minor Act of 1923, girls aged 16 to 21 could be convicted of "immoral conduct" solely on the testimony of their parents. "Immoral conduct" included offenses such as sexual intercourse, thoughts of or curiousness about sexual intercourse, obscene language, masturbation, disrespect toward elders, and provocative wardrobes. Pregnancy resulting from sex outside of marriage would most certainly lead to institutionalization, and girls were more frequently sent to reformatories than boys (West, 1996).

and seeming lack of concern about consent and criminality. For example, in March 2005 the U.S. Supreme Court ruled it unconstitutional to use the death penalty for juveniles. A *Washington Post* article summarizes the argument used to overturn the previous 1989 Supreme Court decision that permitted the execution of juveniles.

> In concluding that the death penalty for minors is cruel and unusual punishment, the court cited a "national consensus" against the practice, along with medical and social-science evidence that teenagers are too immature to be held accountable for their crimes to the same extent as adults. (Lane, 2005)

Although some speculate that it was international pressure that moved the courts to shift, as the United States is one of only a few nations where it is still legal to execute juveniles, or adults who had been convicted of crimes when they were juveniles, this Supreme Court decision clearly confers benefits to those eligible for inclusion into this category of juvenile. Despite this rather positive move to not execute juveniles, Dohrn illustrates that changes in the court system in the late 1990s extended the punitive arm of the state into the life of the child.

> All across the nation, states have been expanding the jurisdiction of adult criminal court to include younger children by lowering the minimum age of criminal jurisdiction and expanding the types of offenses and mechanisms for transfer or waiver of juveniles into adult criminal court. ... The age when a child is legally still considered a child (and when a child becomes culpable as a adult) has become a major element in the expansion of criminal court jurisdiction and the simultaneous constriction and extension of juvenile court jurisdiction. (Dohrn, 2000, 175)

These policy and law changes, both lowering the age at which a child can be held accountable in a juvenile court and raising the number of children moved into adult court, expand the definition of who is culpable, and therefore punishable.

Children are transferred to adult court either automatically or through a process known as the "direct file transfer" where the prosecutor uses "his or her sole discretion in determining whether a child is to be charged in juvenile or adult court" (Dohrn, 2000, 177). A joint investigation in 2000, conducted by *The Chicago Reporter* and the Chicago-based *WBEZ Radio, 91.5 FM*, tracked the racialized consequences of the Illinois Juvenile Court Act of 1987, a law that automatically moves to adult court "15- and 16-year-olds charged with selling drugs within 1,000 feet of a school or public housing development" (Karp, 2000). Despite the fact that drug usage is relatively consistent across racial groups, African Americans were disproportionately impacted by this law. The study identified: "Juvenile drug cases were transferred to Cook County Criminal Court 363 times from 1995 to 1999, and 99 percent of the teens charged were African American or Latino. Ninety-seven percent lived in the city" (Karp, 2000).

Notably, whereas children can be culpable and accountable for crimes, as documented, the state "protects" children through the enactment of laws that stipulate that a 15- or 16-year-old is not able to consent to sex or marriage. Illinois schools teach an abstinence-based sexual education curriculum because those in school are too young to be sexual, and yet the courts in the state don't blink an eye when sentencing children and juveniles to prison or transferring the same child to adult court. The mass media, with headlines such as "13-year-old killer gets 8 years" in the *Chicago Sun-Times*, participates in shaping public sentiment about these natural-born killers (Hussain, 2006).

White supremacy clearly undergirds these shifting meanings surrounding childhood. Historically, not all people had access to participate in these new meanings of the category of child and adolescent. Postman identifies that working-class children did not access the benefits of childhood until much later, but there is muted recognition that these constructs simply did not include nonwhite children. Labor laws were not enforced for nonwhite children in the United States. For example, compulsory school attendance laws and child labor protection laws were not enforced in the southwest (and other regions) because the labor of Latino children was needed in the fields (San Miguel, 1997). This same division about which children merit access to protection under these laws and categories is evidenced today, in the United States, when consumers feel no shame at purchasing items or clothing made by teenagers or children in other countries, generally children of color, who work in untenable labor conditions. These children do not merit protection under the category "innocence."

What emerges from an analysis of race and childhood is that a defining characteristic of childhood, innocence, continues to not be available to all children with significant consequences. For example, in 1998 two African American boys, seven and eight years old, were charged with murdering eleven year old Ryan Harris in Chicago. While charges were eventually dropped when semen was found in Ryan Harris's body and the boys were too young to produce semen, neither the boys nor their families were given any special treatment by the police or in the media coverage, because they were children. An Associated Press story wondered, "How do you punish kids so young if they have committed crimes so vicious?" (Bogira, 2006, 1). Juxtapose these two children with the 1998 Columbine school shootings where the white male teenaged school shooters, Harrris (age eighteen) and Kleibold (age seventeen), were referred to in the press as "outsiders" or "wierdis" and "loners".[6] Questions were asked, like the headline from the *Denver Post*, "Mystery how team players became loners: Friends remember two suspects as bashful, ordinary children" (Simpson & Blevins, 1999). Harris and Kleibold, much closer to adulthood, were constructed by the mainstream media to be outsiders, not predatory deviants, while the two African-American boys, suspected of murder and sexual assault, were not permitted to be viewed as outsiders, much less permitted to be "children." While innocence is "a lot like air in you tires: there is not a lot you can do with it but lose it" (Kincaid 53), innocence is not equally conferred at birth. Just as an earlier chapter identified that preschool, the educational category with the highest rates of expulsion, targets African-American boys for "behavior disorders," race, gender, class and nation of origin clearly impact who gets access to full participation in the category of innocence, a defining characteristic of childhood.

Schools contribute to the construction of this inequitable construct of the child. From the marginalization of works from teacher educational curricula that systemically and rigorously question constructs of the child and the privileges affiliated to these constructs (works by Walkerdine, Aries, Lesko), to the informal discourses used in the everyday practice of the profession of teaching and teacher education that reify meanings about the child. Schools and school-based discourses are a central site of production and naturalization of this artifact.

> The child as a sign within the child-centered pedagogy is not simply a description of a pre-existing child. The practices themselves, in their regulation, produce what it means to be a child; what behaviors, words, etc. are used and those are regulated by a means of an apparatus of classification, and a grading of responses. The "child" becomes a creation and yet at the same time provides room for a reading of pathology. . . . If children become subjects through their insertion into a complex network of practices, there are no children who stand outside their orbit. (Walkerdine, 1988, 203–204)

Race, gender, class, sexual orientation, ability, nation of origin, and more clearly shape what meanings will be attached to "the child" in schools and, subsequently, how deviant behavior is interpreted. White males and those with economic privileges who are violent in schools are more likely to be pathologized than criminalized for their deviant behavior. Pathologization and criminalization are two different, albeit overlapping, institutional practices. Innocence is one key difference that shapes which path a deviant

---

[6] Or, as Therese Quinn reminded me, when Kleibold and Harris were perceived to be "gay" they were demonized as monsters.

body moves through. If perceived to be innocent and yet enacting deviant behavior, the analysis is that he or she can be assisted and is not culpable. If a body is not innocent and has enacted deviant behavior, then he or she is culpable, and there could be a debate as to whether rehabilitation or assistance is warranted. This construct of innocence facilitates who merits not just compassion, but protection under the state. For example, women who are not perceived by the state to be promiscuous get access to police protection when assaulted. Children who are perceived to be good kids are allowed access to participate in the category of the child. They are not transferred to adult court and could get access to rehabilitation, or are not charged and are remanded to their caregivers. Clearly the inverse also applies. Sex-trade workers who are assaulted cannot convince the police to press charges against their assailants. Those who do not get included in the category of the child, African American boys, are not innocent.

The Trouble With Normal

Constructions of deviance/normalcy, or what constitutes a natural sexual practice, is a far from settled debate in the United States. In no way do I argue that the abuse of children is really a normal sexual practice; still, the contemporary establishment of registries to track and to police those convicted of sexual offenses must be considered in a context where deviance is a category historically used to control and marginalize women, non-heteronormative sexual practices, and communities of color. For example, consensual sodomy was criminalized until 2003 in some states, "interracial" marriage and sex was illegal until overturned in 1967 by the *Loving v State of Virginia* decision, and it was legal to rape your wife until the 1970s (as late as the 1990s in some states).[7] Just as there is no unitary category of child, I argue that given this history, a concept of sex offender can be a particularly worrisome category, in particular for educators when the profession has such a long and detailed history of the queers being sexual deviants who are "unfit to teach" (Blount, 2005). Briefly, in this section I want to look at a *queer* history of sex offender registries, and to examine larger discussions about perversity and sexual normativity, as it impacts individuals and families in schools.

The first sex offender registries in the United States, in California in 1947, focused on collecting information on homosexual activity (Humphreys, 1970; Jacobsen, 1999). Prior to the June 26, 2003, *Lawrence & Garner v State of Texas* decision when the U.S. Supreme Court ruled 6–3 that

---

[7] For example, until 1993 North Carolina law stated that "a person may not be prosecuted under this article if the victim is the person's legal spouse at the time of the commission of the alleged rape or sexual offense unless the parties are living separate and apart" (Spousal Rape Laws: 20 Years Later, 2004).

sodomy laws are unconstitutional (overturning the 1986 *Bowers v Hard-wick* decision), sodomy was still a crime in many states for same-sex and opposite-sex partners. Laws against consensual same-sex sodomy were heavily enforced.

[A] 1966 project by the University of California (Los Angeles) Law Review quantified the number of men arrested and convicted in Los Angeles County through anti-gay entrapment and harassment techniques. It found that sodomy laws were enforced frequently; 493 men were arrested for consensual sodomy over a three-year period in Los Angeles in the early 1960s, with 257 men convicted of sodomy and 104 imprisoned. . . . These results correspond with those of other major cities, with substantial numbers of arrests for sodomy and many more for misdemeanor gay-related solicitation offenses. . . . The penalties for convictions of the different offenses varied widely. Consensual sodomy was a felony offense in nearly every state and carried an average maximum prison term of ten years; only murder, kidnapping and rape were penalized more severely.[8] (Jacobsen, 1999, 2433)

Sex offender registries, set up to specifically target and track (and subsequently harass) "known homosexuals," became less popular by the 1980s, largely because they were private documents internal to police forces, and not shared with the public. These internal registries were often broad and encompassed such a range of activities that they were too cumbersome to use (Jacobsen, 1999). In addition, persecution of homosexuality and same-sex practices and desire was an acceptable social practice and other institutions were adequately participating in over discrimination. For example, government agencies tracked the names of "known homosexuals" to deny them employment (Jacobsen, 1999).

Jacobsen argues that the revitalization of sex offender registries in the 1990s was potentially tense for queers for two reasons. First, prior to *Lawrence v Texas*, laws specifically targeted queers and criminalized consensual same-sex sexual practices. Second, when laws are supposedly neutral, or not targeting non-heteronormative sex practices, these "neutral" laws are still disproportionately used against non-heterosexuals.[9] For example, lewdness and indecent exposure charges are still levied against men who

---

[8] See also Humphreys' *Tearoom Trade* (1970, 83–93) for a discussion of the extensive use of police and state resources to monitor public male sex through the use of hidden cameras, decoys, and other mechanisms of surveillance.

[9] Laws disproportionately impact those in poverty. For example, the recent move to display photos of all men convicted of solicitation (purchasing prostitution) in Chicago led to a street sweep. Those placed on the "johns registry" for convictions of prostitution are disproportionately men of color and working-class/poor men. Street prostitution is only 17% of all sex-trade work in Chicago, and generally it is the poor women, those homeless, and with drug problems, who work the streets. The more expensive sex trade that happens in clubs is more protected (Chasnoff, 2006).

engage in consensual same-sex sexual acts in public spaces. Whereas this is not the entrapment of previous decades when police used gay decoys, these laws are still used against men who engage in same-sex sexual acts in public spaces, when males believe that they are not being observed. Current SORs also often require registration for prior convictions. Several states have addressed this issue, such as Massachusetts, by requiring that an administrative hearing be held for every individual before they are assigned to be monitored by a registry. In these states, registration as a sex offender does not encompass consensual sex acts between adults that were criminalized (Jacobsen, 1999).

The reimplementation of SORs in the 1990s is not designed to entrap consensual sodomy or to harass same-sex sexual practices. In no way do I argue that the master plan behind the establishment of SORs is to police or to track non-heteronormative behaviors. Rather, what I argue is that these laws do not operate in isolation. The U.S. Supreme Court decided in 2003 that sodomy laws are unconstitutional and this was not a unanimous decision. The litany of antigay marriage amendments in the 1990s, coupled with a range of other antigay initiatives, for example, the 2005 attempt in Oregon to bar homosexuals from the profession of education, or the ban in Florida and Ohio against gay adults adopting children, and more, illustrates that it would be naïve to assume that all the vestiges of homophobia that are both built into laws and enshrined in practices and applications of these laws, were miraculously waived with this ruling.

This raises possibly thorny questions for some about how (and *if* or *whether*) to demarcate between appropriate and perverse sexual practices, or good or bad families, and more. In our contexts of perverse, persistent heteronormativity, of exploitative capitalism, of misogyny and white supremacy, *perhaps our starting place of normal or family, is a problem.* The first part of the chapter worked to illustrate that the "home" is a space of significant violence and urged the rethinking of "child protection" strategies that erase the significant violence that occurs under the category of nuclear family and patriarchy. In order to think through these relations between the law and rights and sexual normativity, perhaps it is useful to further examine the terms that are at stake. Strategies and policies that turn on our construct of deviance and normalcy might get us into trouble further down the line. At the risk of simplifying Judith Butler's work, one of Butler's interests in *Antigone's Claim* is how communities develop "moral" prohibitions toward certain relations.[10] Specifically, she sees a relationship between

---

[10] In *Antigone's Claim*, Butler applies psychoanalysis and contemporary poststructuralist anthropology to the life of Sophocles' Antigone in an attempt to resuscitate Antigone as a possibly symbolic feminist archetype and to pose interesting questions about cultural norms and "familial" relations (Butler, 2000). Antigone's brother Oedipus unwittingly marries his and Antigone's mother, Jocasta; hence Oedipus is also Antigone's father, and Antigone witnesses, among other things, her father/brother kill her uncle/brother Polynices.

the sentiments expressed by those who prohibit incest and those sentiments directed toward other "nontraditional" families.

> Consider that the horror of incest, the moral revulsion it compels in some, is not that far afield from the same horror and revulsion felt toward lesbian and gay sex, and it is not unrelated to the intense moral condemnation of voluntary single parenting, or gay parenting, or parenting arrangements with more than two adults involved (practices that can be used as evidence to support a claim to remove a child from the custody of the parent in several states in the United States). (Butler, 2000, 71)

This is, of course, evidenced in the infamous quotation by former Senator Rick Santorum of Pennsylvania in an interview with the Associated Press taped on April 7, 2003, and published April 20, 2003. In the interview he is quoted as equating gay sex with everything else ("man with dog" was in his original statement, but this was eliminated from the original print version).

> If the Supreme Court says that you have the right to consensual [gay] sex within your home, then you have the right to bigamy, you have the right to polygamy, you have the right to incest, you have the right to adultery. You have the right to anything. (Associated Press, 2003)

While it seems bizarre to align with Rick Santorum, in the minds of those opposed to non-heteronormative sexual practices, whether we like it or not, the umbrella of perversity is fairly encompassing. As educators, resorting to claims that we are "normal" might not get us too far. Historically educators who have struggled to repeal antigay teaching prohibitions, for example, the 1977 Briggs Initiative, which sought to prohibit out gay and lesbian educators from employment, can't get around the discourses of perversity.

> To defend lesbian and gay teachers successfully, opponents of the Briggs Initiative would need to confront the gay child molestation bugaboo squarely. They would also need to convince voters that lesbian and gay teachers did not otherwise harm the gender and sexual development of their students. (Blount, 2005, 140)

The response to assert normalcy, that gay and lesbian teachers do not harm normative development, though a necessary strategy, can be problematic. What is normal gender development in a white supremacist patriarchal system? What is a normal family, or normal sexual development? What if we view these categories as harmful?

Butler works to unpack the construction of the natural or the normal Western nuclear family and works to ask how prohibitions toward certain sets of familial relations are established. What is so natural about a family or kinship relations? Where does the concept of *unnatural* kinship originate? Butler argues that we have inherited (via Western analytic thought, colonialism, and more) conceptions of kinship that always and already frame normative relations. We inherit this template that appears to have no originary state in nature or culture, but is actively reproduced. Attempts at normalizing the former margins through the integration of gay and lesbian issues into schools, or institutionalizing gay marriage, does little to alter the template of the norm and its preexisting other, the perverse.

> The norm cannot exist without perversion, and only through perversion can the norm be established. We are all supposed to be satisfied by this apparently generous gesture by which the perverse is announced to be essential to the norm. The problem as I see it is that the perverse remains precisely there, as the essential and negative feature of the norm, and the relation between the two remains static, giving way to no rearticulation of the norm itself. (Butler, 2000, 76)

The erasure of laws against consensual sodomy, and the movement of sodomy into a kind of quasi-legal normal state, does not mean that our framework of normal and not normal has adjusted.

Bulter's rereading of this nexus of kinship relations is, as she terms it, a "perverse, promiscuous reading" that I argue is timely. In the United States where many gay rights organizations are earnestly working toward normalization, including the legalization of gay marriage, which often receives more money and resources than the less public work to decriminalize sex acts and practices, Butler's analysis offers a warning. She suggests that moves toward legitimization of same-sex relationships in the eyes of the state will not lead necessarily to the kind of productive changes envisioned. If we move some of the good gays, those in long-term monogamous homonormative relationships, out of the category of "perverse" and afford them benefits and limited protection in the state, without challenging this framework of normal and perverse, who benefits? If arguments in support of queer teachers and gay families turn on the trope that we are good and normal, not deviants, does this further demonize children who are raised in one-parent households? Does this support frameworks of "normal gender and sexual development" of youth that are anything but *normal*? Does our inclusion arrive at the cost of further delineating who counts as not good parents, and who therefore requires monitoring, or who we need to protect the child from?

Where I am left in this discussion is not that the move tomorrow is to abolish SORs, but working to be willing to be uncomfortable with the present system. This chapter has worked to outline several substantive criticisms of the SOR: they contribute to a culture of fear of stranger danger that displaces responsibility from families and patriarchy for violence against children and women. They reify constructs of the child that both afford benefits and privileges to some children and not others and seemingly require the expansion of the punitive arm of the state. The child requires protection from danger and the state needs laws, processes of criminalization, and more surveillance to protect this child. Finally, there are disquieting histories to any discussion of sexual deviances, and perhaps normalcy is not a useful tool in discussions about relationships.

How do we acknowledge and discuss that we continually reproduce constructs of the child that are filled with our own anxieties about sexuality and race and gender? It is no surprise that institutionalized schooling discourses figure deeply in this discussion. Schools are one legitimate site where meanings about the child are reified. We, in schools and in families, as discussed, need the meanings we have attached to childhood more than children do, and these meanings and anxieties might end up getting us into trouble. I wonder, can we imagine colleges of education without children, or more precisely without the meanings we have attached to childhood? The very unit of analysis that structures schools and programs of teacher education, that is, books about pedagogy and more, needs to be not necessarily rejected, but assessed through different frameworks.

> [T]here can no longer be a unitary category "the child," let alone "girl" or "boy." If class and race, poverty and wealth, mental and manual labor produce differently regulated practices, then it is important to examine a multiplicity of subjectivities produced in such conditions. (Walkerdine, 1988, 215)

If schools naturalize these constructs, family and child, which are in fact artificial categories, integral to maintaining state functions of white supremacy and patriarchy, the state also requires mechanisms to maintain and enforce these constructs. Schools are one site that fulfill this function.

This research and writing have moved me to consider how to raise awareness of how the construct of the *normal family* hides not only a highly unnatural set of social relationships, but often violent and dangerous sets of relationships. I bring this chapter back to the theme of the book project, the production of public enemies. Are these SORs producing public enemies at the cost of reducing or minimizing other, more substantial risks? At local community meetings in my former neighborhood in Chicago, a few mothers would print out the photos of the sex offenders who lived in the neighborhood. They would circulate these flyers at monthly meetings and speak of the fear they had for their children's safety. I am not denying that there is fear, but I wonder how comfortable they would feel if flyers were distributed that possessed photos of all their children's male relatives, grandfathers, uncles, fathers, cousins—with addresses—under the title "one of these men is violently assaulting his relative."

I wonder about balancing risks and considering the long-term consequences of strategies that are based on categories that are not just flawed, but have an active history of exclusion. In an attempt to not get stuck in this cul de sac, I read the afterword to Judith Levine's book *Harmful to Minors*, which attempts to work through issues related to children and sexuality (and I read, with worry, the backlash she receives from right-wing groups). I return to the theme of this book project, surrounding the production of fear and enemies. If we are discussing enemies of childhood, or risks for children, *"Poverty is the single greatest risk factor for almost every 'life-smashing' condition a kid might be at risk for, save perhaps compulsive shopping"* (Levine, 2002, 220; emphasis mine). I know this fact, I teach this fact. Yet it persistently gets obscured. In a nation with no adequate or affordable childcare system, no universal healthcare, expensive to prohibitive costs for higher education, and a minimum wage that is not a living wage, we have no registries for the politicians, and employers, who routinely implement or execute policies that actively damage all people, including or even *particularly* children. We have no registries for the men who have histories of "domestic violence," the leading cause of death for women.

> I am still not able to have more than a few minutes' conversation with Michael. I force myself to be casual and neutral. I pretend that nothing has changed. I chat about the weather or the traffic. Instead of an undereducated, probably cognitively impaired man who will most likely spend the rest of his life attempting to get meaningful minimum wage employment, he is a cipher for all my rage, and all my fear, at the women in my life who have been harmed. I will not get in the elevator with him. I will not turn my back to him when I am using the photocopier. However, I will not stop asking myself why he is a legitimate target for my fears.

CHAPTER 5

Political Recoveries

"Softening" Selves, Hard Experiences,
and Organized Resistance

When asked to write autobiographies, participants in an English class at the St. Leonard's Adult High School wrote within a remarkably similar formula:

I was born; I had problems; I made the wrong choices; I was apprehended by the police; I was incarcerated; I found God and He helped me. And . . . My life is now on a better track.

Initially Tim Barnett (my coteacher) and I read the formulaicness of these narratives as a pedagogical failure on our part—we needed to teach and structure the assignment better— or as a comprehension or an ability issue on behalf of the participants. As educators who had taught in a variety of university, high school, and community contexts, we both were aware that students do perform or ventriloquize what teachers request, and we were mindful that for this group, survival (maintaining access to your children or acquiring housing) is dependent on the ability to represent oneself very carefully to the social service organizations that poor and institutionalized people navigate. Participants were all formerly incarcerated, most in 12-step programs for a variety of addictions, and most struggling to address a lifetime of undereducation, underemployment, and poverty.

Despite our attempts at trying different strategies to elicit the narratives (journaling, poetry, oral presentations, and discussions), after a few semesters it was clear that the majority of their autobiographies were often in a similar formula, what we began to term "the redemption genre." The prevalence of this response, coupled with previous educational work with those deeply traumatized by the state-sanctioned violence, moves me to consider what tools are available in institutions to assist those who have survived violence to name and understand these traumas as the rational consequences of unsound environments or as simply individual choices. What roles do institutions, schools and jails, play to recast this experience—concrete evidence of the abject failure of our democratic and public institutions—as individual failure?

Reading autobiographic writing from this high school moved me to examine how negative and traumatic experiences *that are in part the result of annihilating public policies* are recast as private issues. Whereas the expansion of the incarceration-nation actively requires the maintenance of certain kinds of constructs—the "innocent" child and virtuous white woman in need of state protection, or the deranged felon in need of constant surveillance and containment—the PIC also requires that the experiences and the lives of those harmed by institutions and policies be transformed from concrete, potentially revolutionary, evidence into private, individual, failures. In the school to jail nexus, this pathologization or containment of both dissent and evidence is powerful.

> These students leave school in no position to seriously challenge the institutional narratives and media images that represent them as violent and uneducatable and that contribute to the notion that imprisonment is a reasonable, if not natural, option in their lives. (Duncan, 2000, 39)

This shaping of select youth as uneducatable and out of control requires not just participation of schools, but the active management of identities and experience. This process is what I term "the privatization of public issues" and at its core is the ability of institutions to name the "hard" experience of trauma and to soften up selves for surveillance and institutionalization. Clearly, these practices do not go unremarked by those most impacted, and exploring and how institutions participate in the privatization of public issues is a key link in the production of public enemies.

This chapter addresses how knowledge about the self participates in the movement of bodies between oppressive institutions. Children are not born enemies. Enemies are shaped by and through institutions. To investigate, I offer two interrelated discussions: special education and the recovery movement. I select these two lines of analysis because of my locations in teacher education and my work with those formerly incarcerated.

The prevalence and the widespread acceptance of both of these discourses and practices, special education and recovery, at each of my work sites, instigated questions. Further research suggests that these discourses offer parallel opportunities to investigate how institutions work to create identities and manage experience. To be perfectly clear, I am not stating that special education and recovery organizations such as AA are the same, or that they are ineffective. Rather, in the framework of an expanding PIC, these institutional and discursive practices are interconnected, because both special education and recovery movements, such as AA, shape and name "hard" experiences of not fitting in, or of "deviancy" from the norm, and of particular kinds of difference. These hard experiences, however, do possess the potential to radically challenge the effectiveness of institutions and even to call into question our democracy. Naming experience as personal, as an individual problem, absolves us, society and institutions, from recognizing the critical ways we participate in the creation of human beings as different, as deviant or as public enemies.

To examine the institutional "relations of ruling" that participate in this work of naming and shaping experience, I am influenced by D.E. Smith, in her early work on women and psychiatry in the late 1960s, who offered an analysis of the institutional practices that arrange and name feelings.

> Whatever it is that gets called mental illness becomes recognizably and distinctly what it is for the official record, in psychiatric offices, admissions suites of mental hospitals, the intake practices of clinics and etc. ...When she is put on record she is already in relation to the world, which is changed for her. This is the relation of mental illness. There is no phenomenon of mental illness which can be separated from the same procedures which produce the status. The agencies which produce the status also produce mental illness. They don't produce the suffering, the despair, the misery, the loss of self which leads in one way or another to someone's *entry* to the psychiatric process, but they do produce the distinctive behaviors, how they are recorded and understood and that pattern of relating to others *which we call mental illness*. This doesn't mean that what is happening to individuals which leads them into contact with psychiatry is not real. (D.E. Smith & David, 1975, 92–93)

D.E. Smith emphasizes that although the pain or the feeling is real, it is vital to pay attention to how institutions organize and name these experiences and feelings. It is not that students do not have trouble learning, or that the students in my high school program do not have debilitating histories with alcohol and drugs. What is lost, however, when they move into the identity, learning disabled, alcoholic, dropout, or victim (or criminal)?

How are their experiences recast from, for example, symptoms or casualties of radically poor public policies, into poor individual life choices or deviancy?

The position of "survivor" can command resources, empathy, compensation, and can, as the previous chapter notes, actually change public policy, if the trauma is a socially sanctioned one, thus it is keenly important to attend to how institutions shape the experience and agency of those impacted. This chapter argues that a major component of the contemporary state is an acquisition of the ability to *know oneself*, as Foucault argues in *Discipline and Punish* (1977), through highly regulatory and confining discursive practices. The modern criminal system produced the panopticon, which facilitates the acquisition of specific kinds of self-knowledge. Power manifests through the material apparatuses that institutionalize surveillance: the actual panopticon, the presence of officers, electronic monitoring, and the system of parole. Yet power also manifests in the system's ability to not rely on physical systems.

> [T]hat the perfection of power should tend to render its actual exercise unnecessary; that this architectural apparatus should be a machine for creating and sustaining a power relation independent of the person who exercises it; in short, that the inmates should be caught up in a power situation of which they themselves are the bearers. (Foucault, 1977, 201)

Subjects are conditioned, as individuals, to internalize the surveillance. The particular, peculiar work of self-knowledge is central to the disciplinary apparatus. D.E. Smith and David (1975) and Foucault (1977) suggest that the act of confessing and identifying via the language made available through the institution functions in part to erase the ritualized practices of surveillance and power. The act of the confession and the ability to acquire self-knowledge are simultaneously empowering, and possibly revolutionary, at the very same moment as they also serve as a mechanism of deep social control. Who is it that society frames as in need of control?

It is not arbitrary or a coincidence that the individuals caught up in the prison system, or in specific special education categories, are communities of color. These public institutions—school, prison—do not operate independently of a racial foundation—or a *Racial Contract*. Poor people and Indigenous Peoples, Latinos and African Americans, are disproportionately negatively impacted, not coincidentally, as legalized white supremacy after WW II is reframed as individualism. "[A]fter WW II, the prevailing doxy is that racial domination as a system vanishes, and we are left with atomic individuals, some of whom have bad attitudes" (Mills, 2003, 201). Those most negatively impacted by the policies of special education and criminalization are the persistent enemies of the state, people of color, women, the poor, who are convenient scapegoats for economic and political tensions, and their very identities threaten the central fiction of the heteropatriachal, white supremacist nation. Linking this to how state institutions, namely, schools and self-help movements individualize social problems results in the possibility that this nation is busy measuring "difference" or is in need of a higher power; it is not a nation in search of a political recovery and institutional transformation.

To discuss these interrelationships, how institutions name experiences, and the practices of resistance, I continue the practice of "studying up" started in previous chapters, to turn a surveillance gaze upon institutional and discursive practices and structures. I am not interested in exploring the subject in this chapter, but rather what processes make the subject visible and, "repeatedly asking how certain categorizations work, what enactments they are performing and what relations they are creating, rather than what they essentially mean" (Sedgwick, 1990, 27).

In the following section I explore how schools, with an emphasis on the "soft" learning disabilities in special education, contribute to this individuation and self-knowledge through the production of the "self." The next section offers a discussion of the recovery movement, specifically Alcoholics Anonymous, and how experience is named and organized through AA. The third section identifies how experience, especially traumatic experience, can be used in the public sphere. The last section gives examples of movements to resist this individuation using the Boarding School Healing Project and Beyondmedia Education's *Women and Prison: A Site for Resistance*, to discuss how these groups are politicizing experience for healing and for movement building.

Schools as Sites of Self-Knowledge

If schools are a soft extension of the prison state, one of our functions as educators is to prepare the self for the kind of surveillance, hypervisibility, and confession that the PIC requires. Increasingly select schools physically resemble prisons and prepare students for an institutionalized life. Students are required to wear uniforms, to be scanned by metal detectors and frisked by security guards, to use clear plastic bags and backpacks so that their items are visible at all times, and more. Through these physical practices, coincidence or by design, schools prepare youth for the life of other state institutions, including prisons. If a central mechanism of control is to be not merely material apparatuses but the very sense of the self of the individual who enters the prison, then it is useful to examine the role of schools to prepare the subject, the self, in need of surveillance and as an individual who is the product of his or her choices, not shaped, or actively produced in concert with sociocultural forces. As the previous chapter documented, the PIC expands through the very artifacts that schools are organized around, the innocent child. The construction of the category adolescent "can be considered part of a move to a modern nation-state, one in which social sciences and psychology helped make the inner, personal qualities of individuals visible and significant for building a modern society" (Lesko, 2001, 9). In addition to this relationship to the PIC, it is important to track both how schools "soften" up the self, and how institutions manage experience that does not work within the normative frameworks of the school.

Briefly, I want to return to the discussion of special education offered in the first chapter, to highlight how the turn to the individual in the school also produces a self, susceptible to surveillance and to individuation. Similar to the "soft" practices of school discipline, with disrespect and insubordination moving select youth into the juvenile justice system, the "helping" discourses can also function to produce a highly individuated subject that is prepared for surveillance, and a self that is trained to separate the individual from his or her sociocultural contexts. Clearly, these discourses also enable the acquisition of resources that do assist many children in schools. This is not in dispute, rather the expansion of the PIC requires that we view individuals as separate from their contexts, as discrete individuals who need to be managed. The processes of institutional education in the United States fulfill this function, and it is particularly visible in the practices and policies surrounding components of special education.

The Education for All Handicapped Act (EHA) (1975), and the subsequent Individuals with Disabilities Education Act (IDEA) (updated in 2004), provided those who formerly were actively denied access to receive a free, appropriate, and public education. The importance of the goal of IDEA or EHA cannot be understated, as these federal acts made it possible for those formerly actively "left behind" by our public schools to acquire the fundamental right to be educated. The IDEA requires that public schools provide students with federally recognized disabilities needed services and aids to enable learning, and that students are educated in the least restrictive environment (LRE) or with students who are not disabled. Students with disabilities should be integrated, as much as possible, in regular learning environments, and to ensure this goal is addressed, each qualifying student is entitled to possess an individualized education plan (IEP), that links the student to an interdisciplinary team of educational professionals and outlines yearly goals for the student. Because of the mandate of LRE, every teacher in the United States is familiar with the IEP, whether they are a designated "special education" teacher or not.

Educators have naturalized categories of educational disability: "For most teachers, a child so labeled most likely, 'has a disability,' just as, according to one of our study participants, 'some children have blue eyes'" (Harry & Klingner, 2005, 14). Special education preexists the student. The discourses are in schools and in universities, ready to acquire students and to name and organize their educational experiences. There are preset interpretive frameworks waiting to make institutional sense of particular kinds of institutionally important differences, and more. Experts are built around measuring, regulating, and supporting particular individual differences. Failure to perform at the "normative pace of children who have been prepared for certain learning milestones" (Harry & Klingner, 2005, 182) can trigger entry into these practices. Students who call into question these norms, whose identities and experiences do not map neatly into educational institutions, are marked for management. People with "disabilities" (whether the difference is culturally constructed or not is moot at this point) are the population that is most significantly denied access to housing, education, and employment, and this is the population the most "under surveillance" and is "disabled" by physical and social barriers that result in pathologizing, infantilism and poverty" (Reid & Knight, 2006, 18). This line of analysis is frequently difficult for those of us inside the system of the school to recognize.

> A common objection to this kind of interpretation of events might be the question, But are you saying Matthew did not have a disability? Or, Is there no such thing as a disability? We would answer that there is an infinite range of abilities among individuals and that, while there are certainly individuals whose capacities are much more limited than the average, it is societies' decisions related to such individuals that determine whether they will be called disabled. . . . Our concern is what is made of these differences. (Harry & Klingner, 2005, 7–8)

The concern is not only what is made of these differences, but what institutions recognize as difference, how they organize around this identification, what other kinds of relationships are cloaked or masked through this recognition, and more. The problem of the difference is generally only apparent in institutional contexts. For example, the child who can function and resolve problems in everyday life, but cannot in school-based settings. A child can play and behave appropriately in specific cultural or community contexts, but not in classroom settings. These disabilities "are revealed" in school-based, often arbitrary, contexts.[1] There is nothing natural about the

---

[1] See Rogoff, 2003, 37–51.

process through which the differences are identified. "Take away the institution or limit their sphere of relevance and the 'problem' disappears even if the difference does not" (Varenne & McDermott, 1998, 42). This is not to state that these differences are not important or that there are no differences, rather, differences are vital because failure to perform adequately, as this book documents, consigns youth to limited economic, social, and political futures. "Being treated differently can be good, or dangerous, depending on the cultural preoccupations with which it is aligned" (McDermott, Goldman, and Varenne, 2006, 16).

Students' self-knowledge about how their experiences or identities are different is central to the apparatus of the school. Once students are "acquired" by a disability, they often, not always, are provided with important resources, but they are also frequently segregated, documented, and tracked. Their disability has an institutional life. Of particular concern to Varenne and McDermott is the "concern with the individual" (1998, 159) which functions to erase or mask the institutional relations that make that very individual possible. The sociocultural landscape that creates the educational disability is seemingly erased once the student moves into this category. I argue that in Varenne and McDermott's framework, the IEP, the federally mandated individual education plan that every child receiving special education is required to possess, that brings together teachers, parents, and other school- and service-related professionals, moves from being an important tool to assist the child to acquire needed services, to also becoming a blueprint for interpreting and making specific meanings, politically motivated, about difference and what it means for the child, the school, and the wider society.

It is not a surprise that so many students who are poor, or African American, or new immigrants acquire specific educational disabilities, such as "Mental Retardation (MR), specifically Mild Mental Retardation (MMR), also referred to as Educable Mental Retardation; Specific Learning Disability, also refereed to as Learning Disability (LD); Emotional Disturbance (ED); and Speech and Language Impairments (SLI)" (Harry & Klingner, 2005, 2–3). Our discourse of educational "difference" is only a few years removed from the deprivation- or deficit-based theories that were used to justify poor educational achievements by populations that the United States deemed racially or socially inferior (Reid & Knight, 2006; Baker, 2002; Varenne & McDermott, 1998). The origins of educational assessment in the United States have always been intimately linked to eugenics, and connected to practices of race-, gender-, and class-based tracking (Baker, 2002; Stoskepf, 1999). This history of "deficit" theories and biased education assessment has not simply evaporated overnight. For example, frequently, entry into an educational disability is marked by student performance on standardized assessments. A recent study of Latinos in the Chicago Public Schools (CPS) indicated the continuing inadequacy of bilingual services and personnel, a factor that historically has resulted in the overidentification of English Language Learners (ELL) or Limited English Proficiency (LEP) students as special education in other states (Cummins, 1988). The report documents:

> There are 59,078 English Language Learners (Spanish) students in CPS. These students are vastly underserved by the very low number of Spanish bilingual non-instructional professionals: 74 elementary school counselors, 27 school psychologists, 87 social workers, 5 Occupational Therapists and 12 Physical Therapists.
>
> Best practice guidelines require one psychologist per 1,000 students. CPS currently has one psychologist per 1,687 students and only 1 Spanish bilingual psychologist per 6,390 Latino students. There is only one social worker per 1,163 students in CPS and 1 Spanish bilingual social worker per 2,754 Latino students. Illinois State law requires that personnel who evaluate students who have non-English background must be a qualified bilingual specialist. (Aviles et al., 2004, 46)

With Latinos at 36.4% of the total CPS student population (and only 12.6% of teacher and 13.5% of principals), the current availability of bilingual services, especially those in the area of special education, is important (Aviles et al., 2004, 1). Currently, Chicago Public Schools has 19,527 Latinos in preschool programs, and 2,261 of these Latino preschool students are in special education (Aviles et al., 2004, 46). Whereas this category clearly may offer needed resources for preschool students, and undoubtedly all Latino students are not bilingual, it is amazing to conceptualize that 10% of all Latino *preschool* students have been evaluated by a qualified specialist with appropriate assessment tools to have an educational disability, in particular, given the dearth of services for both bilingual and Latino students in CPS.[2]

The concrete links between these practices and the PIC are both wide and diffuse. Evidently, as previously documented, classification as "special

---

[2] I am reminded by disability rights activists that this strategy can result in the further demonization of those students in special education classes. By arguing that these preschoolers are "normal" or "don't belong in special education," the assumption is that this environment is negative, and the folks who really need to be there are somehow negatively impacting the misplaced "regular" students. It is careful work, and in this section I attempt to highlight the construction of these categories while simultaneously acknowledging that in contemporary educational spaces, there are not too many options for students the system demarcates as "nonnormative."

education" in too many cases, and for too many low income and Latino, Indigenous, and African American students, is a ticket, not to educational access, but to undereducation. There is not much "special" in the education offered to the African American students in 1,203 school districts surveyed nationwide in 2002 which identified that "Black overrepresentation in special education programs increased in districts that were operating under court-ordered desegregation" (Harry & Klingner, 2005, 49). There is nothing special in the abnormally high dropout rates for African American students in special education or the reality that African American students in special education are more likely to "have uncertified or provisionally licensed teachers and to graduate with a certificate of attendance or completion rather than a high school diploma (Blanchett, 2006, 26). In addition to this obvious connection, that special education is a documented link in the movement of youth of color toward under education, and that it increases the likelihood of incarceration, as one in three youths in our prison system have received special education services (Offices of Special Education Programs, 1999). Overrepresented in our nation's juvenile justice facilities, the institutional processes of special education also shape and name experience, as *difference*, and "soften" up the individual for surveillance.

These "soft" practices produce subjects and identities and organize difference in institutionally significant ways and attach meanings to particular differences. I write this carefully, fully aware that those whom the system marks as disabled are frequently the first to be targeted for the reduction of services, and are already one of the most economically and politically marginal populations. But as this project is aimed at educators, it is central, as Baker asks, to unpack educational disability discourses.

> What power relations inhere the production of categories such as normal and abnormal? Are these relations worthy of perpetuation? And finally, whether intended or not, is labeling a way of morphing "disability" into the assumptions of an ableist normativity, with all its racial-cultural overtones, rather than questioning certain privileged ontologies and epistemologies to begin with? (Baker, 2002, 689)

The nature of the "special education" categorization perpetuates problematic assumptions about normalcy instead of disrupting them. The range of professionals and expert practices involved in this classification actually function to inhibit the recognition of the immensity of the disciplinary apparatus that is being set into motion. Through one framework these processes are helpful, empowering, natural, scientific, or even "just," and simultaneously these processes can track students away from education, and into invisible and abnormal identities in the blink of an eye. These discourses reify a concept of a normal, perhaps mythic and harmful, that is layered with racial, gendered, and class histories.

For those moved into select "special" educational categories such as "dropout," their experiences are contained.

> [T]he influence of these voices is severely limited because dropouts are perceived as deviant and therefore their perspectives are not worth consideration. The popular image of dropouts as deviant delegitimates their voices and therefore effectively silences their critique of schooling. (Stevenson & Ellsworth, 1993, 260)

The position of "dropout" renders their experience of schooling invalid and positions them as superfluous, possibly dangerous, and perhaps in need of further surveillance by the state. Stevenson and Ellsworth document that dropouts possess an acute analysis about school systems. They state that school policies are unduly harsh, disrespectful, and not relevant, and the curriculum is not preparing them for meaningful employment or postsecondary education, and more, but these critiques are not valid because they are "dropouts." Schools advance with the belief that they are "inherently sound" and the problem lies in the students' family or home life (Stevenson & Ellsworth, 1993). For example, Stevenson and Ellsworth cite, from former Secretary of Education Lauro Cavazos, what I hear frequently from pre- and in-service educators: *Some families (usually Latino or African American parents) just don't care about their children's education* (1993, 261). Sociocultural contexts that shape student performance, such as inequitable school funding schemes that create significantly underresourced schools in poor communities, simply translate into *a student's failure, a dropout*.

The turn to the individual is hardly endemic to schools. From the Personal Responsibility and Work Opportunity Reconciliation Act of 1996 (PROWA) to the meritocratic values embedded in our textbooks (Loewen, 1995), individualism is a core American value. Other socioeconomic changes, notably the growth in the self-help movement, also participate in the promotion of individual and self, and often work to erase the political and economic contexts that actively produce this self.

Recovery

In her work examining how institutional discursive practices shape how we live, the relations of ruling, D.E. Smith framed the work of the "helping professions," specifically, psychological discourses, and I continue this work by examining the role that the self-help or mutual help movement plays in the privatization of public issues. The organizations in this movement, often nonprofits in some cases, do the work that the state once provided, or should have provided. The recovery movement also provides a larger ideological cover to mask the consequences of "hateful" public policies. I offer this critique with the full, perhaps contradictory knowledge that organizations such as Alcoholics Anonymous (AA) continue to radically and positively change people's lives.[3] I do not doubt this; rather, I am working to excavate what other social functions these processes fulfill. Just as the previous section worked to unpack other interpretations of the proliferation of special education, categories that can also radically change students' lives, in this section I investigate, as medical anthropologists Lock and Scheper-Hughes write, the "side effects" of the production of disorders.

> Negative and hostile feelings can be shaped and transformed by doctors and psychiatrists into symptoms of new diseases such as PMS (premenstrual syndrome), depression, or attention deficit disorder. . . . In such a way negative social sentiments such as female rage and school phobias can be recast as individual pathologies and "symptoms" rather than as socially significant signs. . . . This funneling of diffuse but real complaints into the idiom of sickness has led to the problem of medicalization and to the overproduction of illness. *In this process, the role of doctors, social workers, psychiatrists, and criminologists as agents of social consensus is pivotal.* (Lock & Scheper-Hughes, 1990, 67–68; emphasis mine)

Instead of naming these emotions or feelings as criticisms or consequences of public policies, or even simply "outlaw emotions" (chapter 2) that are rational in response to oppressive contexts, professionals have the ability to literally recast these physical and emotional responses as individual and private pathologies. Lock and Scheper-Hughes are pointing to the "medicalization of life." Whereas the recovery movement encompasses more than medical categories and afflictions, and I also emphasize that aspects of the recovery movement do work against oppressive and corporate healthcare practices, the recovery movement emphasizes, in part, the language of disease. In the Lock and Scheper-Hughes paradigm, the role of the professional or the expert who offers a diagnosis is central as this expert acts as the bridge between the discourse and the afflicted body.

---

[3] This chapter's discussion or critique of self-help movements, such as Alcoholics Anonymous and other often consumer-based, nonprofessional self-help organizations, can be interpreted to validate more traditional or conservative therapeutic or healthcare practices, for example, institutionalization or drug therapy. This is not my intent. I reiterate that this chapter attempts to point to some contexts (this, of course, is never neutral) rather than to assess the practices.

Although the recovery movement appears to exist outside of this professional realm, this is often not the case.

In the North American context, the popularization of 12-step groups and support practices can be linked to a similar ideological genesis: the development of the AA movement (Makela, 1996; Warhol & Michie, 1996; Rapping, 1997). AA was formed in 1935 by two white men: a stockbroker and a physician. In their attempts to address their alcoholism Bill Wilson and Dr. Bob Smith began to talk and share their problems with alcohol. A Christian-based core of spiritualism, a man-to-man fellowship, and a definition that placed alcoholism within the disease model, formed a base for the philosophies of AA. The 12 steps that Bob and Bill developed were essentially the steps they used and discussed to clarify and address, in an ongoing manner, their own drinking. Characterized by anonymity (only first names are used and confidentiality is a core component), submitting to a higher power (originally God), and confession, the model of recovery from alcoholism that Bill and Bob developed was antihierarchical and did not require an expert. The model required acknowledging that one was powerless and needed to turn "our lives over to God" (step 2) and for God to "remove all these defects of character" (step 6, AA, n.d.). The steps emphasize the individual and the individual's need to submit to a higher power. Analyzing oppression, identifying common structural inequities that shape the lives of those using alcohol, and working collaboratively to change political and economic contexts that facilitate self-medication are not part of the 12-step foundation. Thus, for white men who have access to social and political power it might be a transformative move to acknowledge a certain sense of powerlessness; however, when one is already positioned as outside the state and in fact criminalized and penalized for existing, acknowledging powerlessness can be further alienating and can be a move to erase existence. A therapeutic recovery, where one leaves an addiction behind, does not "cure" the social ills that led to the addiction in the first place.

Flourishing in part because it advanced alcoholism as a disease, consistent with the medical model, AA developed and prospered between 1940 and 1980, a time of larger cultural, social, and economic shifts in North America.[4] The postwar changes in men's roles contributed to the growth because AA targeted "white Christian males, whose traditional roles and prerequisites were being most severely challenged and usurped, but upon

---

[4] Engaging with the discourse of whether alcoholism or any addiction is a disease or a result of environmental factors is beyond the scope of this project. This section is not intended to offer a response to this question, rather to highlight the structure that has developed to manage these identities.

whom the new system nonetheless depended" (Rapping, 1997, 73). AA modified and did open up to permit women, eventually developing specific resource materials targeted to women and other communities; however, despite this move to include women and minorities, the overriding identification is the identity of the alcoholic, not gender or race. The incorporation of women and minorities did little to acknowledge the social inequalities that might lead women and others to alcoholism; instead, this inclusion was done to illustrate the accessibility and equity of the disease. The AA model prescribes and regulates certain definitions of "the disease" and "the addict" that actually attempt to erase social contexts and race or gender (Warhol & Michie, 1996, 328).

The AA model, initially confined to white males, has expanded. AA is now the largest mutual-help movement worldwide, and it is estimated to have in excess of two million members in 114 countries (Makela, 1996). The term "mutual-help" is more precise than "self-help," as the 12-step process is essentially community based, not solely a "self-help process."[5] The umbrella organization of AA, General Service Office (GSO), gives guidance, policies, and standards, and approves literature and resources to independent small offices in cities all over the United States and Canada. "AA has no real government. Each group is free to work out its own customs and ways of holding meetings, as long as it does not hurt other groups or AA as a whole" (Alcoholics Anonymous, 1972). The global expansion of AA was initially into English-speaking countries with Protestant traditions, and those countries with developed economic and professional relations with the United States (Makela, 1996, 27).

The expanded recovery movement in the North American context grew during the conservative Reagan-Bush years, a time when most state-funded social service programs were being seriously reduced (or privatized). Nonprofits and self-help organizations constitute the "shadow state," or the world of community- and faith-based organizations, which, in the decades of the contraction of the welfare state, offer some similar services once provided by the state (Walch, as cited in Bloom, 2006). As discussed in chapter 3, federal government funding for social welfare programs—for example, housing, unemployment compensation, and food and nutrition assistance—has decreased significantly since 1975. Recovery programs (12-step, self-help) are weaved into educational and judicial systems. People on

---

[5] Self-help is generally defined in opposition to professional help. Mutual-help groups are defined: "to exclude groups led by professionals or others who do not share the defining affliction of the movement, and to exclude advocacy groups. In our usage, a mutual help movement is an association or aggregate of groups whose members meet on a egalitarian basis to counteract through mutual interaction a common affliction or problem in their lives" (Rapping, 1997, 13).

parole are often required to undergo support groups or 12-step programs to ensure and legitimate their recovery (a process called "court carding" in the United States[6]), and disruptive or nonconforming students can be expected to attend support groups to remain in school programs. Some schools, insurance corporations, government agencies, and other institutions have embraced 12-step programs or affiliated practices of support and recovery (Rapping, 1997, 192, n. 7). For example, if an employee is noticed to have a drinking, a drug, or a home life problem that affects his/her work productivity or capacity, many large institutions, instead of firing the employee, will direct the employee to get counseling, go to AA, or contact the EAP (Employee Assistance Program). Makela states that this shift into rehabilitation might be influenced more by economic factors than by healthcare policies:

> The goal of cutting prison and welfare costs may be the most important explanation for the expansion of referrals to AA by courts and Employee Assistance Programs in the United States. In other situations the AA movement may stimulate the growth of private treatment programs. (Makela, 1996, 185)

These are free programs. The state does not participate in oversight or regulation, yet it benefits because it does not have to pay for these services.

Often, formerly and currently incarcerated people attend a myriad of recovery programs.[7] Often attendance is not due to an active philosophical or healthcare choice by the individual. Rather, choice is dictated by what resources are free and available. Also, people are desperate for services and assistance, and recovery models are welcome and opening, and though research may indicate otherwise (Bakalar, 2006), they appear to have a successful track record. This recovery model is also frequently perceived by many to be more democratic, less hierarchical, and less hinged to institutional forces than acquiring counseling services through social workers, therapists, psychiatrists, and so on. In addition, as discussed, people are often *required* to attend a range of programs that require the performance of particular kinds of self-understandings, parenting classes, life skills workshops, goal-setting seminars, and anger management classes, including 12-step programs. A person's failure to attend and satisfactorily

---

[6] This practice persists despite a case in 1996, when the New York Court of Appeals decided that court mandating to AA programs does violate the Establishment Clause of the United States Constitution (Barron, 1996).

[7] As of 2004, AA's membership survey showed that there were 52,651 groups in the United States and 4,872 groups in Canada, totaling 1,280,963 members. Of those, 2,562 groups were located within correctional facilities with a total of 66,576 incarcerated members, or just over 5% of the total AA membership (Alcoholics Anonymous, 2004).

complete the self-improvement, educational, and recovery programs that he or she is often court-mandated to attend can mean a failure to signify rehabilitation and a revocation of parole. Even though AA does not provide letters of reference to parole boards or court officials, roughly 11% of people referred to AA are done so by court order (Alcoholics Anonymous, 2004). The General Service Office acknowledges that pre-parole activity is encouraged and local AA groups can elect to work with parole officers. This is even extended in some areas to include detailed lists of parolees who attended meetings inside correctional facilities. Through court orders, parole requirements, and groups in corrections facilities, AA is interconnected with the PIC.

The reliance of the judicial system on these programs is partially due to economics. As Rapping notes, the expansion and success of AA-type programs could be attributed to the success of AA to "rehabilitate," but also the growth of AA is due to the expansion of referrals by the courts and employee assistance programs (EAPs) to AA and other recovery programs. Courts and workplaces refer individuals to these free programs and it does not cost the state (or the employer) (Rapping, 1997, 85–87). This process functions to facilitate the internalization of power relations. Just as the student who has difficulty learning is shifted through normative and institutional practices into the world of "learning disability," the woman with the drug problem, through normative and institutional practices, is moved into understanding her drug problem through particular individualized, recovery narratives, as opposed to a "rational" response to poverty, violence, or undereducation.

The recovery and self-help programs attended by those who are poor and reliant on state programs, or who were formerly incarcerated, do permit participants to engage in a process of healing. As mentioned earlier, AA changes people's lives, enables them to function, to resume relationships, be employed, and to address what were debilitating, potentially life-threatening addictions. In addition, these programs often have the capacity to signify rehabilitation, personal growth, or learning to the justice system. Experience and the act of speaking out about pain can be radical and revolutionary and AA provides this context. It is not a surprise that feminism, as Rapping notes, played a key role in the development of the recovery movement. Perhaps one of the most powerful movements in the United States, feminism uses experience as a voice to challenge oppressive regimes of patriarchy, heteronormativity, and white supremacy.

> [R]ecovery movement groups . . . institutionalized a way of talking about and dealing with so called "addictive disorders" which was based largely upon insights and ideas borrowed—often explicitly—

from feminist discourse and analysis. Here almost all discussion of addiction, as it were, involved, indeed required—a fairly elaborate form of personal narrative, very different from AA sharing, in which family and other relationship dynamics were introduced and generalized about, as they had been in CR. (Rapping, 1997, 190, n. 4)

Feminist consciousness raising (CR) groups and AA overlapped in that both started from the power of personal experiences and narratives, yet CR and AA had some significant differences. CR groups were used to politically empower women for personal and social change, to analyze collective experiences and to mobilize personal narratives for political or social changes. AA (while not excluding the possibility of political change) is much more individualized and about submitting to higher powers.

As this chapter works to argue, recovery movements can also attempt to rewrite profound experiences from social critiques to private issues. This could be one end to this analysis. Special education is simply a mechanism of state oppression. Schools create and prepare the self for surveillance and to internalize regulatory discourses. The participants in the high school program who are in programs such as AA are cultural dupes who are simply caught in a nexus of the technologies of the prison industrial complex and ventriloquate what institutions dictate. The PIC successfully co-opts the mainstream's perception of the democratic (horizontal, anti-institutional) practices of AA and other self-help programs and utilizes these practices as a front for management of bodies. These cultural systems contain evidence of the structural failure of dominant institutions. Yet it is central to consider what resistance resembles, because there is no institutional practice that doesn't possess a counter-resistance.

Experience and Resistance

Whereas select traumatic experiences have become highly visible in the past few decades, simultaneously their political capacity has been neutralized. Although those marginalized by public policies, such as welfare reform or sexual harassment, are asked to testify in front of elected officials, and those with debilitating illnesses who struggle without healthcare or medicine are included as anecdotes in the president's State of the Union address, these stories appear to have declining affective power. In this moment of the hypervisibility of experience, the stories of the lives of those who struggle have never been so meaningless. For example, in July 2004 the *Chicago Tribune* ran a special three-part series tracing the educational experiences of nine-year-old Rayola Carwell. The series focused on Rayola winning the "educational lottery" in 2004, when she was one of

1,097 students out of nearly 19,000 who had literally won the right, under the federal No Child Left Behind legislation, passed in 2002, to transfer to a district school making Adequate Yearly Progress (AYP). Only 536 students actually transferred. The headline articles tracked Rayola's move to Stockton Elementary School, where she decides to use her middle name, Victoria, because she perceives that Rayola is "too black" for her new school. Rayola does not persist at Stockton. The series is a powerful indictment of the inadequacies of our federal educational legislation, our scandalous minimum wage that is not a living wage, the dramatic consequences of rapid urban gentrification on the lives of the city's working poor, and the endemic and structural nature of white supremacy (Banchero, 2004).

When less than 3% of the students eligible to transfer to a "better" school were able to do so, Rayola's experiences are such clear evidence, in particular, of the failure of federal legislation such as No Child Left Behind. Although the article had some impact, and clearly I was moved, I argue that it does little to continue to produce testimony, or "evidence," of poor public policies, school failures, and more, especially if this testimony circulates in a context where audiences have been trained to interpret through preset frameworks, for example, the "welfare queen" or the "illegal alien." I suggest that a careful reading indicates that Rayola/Victoria seemingly recognizes that this circulation of her story will not improve her educational situation. Throughout the three-part series, the tone (while from Banchero) that comes from nine-year-old Rayola, who is "trudging" and "shrugs and yawns" across schools, is one of resignation. Whereas Rayola telegraphs the poverty and educational failures of the nation, do the details of Rayola's life obscure not the meaning, but the remedy? Rayola disappears from the *Tribune*, and her experiences, front page news for three days, fade. Her educational experiences, while offering a deep critique, do not result in public outcry, do not result in change.

Investigating the landscape that Rayola's experiences circulate within offers insights into relationships between experience—for Rayola, the trauma that results from the abject failure of educational policy—and the politics of disclosure. Whereas language shapes experience, other forces, such as patriarchy and colonialism, impact the landscape in which experience and testimonials circulate, and this landscape defines what counts as a survivor, and what counts as a legitimate "trauma" for different audiences. In addition, disclosures of experience can render bodies more subject to forms of surveillance, disciplining, and social control, as the previous sections suggested. The process of disclosure, or "speaking out" if the experience is not sanctioned and the audience is not aligned with the speaker, can mean that the dominant institutions recuperate or appropriate this act of "speaking out." As feminists have documented, instead of empowering the speaker, those marginalized who speak out, for example, women who speak out against rape or sexual harassment in the work site, can be delegitimated.

> The very act of speaking out has become used as performance and spectacle. The growth of this phenomenon raises questions: Has it simply replayed confessional modes that recuperate dominate patriarchal discourses without subversive effect, or has it been able to create new spaces within these discourses and to begin to develop an autonomous counterdiscourse, one capable of empowering survivors? (Alcoff & Gray-Rosendale, 1996, 208)

For Rayola, the articles offer the feeling that she is all too familiar with this reality of being disempowered.

Yet, despite this landscape, "survivor," in this contemporary era where the Holocaust is an archetype for trauma and versions of recovery are performed daily on TV talk shows, is an important term to evaluate. After World War II, the survivor carries significant cultural and moral weight. "Survivors of traumatic historical events are awarded moral authority and their experience carries the weight of cultural value" (Sturken, in Bal et al., 1999, 241). Audiences reserve a kind of epistemic privilege for the speaking position of survivor. Marita Sturken argues that this position of survivor has garnered such power that it can grant a body the right to speech. "In what ways has declaring oneself a survivor become synonymous with having the right to speak?" (Sturken, in Bal et al., 1999, 242). In order to be heard, she suggests, one has to assert the voice of survivor. Yet survivor and trauma are not neutral categories. All atrocities are not equal and some survivor speaking positions are more privileged than others. Whereas rape or incest survivors' testimonies may be challenged, audiences do not appear to call into question the survivors' narratives from the high school shootings in Columbine, Colorado and Rayola's experiences in poverty do not enable her to use the term "survivor" at all. Patriarchy and colonialism impact the landscape in which these testimonials circulate. In some spheres, to identify as a survivor of a historical trauma such as the Holocaust would carry definitely more moral weight and less social stigma than to identify as a victim of abandonment, rape, or childhood abuse. What is at the core is how these experiences, in particular, traumatic experiences, are narrated both by institutions and by the individuals who are impacted.

What if you are not a survivor of a socially sanctioned trauma that affords a privileged speaking position? What if subjects know that the audience, mainstream North Americans, will not bear witness to their life story in ways that will be politically or personally efficacious?

The desire to demand more from your audience(s) is not diminished by this awareness of their impairments but it does make the work more difficult. The representation of trauma *to* or *for* an audience can often result in an act of epistemic violence where an audience presumes to know too much, or uses the knowledge of another's trauma as a vehicle to understand themselves or humanity "better." Davis offers a clear example of this in a discussion about the U.S. public response to the Abu Ghraib prison torture. The circulation of the photographs of those tortured at Abu Ghraib in the United States functioned to erase the individuals, at the cost of a universal message.

> The human beings represented in the photographs became the abstract objects of forms of torture that were considered an anathema to democracy. . . . Who were these people? Can we imagine them as workers, artists, educators, parents, children? Can we imagine ourselves in their places? I don't think we were encouraged to think about the images in this way. (Davis, 2005, 80)

Davis suggests that these representations functioned to erase the particular, the real people who were tortured, but were used to symbolize fundamental questions about U.S. democracy. The "interpretive schema offered to the public . . . foreclosed solidarity with the victims" (Davis, 2005, 80).

Knowing this context, an awareness of "interpretive schema" that folks will bring to interpreting your life, or an awareness of epistemology of ignorance, can move subjects to exert more control over how their experiences are understood. Or, Sommer (1999) argues, in *Proceed With Caution, When Engaged by Minority Writing in the Americas*, perhaps the knowledge of a fundamentally incompetent audience that possesses significant power may translate into the development of creative strategies to signify to this audience that their incompetence is a flaw that will not go unnoticed. Readers may have the privilege to be ignorant on issues that are vitally central to the lives of too many, but this ignorance will not go unremarked. Toni Morrison asserts that readers may never know what it is like to be a slave, yet they have an historical burden to acknowledge and understand to a reasonable degree the legacy of slavery. If readers fail to possess this "reasonable" level of knowledge, they will not be permitted to be voyeurs.[8] Perhaps the reader becomes the "butt of a textual joke" where the author at least derives some pleasure from the cognitive impairment of the reader.

---

[8] For example, Sommer discusses how carefully, in Morrison's *Beloved*, Sethe and Beloved disclose their histories of trauma: "The story of slavery is public, it needs to be, but she [Morrison] won't have readers warming their cold bones on harrowing confessions of degradation and death" (1999, 164).

Sommer identifies a variety of narrative strategies that the authors she ana-lyzes use to deal with interpretive dilemmas partially inscribed in Western ways of knowing: empathy, universalizing experiences, apolitical readings, and more. She inverts Spivak's question to raise an issue, central to trauma and experience: "To ask if the subaltern can speak, as Gayatri Spivak had asked, misses a related point. The pertinent question is whether the other party can listen" (Sommer, 1999, 20). Speaking truth to power, as the adage states, can be empowering for the speaker, but if the audience is not able to listen, power is limited.[9] Sommer argues that the author's knowledge of the epistemic location of her reader incites authors to be crafty. If the author knows that the reader is not a competent reader, authors need to craft a particular tale to achieve their desired ends—to disturb the readers and bring their realities, their struggles, their traumas into existence, making the deep and lasting social reality of the trauma real to themselves and oth-ers, and bringing the social and political into existence.

Boarding School Healing Project and Women and Prison: A Site for Resistance

Contexts of endemic indifference and incompetence when audiences lack an awareness of the historical, economic, and political conditions that shaped the author's experiences, are moved, by necessity, to complicated strategies of disclosure that do not merely reproduce existing indifference or pathology. "Telling the simple truth" is not useful if an audience is not interested or is not able to hear the truth. These strategies of calculated dis-closures and this awareness of how specific kinds of violence delegitimize or disqualify their speaking position are evidenced by any marginalized population: students in schools, women in the prison system. Those poor and marginalized will need to ventriloquize for the job market, for social service agencies, and for a myriad of new institutional structures. It is use-ful to possess a variety of stories about trauma and life for the employ-ment market or to protect yourself from the pain of narrating a traumatic experience that is outside the comprehension of your everyday audience, or when the larger contexts view your trauma as the result of your individ-ual poor choices, instead of connecting this experience to harmful public policies. Examining the relationships between the recovery movement and the PIC indicates that the prevailing tools that those incarcerated acquire to understand their experience are tools and frameworks that work to advance ideologies of individualism, and to emphasize personal respon-

---

[9] I use the metaphor of aurality, following the writing of Spivak and Sommer, but would prefer other metaphors.

sibility over environmental contexts, and personal growth over collective empowerment and political advocacy.

At a 2004 discussion, *Gender, Race and Incarceration*, in Chicago, Pilar Maschi from Critical Resistance asked what a political recovery model might look like for women in the PIC. She suggested that the dominant model of recovery available for those who experience state violence was a highly individuated therapeutic model that generally did not empower women to emerge as communities of activists to challenge the oppressive and punitive environments that moved them into the PIC. She spoke about the limitations of the therapeutic model, and her recovery through politicization and community building:

> Before I became politicized I had never heard of the concept, prison abolition. I knew the police were only in poor neighborhoods like mine. I knew they were caging and beating my friends and families inside and outside jails and prisons. I knew my friends and families were disappearing to the state, while newly built high rises were replacing Latino and African American owned family businesses. And at worst, I hated the police for shooting and killing my father with a 9 millimeter, when I was 17. I spent most of my life fighting the police and other institutions the best way I knew how. I was angry and the only resistance I knew was using drugs and remaining numb. I knew the police were only pawns of a larger force that I was against, but I also felt responsible for the choices that I made in the course of my life. I often was told by mostly everyone that I deserved being caged and I internalized it. I thought that was the price I had to pay for being a bad person. With support from people who believed the PIC needed to be dismantled, I realized I did not have access to the same choices those in power did and I didn't have to accept it. Being politically active is a form of recovery, and truly a form of resistance. It is the closest feeling I have to freedom. It is a place where my hopes are manifested. (Maschi, 2004)

Maschi, by clearly critiquing the therapeutic model, names a political recovery that does not ask her to individualize, does not ask her to separate her experiences from a context and a history, and actively values her impetus for change. These opportunities for political recoveries are rare, but I offer an overview of two initiatives, the Boarding School Healing Project (BSHP) and Women and Prison: A Site for Resistance, that work to reappropriate the discourse of survivors, in this saturated landscape, to recast experiences, and to politicize trauma in the framework of movement building for community change.

Established in 2000, the BSHP (http://www.boardingschoolhealing-project.org/) is designed to heal Indigenous Communities from the genocide in the United States, induced by the U.S. government and religious orders, that was carried out in part through formal education. Starting with the Carlisle School in Pennsylvania in 1879, the U.S. government, often in partnership with religious institutions, with the mission to "Kill the Indian and to Save the Man" (Adams, 1988; A. Smith, 2005), established a network of schools across the United States (and Canada). The schools trained students for low-wage domestic labor positions in violent, prisonlike environments. Sexual and physical abuse was rampant. As A. Smith (2005) and Adams (1988) document, attendance at these schools was mandatory. These schools were federal policy in the United States and began to decline, slowly, only after the publication in 1928 of *The Meriam Report*, which recommended that boarding schools be closed.

The BSHP "seeks to document boarding school abuses and demand justice from the U.S. government and churches. The four components of this project are healing, education, documentation, and accountability" (A. Smith, 2005, 44). The process of recovery from these state-sanctioned traumas requires support groups for survivors, but it also requires community consciousness raising, and politicization. Whereas the first step for the BSHP was to establish support groups for survivors, this second step, documentation, includes political education with communities and survivors.

> Part of the documentation process entails asking participants what types of remedies they would like to see from both churches and the U.S. government, so they can be involved in the political strategy as well. (A. Smith, 2005, 45)

The process to raise awareness involves a grassroots educational campaign that relies on trained educators recruited from the community. The process of community-based education and documentation has resulted in the reevaluation of experience, as many survivors of the boarding schools did not necessarily language the violence they endured as a human rights violation (A. Smith, 2005, 45). Through this process, experience is reclaimed, not just by the individuals, but by a community. The experience of those that survived boarding schools is no longer defined and owned by the state. Finally, the fourth principle of the BSHP is accountability, and to date the BSHP strategy has been to pursue accountability most aggressively through the courts. Healing means addressing sovereignty issues, and making reparations that are not merely individual monetary compensations is a powerful move. Reclaiming experience, training community members, and collaboratively investigating avenues for reparations, are all connected to recovery.

Launched by Beyondmedia Education in 2005, the mission of this multimedia site (http://www.womenandprison.org) is to provide communities widespread access to the realities of the lives of women in prisons in the United States.[10] The site was established to counter the relative invisibility of the issue of race, gender, and incarceration in the United States, and also to prioritize the experience and analysis of former prisoners. Combining interviews, video and audio clips, links to reports by a number of human rights organizations (for example, Amnesty International and Human Rights Watch), poetry, and a few academic articles that offer additional theoretical insights, the site is intended to provide a space for organizing and educating around women and prison. Explicitly, the site

> [M]akes visible women's experiences in the criminal justice system. Documenting these stories is integral to this project of resistance. The stories are supported by a collection of resources, such as organizations, reports, essays, and links to a wide range of information on women and prison. . . . This site serves as a dedicated space for prisoners, those previously incarcerated, activists, students, academics, and everyone who strives for social justice. Through the use of this website, we hope to promote strategies and actions that challenge the system and the ways that it reproduces all forms of discrimination, violence, and social injustice in the treatment of women and their families. (Women and Prison, 2006)

Making women's experiences visible means prioritizing the voices and analyses of those directly impacted. In *A Site for Resistance*, this includes academic and journalistic articles, poetry, letters, and hopefully grievances and other kinds of state documentations authored by women. The site also includes interviews. As of 2006, the site has 13 in-depth transcribed interviews. Each woman who is interviewed is named, and in some cases there are photos. Their participation is entirely voluntary and when resources are available through grants that have been acquired to support the site, stipends have been available for women to participate, and for the women who gather stories. As a member of the collective that initiated this project I have some stake in it and I am not unbiased in my evaluation, but *Women and Prison: A Site for Resistance* offers a model of representing experiences that is not simply individuated and therapeutic, but linked to change and advocacy.

---

[10] I am, as previous references in this book attest, personally invested in this organization. Beyondmedia Education was started by Salome Chasnoff in 2000. I was an active board member from 2000 to 2005, and as a member of the group that started the site, I continue to be a supporter, and more. The real labor of constructing the site was done by technowizard Kelley Noah and numerous interns such as Amber Smock. As of 2006 Jessi Jackson is the site coordinator.

The interviews, currently available via audio and transcription, with video links forthcoming, offer powerful personal experiences of life before, during, and after prison, in addition to central critiques about the PIC and analysis of various issues related to the PIC: healthcare, parenting, limitations of rehabilitation programs, and more. For example, Pamela Thomas, in her interview, offers an analysis about the lack of educational resources in prisons.

> They say people in prison don't want to go to school. They would be locked up for ten years and don't have a G.E.D. That's 'cause they take ten years to get your name off the waiting list. You might have 500 people, and you have got 6 spots open. It's not that people don't want to get educated. It is hard to get into the school. You get lucky, 'cause you have to know somebody or somebody pulled your name out or something like that. I don't see how it benefits anybody. (Thomas, n.d.)

Not only does Thomas offer an analysis of her experience, but her critique of the societal interpretation of women in prison is powerful. If a reader is interested in educational issues in prison, they could link to reports on the site that offer more context on education in prisons, written by human rights organizations or other women. Or, when Iyrania Hill described her experiences in segregation:

> I just felt like I was crazy cause you stay in your room for twenty-three hours a day, you come out for one hour. You got one hour to take a shower, wash your clothes if you got some clothes that need washing, comb your hair. You got one hour to do just some of everything. Then after the one hour's up, you're back in your room twenty three hours, no TV. (Hill, n.d.)

Hill's words stand alone as critique and analysis, but if Web users need more, *Surviving Solitary*, by former political prisoner Laura Whitehorn (1997), offers more context to the experiences of segregation. Reports from human rights organizations also offer resources, and more data.

I emphasize how the interviews are placed and used, because while Hill and Thomas are set within an interpretive schema, they are positioned on a Web site called "A Site for Resistance." I would argue that their words *contribute* to this interpretive schema, they are not interpreted. Instead of being used within a project for other authors (such as this book), or rendered anonymous in reports or surveys, or used to support an interpretive framework offer by a researcher, Hill and Thomas are agents of knowledge production who are active participants of the site, which seeks to reframe the experiences of women in prison as vital critiques of the state.

The site includes a glossary, and there are spaces for feedback and to submit work. It offers links to organizations, and it is constantly growing. This site disseminates experience, in a politicized context. To name the site as resistance shapes how viewers will interpret the site, or even how it will be located on the Web. Although the medium of the Internet does not ensure access for everyone, *Woman and Prison: A Site for Resistance* has the potential to be a dynamic organizing tool.

These two organizations are not the only models, nor are they perfect, but both *A Site for Resistance* and BSHP offer concrete examples of collaborative processes that struggle with the centrality of translating experience into documentary evidence within an explicitly political framework. As Maschi (2004) clearly identified, recovery is not through an isolated speech act. Recovery requires sovereignty, politicization, control over self-representation, and more. These frameworks differentiate BSHP and *A Site for Resistance* from other mutual or self-help groups and research or documentation projects. These initiatives start from a recognition that survivor is a powerful speaking position, that experience is central, and that the state apparatus seeks to contain and manage these experiences. BSHP and *A Site for Resistance* aim to create community spaces that support experiences to be used in politically empowering ways that are also individually healing.

The Revolution Will Not Be Funded?[11]

Special education and recovery movements can function both to mask powerful critiques of what passes for natural and normal and "right" within our institutions, and to track the individual, demarcated by her difference, more and more into the grasp of punitive surveillance structures. The individual differences, or outlaw behaviors and emotions, or deviancies that are the core of both recovery movements and special education do possess the potential to radically challenge the effectiveness of institutions and even to call into question fundamental tenets of our democracy. What if we were asked as a nation to reconceptualize ability and disability, to acknowledge these as constructs? How would our institutions have to change? What if we had to take seriously the poverty or compulsory heteronormativity, or system white supremacy, that, for some, shapes our nation's desire to self-medicate? What if all this rage, and sadness, and "difference" were not managed by the state, but, like the Boarding School Healing Project, or the Women and Prison Web site, these experience are used to incite a new state?

---

[11] I borrow this heading from the INCITE! conference in May 2004.

CHAPTER **6**

Horizons of Abolition

Strategizing for Change through the
Good, the Bad, and the Innocent

I am talking to educators about the school to jail "pipeline." It is a hot September day and folks are fanning themselves with my handout. A woman is visibly sleeping in the third row.

I sketch for the audience how schools facilitate the movement of youth of color into more punitive institutions such as prisons. I don't feel as if I have the audience—they are drifting. It is the weather, or perhaps it is because I am talking right after lunch. At the end of my talk I offer a short discussion about the concept of prison abolition and people visibly perk up. I talk about how the relationships between schools and jails moved me to consider the concept of prison abolition, or imagining worlds without prisons. I am careful to say that for me abolition does not mean opening the doors to San Quentin tomorrow, although I do not state that I am not certain this is such a bad idea, but rather I want to work toward reducing my, and my communities', dependence on police, surveillance, and other punitive structures.

The word abolition jars the audience. When I say this word, I feel the tone in the room change. People wake up. They twitch in their molded chairs and refocus on what I am saying. People make eye contact with me and the room becomes more engaged, more restless.

After I finish my talk, the first questions are slightly hostile, or at least I perceive them this way, and they are all centered around fear and abolition, as they are at the end of most of my talks on the role

165

of education in the incarceration-nation that introduces abolition. People ask:

What about the child molesters? What about the rapists? The real sociopaths? Don't we still need prisons for these really bad people?

I have just spent almost one hour documenting that schools actively produce categories of "bad" people, and these categories are deeply racialized, embedded in historical practices of disqualification, and the question that preoccupies people is simply:

What about the bad people?

I am pretty dejected. I wonder whether I am an effective speaker. If I offered enough facts, or shaped the argument. Or, what are these fears and investments in "bad people"?

The persistence of these kinds of questions, "what about the bad people," despite all kinds of qualifiers and discussions moved me to consider that educators, and other audiences, have investments in constructs of good and bad people. In particular, attempts on my part to analyze the relationships between schools and jails, or to critique these systems periodically ended up being interpreted as support for the perpetrators and diminishing the natural rights or the experiences of victims. To be fair, these questions also arose in contexts with those that were disproportionately impacted by incarceration. For example, for two semesters in my social studies class at the high school we read chapters from Angela Davis's *Are Prisons Obsolete?* Students, all formerly incarcerated except myself and my coteacher Ajitha Reddy, are quick to say that Amendment 13 is unjust, *Neither slavery nor involuntary servitude, except as a punishment for crime whereof the party shall have been duly convicted, shall exist within the United States, or any place subject to their jurisdiction,* because it permits those incarcerated to be, literally, slaves. They widely acknowledge they are routinely denied their basic bill of rights guaranteed them in the Constitution, and that the prison system is unfixable, corrupt, and brutal. Yet, simultaneously, with a few detractors, they do not support Davis's argument. Participants respond that they could not imagine a world without prisons, because the "really bad people" need to be placed somewhere. There really are bad people who belong in prison (but just not them).

This construction of "victim" and "perpetrator," of those good and those bad, with conflicting and usually absolutely dichotomous interests, has bled into our legal and popular conceptions of justice. These categories are not adequate. Bad people, as my friend and colleague Alison Bailey states, are never the Enron executives. Bad people are always those targeted and arrested by police and without the resources to get a good lawyer: the women in jail for prostitution, the kids on the corner picked up for selling drugs. Our law and order system does not catch all the bad people, nor does it actually recognize as a crime all the kinds of harm and violence that individuals experience. In fact, our law and order system has historically protected those with power and privilege from scrutiny and does not recognize their harmful actions as crime. However, the purpose of my discussions around prison abolition, or reducing our reliance on incarceration and punishment as responses to significant social problems, is not to end up in a debate about who is "really bad" or to quibble over who is "badder." Even to admit to the obvious, that we are all flawed, misses the point. The system does not work. It does not provide rehabilitation. It targets poor people and people of color and lends itself to interlocking relationships with other institutions. It is directly connected to the histories of race and oppression in the United States and it is difficult to talk about our contemporary prison system in isolation of slavery. It forecloses other avenues for conceptualizing and addressing the trauma of violence, and, arguably, does little to improve the lives of communities and individuals who experience harm. Educators need to be linking schools to the expanding PIC and this requires us to unpack natural categories such as the child or school discipline and to clearly link these categories and practices to the PIC, and to widen our landscape of what are relevant knowledge bases and skills sets for educators to possess.

However, what became clear to me as a result of my, however nascent, attempts to discuss prison abolition and how we are complicit in the production of public enemies, is that this project must include discussion about our investments in bad people (without which there can be no good people) and some strategies to work through and around these constructs of the good, the bad, and the innocent. These constructs have significant implications for educators, who have equally deep investments in success and failure in school. Our entire project, as educators, is predicated on failure. We teach, and some students, always, fail to learn. Failure is one *successful* path through school.

> In America, no particular person need fail, and failure need not be confined to the children of any particular groups. But half the children must fall below average, and therein lies the problem that concerns us. (Varenne & McDermott, 1998, 209)

Just as our schools produce gifted children, successful learners, good kids, we simultaneously require and produce the inverse, remedial learners, educational failures, bad seeds, and more. Investigating our investments in these educated outcomes offers an opportunity to conceptualize different strategies for change.

In this chapter I examine some contemporary strategies that are working to interrupt the school to jail track, and consider these strategies in the context of both prison abolition work and investments in *the good, the bad, and the innocent*. In the last part of this chapter I offer discussions about solidarity and movement building for change. The emphasis in this chapter is on strategies for change and examining and complicating practices that have had limited success, and mobilizing "us" educators in elementary, secondary, and university classrooms to participate in movements that work toward abolition. First, briefly, I define prison abolition and how and why it intersects with education.

What Is Abolition?

The term "prison abolition" literally means to work to abolish prisons. It is a relatively small movement supported by national organizations like Critical Resistance, centered in Oakland, California, and by networks of antiprison activists such as the Anarchist Black Cross. Prison abolition, for most of these organizations, does not mean there will be no problems or violence, rather that prisons are not a just nor an efficient or moral solution to the problems that lead folks to commit crimes. Or, as Davis writes:

> What I have tried to do—together with many other public intellectuals, activists, scholars—is to encourage people to think about the possibility that punishment may be a consequence of the forces and not an inevitable consequence of the commission of crime. Which is not to say that people in prisons have not committed what we call "crimes"—I am not making that argument at all. Regardless of who has or has not committed crimes, punishment, in brief can be seen more as a consequence of racialized surveillance. (2005, 40)

As Davis (and others) suggest, prison abolition is not arguing that crimes do not occur, or that people do not do "bad things." Rather our system of punishment, and who is most impacted by this system, is a result of racialized surveillance. African Americans, Latinos, and poor people are disproportionately scrutinized by a number of state agencies: schools, police, Immigration and Naturalization Services. This is evident from discussion in Chapter 2 that clearly outlines how poor people and people of color are under surveillance: scrutinized for educational disabilities and disrespect in schools, and targeted for drug searches and traffic violations, and more.

For myself, working toward abolition means creating structures that reduce the demand and need for prisons. It is ensuring that communities have viable, at least living-wage jobs that are not dehumanizing. It means establishing mechanisms for alternative dispute resolution and other processes that address conflict or harm with mediation. It means ensuring that our most vulnerable populations, for example, those who are mentally ill or undereducated, do not get warehoused in our prisons and jails because of the failure of other institutions such as healthcare and education. It means practicing how to communicate and to live across differences and to rely more on each other instead of the police. Working toward a horizon of abolition requires an acknowledgment that prisons have been used, as Davis writes, as "a way of disappearing people in the false hope of disappearing the underlying social problems they represent" (Davis, 2005, 41). Our prison and jail cells fill up with high school dropouts, the homeless, those self-medicating with alcohol and street drugs, and people with mental illness. As we have reduced social welfare programs, and criminalized the options that poor people possess to cope with untenable situations, it is important to remember that the majority of those in prisons and jails *are* poor people. These are not bad people; there are simply few other institutions that they can inhabit.

Expanding what counts as education reform is central, not solely because of my location as a preservice teacher educator, but because schools are, as documented, feeder institutions for jails and prisons. When schools look like prisons, the curriculum is geared *not* toward college, but to service-labor, and the schools are full of police or other structures that serve only as punitive functions at specific schools to prepare youth to be institutionalized. Education reform is not just a central component of rethinking our systems of punishment and justice, but also our democracy. If schools continue to emphasize security and discipline, seemingly at the expense of civic and intellectual development, what are the consequences?

Working toward a horizon of abolition forces me to continue learning and considering the depth of how prisons and incarceration are naturalized in our communities. However, this multifaceted goal of prison abolition does not mean *not* doing reform work. The horizon of abolition does not preclude working for reforms and changes. Reform work and service providing are required because there are real bodies who need immediate assistance. As longtime feminist prison activist and scholar Karlene Faith writes:

> Every reform raises the question of whether, in Gramsci's terms, it is a revolutionary reform, one that has liberatory potential to challenge the status quo, or a reform reform, which may ease the problem temporarily or superficially, but reinforces the status quo by validating the system through the process of improving it. We do liberal reform work because real women in real crises occupy the prisons, and they can't be ignored. Revolutionary reform work is educative: it

> raises questions of human rights (and thereby validates prisoners as human beings) and demonstrates that the state apparatus, which is mandated to uphold human rights, is one of the worst rights abusers. (Faith, 2000, 164–165)

Faith reminds me of the necessity of doing the "both/and" where everyday local work may involve service providing or working for reforms, but it is also useful to place, understand, and connect this labor to a larger movement. For example, I cofacilitated domestic violence workshops at the Cook County Jail because there are real women in prisons and jails with real needs. We distributed information about the resources available to women including housing and advocacy services. Yet, despite offering information to women who generally were not informed about these resources, this service-providing was also problematic if analyzed through a wider framework. Our work was free and removed responsibility from the jail to provide these services. Our program made the jail "look good" because a group of university academics volunteered their time and provided services and did nothing to challenge the existence of the jail, in fact our work potentially strengthened the jail's legitimacy. This creates a clear contradiction, as how do we challenge the legitimacy of the jail, yet recognize that there are women who require immediate resources? There are significant tensions between these frameworks, reform or service-providing and abolition, and I don't think that these tensions are necessarily a negative. For me, these tensions about how and where to work, and the conflicts surrounding short- and long-term strategies for change, can make both the "direct service" and "abolition" work stronger. I specifically use the term *the horizon* of prison abolition because this is a goal that shifts yet simultaneously frames all of my work. Abolition is also a concept that is grounded in histories of successful struggles for racial and economic (and gender) justice, and invoking these histories is useful.

Abolition and Education: Antecedents

The elimination of corporal punishment, though perceived to be "unthinkable" today, is directly connected to a legacy of other struggles for justice, specifically racial and economic. In the United States there have been successful movements to abolish slavery, lynching, and the death penalty. Abolitionism, the political and social movement that labored to legally abolish slavery and the slave trade, resulted in Amendment 13 (1865). Currently, there is still a nationwide campaign in place to abolish the death penalty. Although abolitionist movements have complicated consequences, for example, an argument can be made that lynching was replaced by the death penalty, invoking the term *abolition* in antiprison organizing and writing connects contemporary struggles to these histories of race, and to these legacies. The word abolition is powerful because of this history.

Education also has a history with the term *abolition*, and with discussions about state-endorsed violence. Although corporal punishment has not been completely eradicated from schools, in the last half a decade there has been a significant shift in public opinion and in policies and practices surrounding corporal punishment.

> In 1976, Pennsylvania reported 35,712 incidents compared to ninety in 1997. . . . Texas, the paddling capital of the country, has severely reduced its use of corporal punishment in the schools. In 1976, 262,663 incidents of paddling were reported, while in 1997, it was reduced to 81,373. (Hyman et al., 2002, 78)

In 2006, it is reasonably unthinkable in my urban public school district, Chicago, for any teacher to smack or spank or cane a student, regardless of how heinous the act committed by the student. Illinois outlawed corporal punishment in public schools in 1994. This kind of physical contact would, at the least, be grounds for immediate dismissal of the teacher, perhaps criminal prosecution. Corporal punishment such as caning or paddling, even though it is still practiced in private and parochial schools, and is not banned in all school districts, is a rarity. Yet, the United States and parts of Australia are still among the "thirty-five industrialized countries who do not ban this disciplinary technique" (McCarthy, 2005, 235). Starting in 1970, by 2005 over half of the states abolished corporal punishment in schools. The disuse of corporal punishment in schools in the United States has been a slow process transpiring at the local and the state levels, and there is still little consistency, or agreement, on this practice as some districts have banned it, while the state permits it (McCarthy, 2005; Lyman, 2006). Yet, although the practice is still disputed in the United States, public polls clearly indicate that the majority of parents are not in support of schools possessing the right to engage in corporal punishment.

> A good example of public reaction to the shocking results of legally sanctioned paddling occurred in 1996 in California where Republican legislator Mickey Conroy introduced AB 101 which would have allowed corporal punishment of California students. At a public hearing on the bill, pictures of the battered behinds of students who had been legally paddled in other states were displayed by child advocates. The pictures were so shocking that most Republican legislators disassociated themselves with this bill, which ultimately died. (Hyman et al., 2002, 75)

Whereas the eradication of corporal punishment in schools accelerated in the last half century, most dramatically in the last 20 years, the frameworks for this initiative were established a century earlier (Aries, 1962; Lesko, 2001). Enlightenment philosophers such as Locke (*Some Thought Concerning Education* [1683]), critical of corporal punishment in child-rearing, slowly ushered in concepts of the nature of the child, *tabula rasa*, that moved away from the religious doctrine that conceptualized the child's fate as predestined and the child as born in sin, infant damnation. Enlightenment constructs of the child, with corresponding educational philosophies, were restricted to sons of gentlemen, the unremarked white male child. Historically, arguments that paddling or caning was detrimental to student learning, or that corporal punishment did not function as a deterrent, have not been the most effective strategies. Rather, changed perceptions of the nature of the child assisted in the decline in the use of caning, paddling, and other forms of corporal punishment in schools. By no means is this shift neat and complete, nor, as documented in previous chapters, is this conception of the child accessible to all. In contemporary communities, schools and parents in the United States still adhere to the Calvinistic "spare the rod and spoil the child" philosophy where the lack of corporal punishment will result in the child who is too indulged, and spoiled. Rather, the shifts in the meaning of the child and childhood, including increased emotional investments in the child, produced in relation to their changing economic value, translated into an increase in the number of parents (and then subsequently schools) *not* participating in the "spare the rod" philosophy.[1]

Ironically, the decline of corporal punishment in schools occurred through these shifting definitions of the child that, as previous chapters illustrate, simultaneously necessitated the expansion of the PIC. In addition, the construct of the child as vulnerable, as innocent, and "in need of" protection, did not enable progressive change regarding corporal punishment through the court system. The courts actually offer less protection to children. For example, perceived as *in loco parentis*, schools are afforded much more cover than prisons to engage in corporal punishment. The courts have historically been mixed in their recognition of the child's

---

[1] These changing meanings about the child significantly impacted other social and economic practices. A shift in the core belief of the nature of humanity, from infant damnation and Calvinism, to the framework of Locke and other Enlightenment philosophies, impacted the status of woman. She shifted into the "republican mother" responsible for the morality of the nation and this was the wedge used to access the "semi-profession" of teaching, as the role of educator was simply a natural extension of the inherent characteristics (white) women possessed. This new status, however, meant low wages and limited access to the public sphere (Martusewicz, 1994).

right to constitutional protection, for example, to be protected under the 8th Amendment from "cruel and unusual punishment" (Levy & Levine, 1983; Roy, 2001). In the 1977 *Ingraham v Wright* decision, the Supreme Court denied the plaintiffs, youths who were violently beaten in school by teachers for being slow to respond to a question and "tardy," the right to protection under the 8th Amendment.[2] In addition to failing to account for the shifts in the nation's understanding of the child, "The Court's statements reflect nineteenth century thinking about the nature of children, schools, and discipline, and clearly ignored available social science data, even in 1976" (Hyman et al., 2002, 79), what is also notable is the rationale for denying students protection under the 8th Amendment. Schools are public sites, unlike prisons.

> The Court drew the distinction of openness as its final reason for denying school children the protections of the Eighth Amendment. A school, unlike a prison, is open. Parents can talk freely with their children, teachers, and administrators. Parents can also participate in parent-teacher associations and can vote in school board elections, thereby making their opinions known. The Court maintained that the openness of public schools and their supervision by the community afford significant safeguards against the kinds of abuses from which the Eighth Amendment protects the prisoner. The threat of civil and criminal liability for excessive use of force serves as a powerful curb on the consequences of excessive corporal punishment. Therefore, the Court concluded, as long as the schools are open to public scrutiny, there is no reason to believe that these common-law constraints would not effectively remedy and deter excess use of force in administering corporal punishment. (Roy, 2001, 558)

The construct of the school as open, as public, as a transparent institution is notable, in particular as it is juxtaposed with prisons as less open. Both are publicly funded *public* institutions. As Jenson notes in her work on gender and technology in public schools, it is important to continue the work of "chipping away at the private life of our purportedly 'public' schools" (2004, 155), because these facades of public cloak deeply private practices. Public schools "have closed their doors and abided, not by public policies or even discourses, but by their own peculiar, largely privately driven

---

[2] Whereas *Ingraham v Wright* is the only case heard by the U.S. Supreme Court that addresses corporal punishment in schools, at the state levels, there have been more recent cases that address issues related to due process that have had more success (McCarthy, 2005).

policies and agendas" (135).[3] Public schools, unlike the difficult to enter prisons, are perceived to be accessible and accountable, and this provides a cover to conceal the private practices that transpire in classrooms and other spaces in the public institution of schools, but it is also a cover for the practices of violence and control at the school that are conducted in plain sight. Whereas a prison can discipline the body in a public institution in "private" solitary confinement and through sensory deprivation and other strategies, the school can rely on practices conducted in "public."

In addition, this discussion of the abolition of corporal punishment in schools is instructive for several reasons. Abolitionist histories are always important to track as they offer concrete examples of contextual social change and understanding the forces that impact public perceptions of the role of violence and punishment offers those invested in changing these public sentiment into how change happens, and what investments the public possesses in these constructs. Also valuable is that the mechanisms used to abolish caning and spanking in schools, these new discourses of childhood, resulted in the enactment of other disciplinary practices and methods. Also central to acknowledge is that bodies continue to be disciplined in schools and regulated by gender, race, and sexuality, yet these practices have moved to other sites. If abolition may result in the reconfiguration of power, it is useful to connect the eradication of paddling and caning to the establishment of the Amber Alert and other child protection curriculum. The disciplinary mechanisms persist but conform to new sociopolitical contexts. The child continues to be disciplined through hidden curriculum, and other forces, as this book documents. The conceptions of the child that enabled this shift away from corporal punishment, to the construct of the child as in need of protection, or vulnerable, reflects another kind of disciplining, other mechanisms of control and power.

The move to eradicate corporal punishment in schools is also a relatively contemporary consequence of a shift that started to occur over a century earlier. Changing meanings of the child had long-range implications. Perhaps the same is true of other abolitionist strategies. Core discursive and ontological changes, established now, could incite all kinds of future shifts, some of which are unimaginable. For example, shifting the discourse of what "discipline" means could alter other responses to vio-

---

[3] "As teachers readily remind us, they 'close their doors.' Never mind curriculum, pedagogy, textbooks, research or policy—once those doors are closed, what happens is no longer 'public'; the teacher-controlled private realm, mediated as it may be by peculiar institutional orders and traditions, is only marginally influenced by the 'outside'" (Jenson, 2004, 154).

lence, thus potentially dramatically impacting the futures of institutions and reframing relationalities that we cannot yet imagine.

Investigating education's relationship to corporal punishment and abolition also illustrates that strategies for change need to be evaluated carefully. If arguments for eradicating corporal punishment in schools were not necessarily advanced by evidence that illustrated that caning was detrimental to student learning, or that paddling was not an effective deterrent, it is useful to examine contemporary strategies that work to link education to incarceration, and to educate the public and to shift public sentiment toward prison abolition. What core beliefs do these strategies use? Given the landscape that this book offers, connecting public sentiment to public policy, examining our investments as educational professionals, and theorizing the landscape of racial ignorance, what is working? If mass media, including *OZ*, reproduces new masks for old ideas about race and contributes to the maintenance of an educated ignorance surrounding crime, what moves are possible? What are the dangers when working within this landscape where audiences possess firm investments in the "good, the bad, and the innocent"?

Educate Not Incarcerate and Innocence Projects

I turn to activists, artists, and writers who advocate a kind of crafty public activism, the manipulation of public sentiment; and I offer two examples of interesting strategies, Educate Not Incarcerate and Innocence Projects, which work to invoke histories of abolition in the public sphere. These strategies, with limitations, attempt to do the treacherous work of trying to traffic ideas and create change on a landscape that is saturated with stereotypes and fears.

In the last decade, several grassroots youth- and school-initiated educational campaigns have emerged that directly link schools to jails. Frequently called *Schools Not Jails*, or *Educate Not Incarcerate*, or prominently featuring these phrases, these educational and organizing campaigns work to mobilize youth and communities around the abjectly flawed economic strategy of allocating resources toward incarceration, and not into education. In the mid to late 1990s, these initiatives began springing up across North America (Acey, 2000). Started by university and high school students in California in response to Proposition 209,[4] the framework "schools not jails" originated from the participating youth who named the purpose of high school explicitly "to get you ready for prison," and the basis of this

---

[4] In 1996, Proposition 209, co-opting the language of civil rights, successfully sought to amend the California state constitution to eradicate all affirmative action programs.

movement was a youth-led "staunchly anti-school critique" (Acey, 2000, 208). However, the movement sometimes loses this antischool analysis and posits education as simply the response to incarceration, when clearly the response is not this simple. Education, as this book documents, can function as a feeder institution to prisons; therefore, simply advocating "educate not incarcerate" negates the ongoing history that the schools have always been used as mechanisms to prepare select populations for underemployment, containment, or incarceration. Yet, simultaneously, education does empower, and it can move us to critically engage in our worlds as radical political change agents. Organizing around this concept of *Schools Not Jails*, despite the critiques of this movement professionalizing what was originally a youth-driven project and "mainstreaming" a radical agenda (Acey, 2000), grew in the decade after the initial Proposition 209 youth mobilization in California.

The framework of education not incarcerate, or schools not jails, has functioned as an effective mobilizing tool to bring together coalitions to address many of the issues this book has highlighted: school disciplinary inequities, state resource allocation injustices, and more. In Chicago, a coalition of educators, youth, and activists formed the *Stop the Schoolhouse–Jailhouse Track*, and worked to highlight how school disciplinary policies target youth of color and shape their participation in the criminal justice system. This Chicago-based organization is linked to a national structure (*Stop Schools to Jails*). In 2006, a coalition in Ontario, Canada, used the framework of educate not incarcerate to halt (perhaps only temporarily) the proposed construction of a new "superjail" for youth, in Brampton, Ontario (81 Reasons, 2006).

Although relatively small movements, these coalitions and initiatives that are formed around the framework of *educate not incarcerate* have met with some success. They have received media attention, attracted youth and activist participation, and mobilized educators. For example, in 2003, the National Education Association supported an *Education Not Incarceration* curriculum that was used in classes in Oakland, California, to educate students about state budgets and resource allocation, prison construction, and more. The curriculum incorporated experiences that were already a reality in the lives of the students: the incarceration of friends and family members, the daily budgetary shortfalls, and the school. As reported by one ninth-grade teacher, Dannenberg, in an article for the National Education Association, bringing incarceration and debates about state budgetary allocations into the curriculum was not something foreign and therefore disturbing to students; these were experiences from their communities. The curriculum expanded vocabulary and analytic skill sets for students, by introducing terms such as "recidivism" and "moratorium," and generated discussions about civil rights and compassion in the students' daily, not historic, contexts. The culmination of the short curriculum component resulted in a letter drafted by each student to a state legislator (cc-ing the governor) and hand delivered to state senators in Sacramento (sadly, few of the letters received a response). These assignments fulfilled state competency requirements, in this case the California State Framework Reading/Language Arts requirements (Dannenberg, 2005).

Groups working to uncover "innocence" are another example of creative and successful strategies. The Innocence Project, founded in 1992 by Barry Scheck and Peter Neufeld at the Benjamin N. Cardozo School of Law in New York, uses law students to investigate the cases of those in prison who believe that they were unjustly convicted. There are now approximately 30 centers, institutes, or programs modeled on the original Innocence Project in journalism and in law schools across the country. As Larry Marshall, director of the Centre for Wrongful Convictions at Northwestern University, a leading Midwest organization pursuing cases of wrongful conviction, stated at a 2002 Death Penalty Symposium in Illinois, when attempting to reform regressive and punitive laws and practices, the pervasive and very well documented racism in the justice system does not move the mainstream. Reform of the death penalty would not arise from the circulation of narratives or representations of the systemic white supremacy in our criminal justice system. Innocence, a trope, works because people identify with the story of innocent men behind bars.[5] The use of this innocence trope in contemporary prison reform spaces, such as the Innocence Projects, has resulted in some gains; for example, it has required the use of DNA testing in some states, and the Justice for All Act, signed on October 30, 2004, awards any person in prison who is convicted of a federal crime the right to petition a federal court for a DNA test to support a claim of innocence (Rothstein, 2005). It has also popularized awareness of the limitations of eyewitness testimony, particularly cross-racial eyewitness testimony, and the use of "jailhouse informants" to secure convictions.

However, the juxtaposing of incarceration and education, through the mobilizing of students, particularly in middle or elementary schools, to act as education and anti-prison advocates, and through the use of the trope of innocence directly to mobilize the mainstream's fears of unjust persecution, have limitations. Both of these strategies trade on the trope of

---

[5] In the late 1990s the *Chicago Tribune* and undergraduate journalism students participated in overturning death penalty cases in Illinois and advancing a movement that culminated with the issuance, by Republican Governor Ryan, of a moratorium on the death penalty and the subsequent commutation of 160 death row sentences to life in prison.

innocence. The Innocence Projects do so explicitly, and the Educate Not Incarcerate framework does so more indirectly, with the use of the innocent child who does not deserve the future that the state has constructed via impersonal, yet highly intimate, public policy decisions. The use of the child in schools, not youth groups, or sports teams, is key, as this subject position of *child student* is perceived to be innocent and good. They are not perceived as politically tainted, as perhaps those who were formerly incarcerated or who are graduate students might be, and they are not perceived to be undeserving of public resources. College or even high school students could be seen as less deserving or less innocent, but elementary and middle schools students are closer to the concept of child.

While achieving some success, these strategies have troubling consequences. Innocence requires guilt, just as good requires bad, success needs failure, ability is framed by disability, "gifted" is produced in relation to "remedial," and more. If we have innocent men and women trapped behind bars, we clearly also have guilty or culpable individuals who need to be behind bars. If children are exempt from incarceration, perhaps adults who are culpable are not. If innocence merits resources, the guilty do not. The popularization of this innocence trope in the last decade, in part due to the exonerated movement and the success of the original Innocence Project, has moved into mass media with 2005–2006 TV shows such as *InJustice* or *Prison Break* sensationalizing stories of innocent and emphatic men and a few women caught behind bars in worlds of dangerous felons, who are culpable, and are "bad." Innocence is a safe strategy that can be used for some changes yet it can also be mobilized for regressive ends. Senator Kay Bailey Hutchison argued that Pell grants should be removed from prisons because, essentially, the innocent working class family cannot afford higher education, and these families are being denied access to higher education because those convicted and in prison are taking up valuable resources. Innocent is invoked adroitly to deny the "bad" or guilty people resources, yet the purportedly "innocent" working class families do not receive any new resources, as an earlier chapter articulates. Innocence is not a neutral strategy. Race, sexuality, gender, and more shape this category, and impact who gets access to full participation as innocent.

And, as we jaywalk, or cheat on taxes, or download songs for free from the Internet, or lie to the boss, or "borrow" paper from the photocopier at work for personal use, or use a variety of legal and illegal drugs, and more, what precisely does this category *innocent* mean? Invoking it is worrisome as it reifies an identity that is not possible, yet fictions still persist. Innocence also exists in a legal and cultural landscape where what is defined as a crime has been, and continues to be, explicitly racialized. In addition, in a nation where select communities are under watch, whose lives will be scrutinized and under surveillance to expose these failures to inhabit a category that is fictitious? Those with more power can protect themselves from having their parenting strategies evaluated, their housekeeping or cooking abilities assessed, their behaviors and emotions scrutinized for signs of insubordination, anger management problems, or learning disabilities, their workforce productivity measured, and more. Those with power can protect themselves from the kind of surveillance that would indicate, probably immediately, that they are not innocent, or always good.

Arguing that flawed public policies and laws harm the "innocent" is not a new strategy. As documented in the Freedom Center Collection in Cincinnati, when campaigning for the end of slavery, white, northern abolitionists acquired (purchased) children who were slaves who passed for white. These children would be then dressed up in "white clothes," moved into normative "white civilized" poses, and photographed. These images of *white-looking* African American children, formerly enslaved, would be placed on abolitionist postcards that were used to mobilize the sentiments of whites to abolish slavery. One interpretation of the motivating logic behind this was that identification and empathy are required in order to make changes. The use of children who could pass for white is significant, as they could generate empathy in white audiences. For those who are working to advocate a potentially unpopular issue, to be an effective speaker is to "know the horizon" (McBride, 2001, 151) of your desired audience. McBride, in his analysis of testimonies of men and women who were enslaved in the United States, highlights the moves these authors take to compel white audience support for the abolitionist cause:

> As is the case with the producers of any narrative, slave witnesses had to understand clearly the terms of this discursive terrain to which they addressed themselves. Once they did, they had to determine how best to mold, bend, and shape their narrative testimony within these terms to achieve their political aims. The narrative challenge, then, was to relate one's story in terms that would "make sense" for one's readership (which I understand here less as a group of "real people" than as a complex of discursive concerns). (McBride, 2001, 7)

McBride writes that successful discursive acts (literally "to have political efficacy for the cause of abolitionism") require the ability to establish reliability within the audience's paradigm and to move the audience from spectator to engaged witness. The author/speaker must know and work within "the very discourse that creates, allows, and enables, the situation for the slave to be able to speak at all" (McBride, 2001,172). Just as white folks are going to be persuaded to reform the death penalty, or implement

DNA testing for all accused of a capital crime, because they see themselves possibly as potential future victims of our law and order state, liberal white northerners might be invested in abolishing slavery if they saw that innocent children and those that resembled their children were trapped by the practice.

The many lawyers, journalists, and students who pursue and support the Innocence Projects, and the youths and teachers who participate in a range of Educate Not Incarcerate campaigns, are neither ineffective nor, probably, unaware of the limitations of their strategies. One of Dannenberg's follow-up "big" questions to her curriculum component is, "How does the culture of imprisonment become a norm in the community?" (Dannenberg, 2005). She understands that forces outside of schools shape the meanings associated with incarceration. I elect to describe these initiatives precisely because they are powerful and relatively successful strategies that have been used in the last few years and that have effectively mobilized diverse coalitions. In addition, they invoke histories of the abolition movement, and this work in the United States is always and already premised on a foundation of racial, economic, and gender justice. But, as both of these strategies rely on and invoke investments in the innocent, I worry about their consequences. Just as the previous discussion on the abolition of corporal punishment in schools relied on changing core meanings associated with the child, I wonder if prison abolition requires changing our "core" definitions and values related to, perhaps, how white supremacy is integrated into our understandings of law and order, or, perhaps, shifting our investments in, and understandings of, discipline.

Also, these critiques of innocence as a strategy are intended to raise questions of abolition versus reform, or the differences between working toward systemic shifts that expose inherent flaws that cannot be repaired or fixed, and reform, which has as one goal, to change parts, but leaves the system intact. There are real women and men in prisons who need services. Pell grants need to get back into prisons. Jails need to *not* be too cold or too hot, with inadequate medical treatment and indigestible food. School discipline policies need to change to make sure that categories such as the vague "disrespect" are not grounds for suspension. But, if these reforms do not account for the larger contexts, the underlying Racial and Sexual contracts, they may result in simply inviting power to manifest in different places. Consistently offering services that meet the real needs of deeply impoverished men and women while advocating for reforms is required because there are real bodies at stake, but simultaneously this analysis calls for placing this labor in larger contexts to expose systemic failures that will not be improved simply through reform. At the core, the system will not be fixed with reforms or changes in the laws, or better trained teachers, or even more equitable resource allocation. These reforms will make significant differences, and therefore, for some of us, this is the work we will continue to do because there are real bodies in schools and in jails.

The Limits of Solidarity

In the event that someone is able to diffuse the "what about the bad people" maelstrom, a second question I am most frequently asked in relation to this work, generally in academic spaces, is how did I get involved? Who am I in relation to this work? After eight years, I believe that the underlying question is what is my relationship to incarceration. Generally, it is usually asked genuinely to ascertain my commitment level. Am I an exploitative academic who, as my friend and colleague Mary Hermes (2002) points out, works to "hit and run" and to rip off the stories and the lives of the poor people for academic profit? Or do I have the legitimate street credentials, the personal relationship to the topic? Frequently, the framework for those in university spaces is that we work on issues because of our personal investments. A few years of questions about "why I do this work" or "how did I get involved?" motivated me to consider questions about solidarity and the limits of affiliation.

In particular, I want to trouble the categories of an US and a THEM: those that have been in prison and those that have not been in prison. I want to argue for a "both/and" framework. Incarceration aggressively harms poor communities and people of color and it matters whether you have direct experience with incarceration, but simply framing the discussion in terms of who has direct experience is limiting. I argue that acknowledging who is impacted is central, yet perpetuating a demarcation furthers an isolation and places the nonincarcerated neatly outside a sphere of influence or responsibility, and it negates the reality that the epidemic of incarceration in the United States shapes the lives of all. Barkley Brown wrote explicitly that white women were (and are) able to live the lives they did because black women lived the lives that they did (1997, 275). The "free" live the lives they do, because the incarcerated live the lives they do. As documented in this project, our nation appears to require the employment prisons provide, the manner in which jails attempt to wipe from our landscape the abject failure of our mental healthcare system, and more. Not only does the class and race expansion of the PIC benefit those in "the free world," but also, I want to argue, those wealthy, or not targeted for surveillance by schools or police forces, are impacted in other ways by the expansion of the PIC.

Prisons, punishment, and crime shape our democracy. In particular, the spectacle of punishment is an instrumental component of our social order.

Although sheltered from scrutiny, prisons form a central component of our lives, even if we have not been incarcerated. Prisons contribute to shaping the everyday life of the majority of our institutions in the United States: social services, schools, immigration services. Prisons function as the logical repository for the racialized surveillance practices in our schools. Prisons also provide and naturalize value systems. Prisons, *like detention in schools*, provide a place for the "bad" people to go, thus extending a value system that isolation and punishment are "just" responses to outlaw emotions or acts of violence. These spectacles of punishment regulate the lives of all people in the United States, not simply those who are housed in prisons and jails.

Illustrating this interconnectedness requires a willful muddling of an US and a THEM and a recognition that these divisions, while vital, also simultaneously maintain the invisibility of other sets of relationships. For example, reframing who is impacted by incarceration to include the people in the communities where prisons are the central industry can broaden a movement for change. Britton, in her work looking at female employees at prisons, raises an interesting question:

> [I]n her best selling book *Kind and Unusual Punishment*, Jessica Mitford asks, "For after all, if we were to ask a small boy, 'what do you want to be when you grow up?' and he were to answer, 'A prison guard,' should we not find that a trifle worrying—cause perhaps, to take off to a child guidance clinic for observation and therapy?" (Britton, 2003, 51)

Viewing these communities as also "harmed" by the expansion of the PIC permits other relationships and subsequent possibilities for mobilization. I expand the conceptions of who is impacted by the epidemic of incarceration to include those who work in these dehumanizing institutions, live next to prisons, or teach elementary school in communities where there are many prisons, but few college classrooms.

Expanding the framework of impact is vital. In her discussion about the consequences of the *Brown* decisions, Ladson-Billings argues that de jure and de facto segregation hurt not just poor children or children of color, but white students who typically continue to attend the most racially segregated schools, those with a white majority.

> Might it be a place to begin to examine not just the mis-education of children of color and the poor but also that of White, middle-class children whose limited perspectives severely hamper their ability to function effectively in the global community? (Ladson-Billings, 2004, 11)

Just as Ladson-Billings asks why white children going to all-white schools are rarely perceived to be cognitively impaired, or educationally diminished, when frameworks about impact shift, so do communities' and individuals' investments in asking better questions, and in working to formulate responses that reflect their community. The epidemic of incarceration harms not just those directly targeted and tracked by the surveillance mechanisms of the school and the police, but those who live in relation to these state-sanctioned practices.

Adopting a strategy of "we are all prisoners," like the front page of France's *Le Monde*, "We Are All Americans" (*Nous sommes tous Américains*), displayed after September 11, 2001, is not the response. Erasing the particularity of the consequences of mass incarceration and of the Racial Sexual Contract is not the goal; rather, my desire is to reframe the terrain on which our discussions about school failure, punishment, and education circulate. This also requires an acknowledgment that the PIC significantly impacts all, in a variety of ways. More people speaking out about the roles incarceration plays in their lives can challenge the gendered and racialized indifference that perpetuates the movement of too many into prisons and jails.

This kind of solidarity is tricky, though. When my father died in 2002, at the age of 66 in his house in semirural Canada, my sister and I sorted through his papers and cried. Aside from an enormous, obsessive, and worthless stamp collection, he left an old hard-sided briefcase that contained what I called his "criminal paperwork." My immigrant father had been arrested. Mostly he had been picked up for drunk driving in his early 1980s diesel pick-up truck, but he had also been arrested for theft, shoplifting at a local grocery store. My sister and I were not that surprised, but it was still odd to see the paperwork; the small pretty-colored carbon copies of paper. He lost a job because of his theft conviction. Being a tall white man with impeccable English (and also being Canadian), he received a fine or a license suspension for the majority of his convictions. I have no memory of any of my father's arrests. I do remember him disappearing for stretches of time throughout my teens, and I remember that he frequently had no car, which was notable in our town with a lack of adequate public transportation. As a child, this reality was actively erased, a somewhat difficult thing to do in a small community. Yet what is central to note is that despite being a foreigner with beautiful socialist tendencies, my father would never have been profiled as a public enemy. He was under no surveillance by the state, and he even managed to evade being "court carded" to join Narcotics Anonymous or Alcoholics Anonymous.

For me to write that my father's or my experience is equivalent to some of the people cited in this book is trivializing to their lives, and simply silly.

Yet, my confession indicates that the reaches of the PIC touch those of us who might perceive ourselves as "outsiders," and that the secrets inside too many families perhaps hold examples of the PIC's intimate regulation of the quiet traumas of our lives. This confession also clearly demonstrates that whiteness, gender, and perhaps the corresponding illusion of class status that is linked to speech, or posture, and education, directly shape how each of us intersects with the PIC. While expanding frameworks of impact are vital to generate mass support to interrupt the movement between schools and jails, it is equally central to name a distinction between not just those currently or formerly incarcerated, but those the state actively targets for surveillance. Those who have been affected can offer the salient analysis, and can function to mobilize public sentiment to shift public policy. My father's outlaw emotions were punished, but at a fraction of the intensity that would have been leveled on a different body, in a different space. Poor people and communities of color, increasingly poor women of color as this project documents, are those the state profiles for incarceration, and for physical and civil death.

Concluding Actions

This project worked to link two sites that occupy a significant portion of my professional and personal life: a high school program for formerly incarcerated men and women, and a teacher education program in a university. Investigating the frameworks that produce the gender, race, and class discrepancies between these two sites, I wanted to illustrate that these two sites are *interconnected processes* of explicitly racialized and gendered systems. Schools participate in the production of public enemies; for example, we legitimate and enhance select fears that in turn require the intervention of the PIC and we enact a kind of racial profiling that anticipates the work of other state institutions. The seemingly tiresome focus on structures and systems in this book is my attempt to turn a part of the surveillance gaze onto us, educators, "those acquired by positions of privilege and power" (Varenne & McDermott, 1998, 215), and to work to be relentless in moving us to question seemingly natural or normal educational categories and practices, such as school discipline, the concept of the child, and to push for an expanded conception of educational policy that encompasses the PIC. This methodological and epistemological choice to focus on our practices is in part motivated by a sense of urgency. Perhaps it is arrogant to frame this project as urgent, but I perceive this project to be a part of my accountability to the men and women I teach and learn with at the high school for formerly incarcerated women each semester, the many family members of those in prisons and jails that organize for change, and those I have met in prisons and jail cells across Illinois.

Interrupting this movement, as this project documents, requires multi-faceted approaches, and clearly, as this book documents, some resistance is in place, organized by a range of activists, both youth and educators. For educators new to the topic, the project of how to get involved or what to do can seem overwhelming. This book suggests that those invested in moving the relationships between schools and jails need to track state budgetary allocations and link educational policy discourses to prison expansion. We must unpack the natural educational labels, such as special education, and name the profession's historic and ongoing goal to enact racial surveillance. We must be examining and changing school discipline policies and the corresponding informal practices that tie them to the PIC. Educators need to be consistently paying attention to how mass media portrays crime, and youth, in addition to the work in classrooms to foster media literacy for ourselves and for students, and to create spaces and tools for media construction. We should name and challenge how schools produce and legitimate particular fears, through the reification of constructs of the child, and be vigilant about how schools (and prisons) work to shape and name experiences. Each of these trajectories is central, dynamic, and interrelated, and it would be difficult to prioritize one aspect to tackle.

With this list, and I suggest that it is only partial, the tasks appear overwhelming. At the close of this project, in addition to worrying about all the pieces that I edited out, I worry that the relentless focus on our limitations as practitioners will be simply too much, and cause us to retreat. We will stay in, or move back to, our university, or our elementary or high school classrooms, and think that the challenge is too much, the issues are too complex, and the sites to change are too diffuse. We educators will just shut our doors and retreat to what we perceive as our private space, the classroom.

I can even name three easy and "right" next steps, and it is to get, or to stay, educated on these issues, to join groups working for change, and then to form alliances across associations and groups. Join with colleagues, teachers, parents' associations, youth, labor unions, churches, and neighborhood community-based organizations. For each of the issues named in the book, and more, including the antimilitarization of schools or how gentrification is impacting your neighborhood school, there is an active group in your area. These gritty and slick organizations are flyering the telephone poles on streets where those most directly impacted live. There are palm cards advertising meetings and promising free snacks and music at your local independent coffee shop. Youth are connecting and plotting online in chatrooms and e-groups and on Myspace. There are the grandmothers and uncles in church basements on Sunday afternoons, and in storefront arts organizations on Wednesday evenings. There is a group working for change in your neighborhood. Some of these meetings will be dull and drag on, with too many male speakers who pontificate, and too few follow-up action steps; but some will be vibrant, with participation from youth, artists, teachers, and church people. When people who, by geography and design, ordinarily do not have conversations and do not work alongside one another, collaborate to address a common goal, there are possibilities for change. In the United States, in cities starkly divided by race, class, language, religion, and more, initiatives that mobilize people to reclaim public issues they have a stake in, and to dialogue, argue, and struggle to educate one another, are increasingly rare and valuable. These groups, fraught, tenacious, or limited, with a horizon of abolition that mobilizes the histories of people who fought for principles not achieved in their lifetime, enable me to continue to participate in local projects that struggle for justice: the high school, Beyondmedia Education, and more.

Somehow, as attractive as this incentive to participate in local movements for change is, this call to a movement has met with some, but limited, success from educators. Perhaps it is the linkages to the histories of our profession, or perhaps it is that we have yet to see ourselves as directly impacted. And we are inundated with work, our time is finite, and too often educators are "blamed" or used as scapegoats for cultural and political problems from obesity to our nation's moral and economic "crisis". Yet, as this book works to document, educators cannot afford not to participate. When the research gaze moves from the students and those directly impacted, to the educational policies, practices, and informal knowledges that participate in the movement of bodies from schools to jails, we are responsible.

References

ABC News. (2005). Sex Offender Nabbed After Oprah Show. Retrieved February 5, 2006, from ABC News Entertainment Web site: http://abcnews. go.com/Entertainment/wireStory?id=1193647&CMP=OTC-RSSFeeds0312.

Abolish (1989). Retrieved April 3, 2006, from *OED* online (2nd ed.). Oxford: Oxford University Press.

Abolition. (1989). Retrieved April 3, 2006, from *OED* online (2nd ed.). Oxford: Oxford University Press.

Acey, C. E. S. A. (2000). This Is an Illogical Statement: Dangerous Trends in Anti-Prison Activism. *Social Justice*, Vol. 27, No. 3, 206–211.

Acker, S. (1983). Women and teaching: A semi-detached sociology of a semi-profession. In S. Walker & L. Barton (Eds.), *Gender, Class and Education*. London: Falmer Press, 123–140.

Adams, D.W. (1988). Fundamental considerations: The deep meaning of Native American schooling, 1880–1900. *Harvard Educational Review*, 58(1), 1–28.

Advancement Project & The Civil Rights Project. (2000). Opportunities Suspended: The Devastating Consequences of Zero Tolerance and School Discipline Policies. Retrieved October 27, 2005, from The Civil Rights Project Web site: http://www.civilrightsproject.harvard.edu/research/discipline/opport_suspended.php.

Alcoff, L. & Gray-Ronsendale, L. (1996). Survivor discourse: Transgression or recuperation? In S. Smith & J. Watson (Eds.), *Getting a Life: Everyday Uses of Autobiography*. Minneapolis: University of Minnesota Press, 198–225.

Alcoholics Anonymous. (n.d.). A Brief Guide to Alcoholics Anonymous. Retrieved October 21, 2005, from Alcoholics Anonymous Web site: http://www.aa.org/default/en_pdfs/p-42_abriefguidetoaa.pdf.

Alcoholics Anonymous. (2004). 2004 Membership Survey. Retrieved October 21, 2005, from Alcoholics Anonymous Membership Web site: http://www.aa.org/default/en_pdfs/p-48_04survey.pdf.

Allard, P. (2002). *Life Sentences: Denying Welfare Benefits to Women Convicted of Drug Offenses*. Washington, DC: The Sentencing Project.

Alper, L. & Leistyna, P. (2005). *Class Dismissed: How TV Frames the Working Class, Media Education Foundation* [documentary film].

American Civil Liberties Union (ACLU). (2005). ACLU Applauds Senate Reintroduction of Racial Profiling Bill, Urges Congress to Finally Pass Comprehensive Legislation Next Year. Retrieved December 19, 2005, from the American Civil Liberties Union Web site: http://www.aclu.org/racialjustice/racialprofiling/23090prs20051219.html.

America's Missing. (2005). Broadcast Emergency Response (Amber). Press Release, September 14, 2005. Retrieved July 15, 2006, from America's Missing: Broadcast Emergency Response (Amber) Web site: www.amberillinois. org/PDF/PressReleases/release091405.pdf.

Amin, A. (1994). Models, fantasies and phantoms of transition. In A. Amin (Ed.), *The Post-Fordist Reader.* Oxford, England: Blackwell, 1–40.

Amnesty International. (1997). Cold Storage: Super-maximum security confinement in Indiana. Retrieved August 21, 2006, from http://www.hrw. org/reports/1997/usind/.

Amnesty International. (1998a). Human Rights for All. Retrieved August 21, 2006, from http://www.globalissues.org/HumanRights/HumanRightsForAll.asp? p=1.

Amnesty International. (1998b). Nowhere to Hide: Retaliation Against Women in Michigan State Prisons. Retrieved August 21, 2006, from http://www.hrw. org/reports98/women/.

Amnesty International. (1999, March 1). "Not Part of My Sentence": Violations of the Human Rights of Women in Custody. Retrieved August 22, 2006, from http://web.amnesty.org/library/Index/ENGAMR510191999? open&of=ENG-360.

Anderson, J. (1990). *The Education of Blacks in the South, 1860–1935.* Durham: University of North Carolina Press.

Anyon, J. (1980). Social Class and the Hidden Curriculum of Work. Retrieved August 21, 2006, from *Journal of Education,* 162(1) Web site: http://rlab. cs.utep.edu/~freudent/stem-ed/papers/hiddencurriculum.pdf.

Anyon, J. (1997). *Ghetto Schooling: A Political Economy of Urban Educational Reform.* New York: Teachers College Press.

Anyon, J. (2005). *Radical Possibilities.* New York: Routledge.

APA Online. (2003). General form for electronic references. Retrieved April 09, 2006, from Electronic References Web site: http://www.apastyle.org/elec-general.html.

Apple, M.W. (1979). *Ideology and Curriculum.* Boston: Routledge.

Aries, P. (1962). *Centuries of Childhood: A Social History of Family Life.* New York: Knopf.

Arnold, M. & Lassmann, M.E. (2003). Overrepresentation of minority students in special education. *Education,* 124, 230–236.

Associated Press. (2003). *USA TODAY,* Excerpt from Santorum interview. Retrieved April 23, 2003, from http://www.usatoday.com/news/washington/ 2003-04-23-santorum-excerpt_x.htm.

AVERT. Age of Consent Laws. Retrieved October 2 2006, from http://www. avert.org/aofconsent.htm.

Aviles, A., Capeheart, L., Davila, E.R., & Pérez Miller, A. (2004). *DANDO UN PASO ¿PA' LANTE O PA' TRAS? LATINOS IN THE CHICAGO PUBLIC SCHOOLS.* 2nd Legislative District Education Advisory Committee of The Honorable Senator Miguel del Valle. Retrieved August 2, 2006, from Illinois Senator Miguel del Valle's Web site: http://www.senatedem.state.il.us/del-valle/Dando%20un%20Paso%20Sep2004%20Draft%20Eng.pdf.

Ayers, W., Dohrn, B., & Ayers, R. (Eds.). (2001). *Zero Tolerance: Resisting the Drive for Punishment in Our Schools.* New York: New Press.

Baca, J. (2001). *A Place to Stand.* New York: Grove Press.

Bakalar, N. (2006, July 25). Review Sees No Advantage in 12-Step Programs. *New York Times*, D6.

Baker, B. (2002). The hunt for disability: The new eugenics and the normalization of school children. *Teachers College Record*, 104(4), 663—703.

Bal, M., Crewe, J., & Spitzer, L. (Eds.). (1999). *Acts of Memory: Cultural Recall in the Present*. Hanover, NH: University Press of New England.

Banchero, S. (2004, July 18). Chapter One: One Girl's Struggle to Find a Future. *Chicago Tribune*.

Banchero, S. (2004, July 19). Chapter Two: Falling Back. *Chicago Tribune*.

Banchero, S. (2004, July 20). Chapter Three: Starting Over. *Chicago Tribune*.

Barak, G., Flavin, J., & Leighton, P. (2002). *Class, Race, Gender and Crime: Social Realities of Justice in America*. Los Angeles: Roxbury.

Barkley Brown, E. (1997). "What Has Happened Here." In *The Second Wave: A Reader in Feminist Theory*. Ed Linda Nicholson. New York: Routledge, 272-287.

Barron, J. (1996, June 12). N.Y. Court Lets Inmate Refuse Alcohol Program. *New York Times*.

Batiuk, M.E. (1997). The state of post-secondary education in Ohio. *Journal of Correctional Education*, 48(2), 70-72.

Bell, D. (2006, July 10). "They Deserve It." *The Nation*. Retrieved July 13, 2006, from *The Nation* Web site: http://www.thenation.com/docprem.mhtml?i=20060710&s=bell.

Berlant, L. (Ed.). (2004). *Compassion: The Culture and Politics of an Emotion*. New York: Routledge.

Berlak, H. (2001). Race and the Achievement Gap. *Rethinking Schools Online*, 15(4). Retrieved January 30, 2004, from http://www.rethinkingschools.org/archive/15_04/Race 154.shtml.

Bernstein, J. & Shapiro, I. (n.d.). Unhappy Anniversary: Federal minimum wage remains unchanged for eighth straight year, falls to 56-year low relative to the average wage. Retrieved April 3, 2006, from Economic Policy Institute Web site: http://www.cbpp.org/9-1-05mw.htm.

Best, J. (1990). *Threatened Children: Rhetoric and Concern About Child-Victims*. Chicago: University of Chicago Press.

Best, J. (2004). *Deviance: Career of a Concept*. Belmont, CA: Thomson/Wadsworth.

Bhattacharjee, A. & Silliman, J. (Eds.). (2002). *Policing the National Body: Race, Gender and Criminalization in the United States*. Cambridge, MA: South End Press.

Biehl, A. (n.d.). Foundation Trust. Retrieved August 23, 2006, from: http://www.amybiehl.org/.

Bilchik, S. (1999). *Juvenile Justice Bulletin: Minorities in the Juvenile Justice System*. National Report Series. U.S. Department of Justice, Office of Justice Programs, Office of Juvenile Justice and Delinquency Prevention, Washington, DC.

Blackmar, E. (2005). Appropriating the "Commons": The tragedy of property rights discourse. In S. Low & N. Smith (Eds.), *The Politics of Public Space*. New York: Routledge.

Blanchett, W.J. (2006). Disproportionate Representation of African American Students in Special Education: Acknowledging the Role of White Privilege and Racism. *Educational Researcher*, 35(6), 24-28.

Bloom, L. (2006). "When one person makes it, we all make it." Community support in the lives of low-income mothers attending post-secondary education. Unpublished manuscript.

Bloom, L.R. & Kilgore, D. (2003). The colonization of m(others) in poverty in a welfare-to-work education. *Educational Policy*, 17(3), 365–384.

Blount, J.M. (2005). *Fit to Teach: Same-Sex Desire, Gender and School Work in the Twentieth Century*. New York: State University of New York Press.

Bogira, S. (2006). Who Killed Ryan Harris? *The Chicago Reader*. Retrieved October 21, 2006 from http://www.chicagoreader.com/features/stories/floyddurr/.

Bohrmann R. & N. Murakawa. (2005). Remaking Big Government: Immigration and Crime Control in the United States. In J. Sudbury (Ed.), *Global Lockdown: Gender, Race, and the Rise of the Prison Industrial Complex*. New York: Routledge, 109–126.

Britton, D. (2003). *At Work in the Iron Cage: The Prison as Gendered Organization*. New York: New York University Press.

Bureau of the Census. (1996). Large farms are thriving in the United States. Retrieved January 9, 2006, from Agricultural Brief Web site: http://www.nass.usda.gov/census/census92/ab_9601.pdf.

Bureau of Justice Statistics. (1998). National sex offender registry assistance program. Retrieved February 5, 2006, from Bureau of Justice Statistics Web site: http://www.ojp.usdoj.gov/bjs/pub/pdf/nsorap98.pdf.

Bureau of Justice Statistics. (1999). State prison expenditures, 1996. Retrieved January 9, 2006, from Bureau of Justice Statistics Web site: http://www.ojp.usdoj.gov/bjs/pub/pdf/spe96.pdf.

Bureau of Justice Statistics. (2000). Sexual assault of young children as reported to law enforcement: Victim, incident, and offender characteristics. Retrieved February 5, 2006, from Bureau of Justice Statistics Web site: http://www.ojp.usdoj.gov/bjs/pub/pdf/saycrle.pdf.

Bureau of Justice Statistics. (2003a). Recidivism of sex offenders released from prison in 1994. Retrieved February 5, 2006, from Bureau of Justice Statistics Web site: http://www.ojp.gov/bjs/pub/pdf/rsorp94.pdf.

Bureau of Justice Statistics (2003b). Education and Correctional Populations. Retrieved October 20, 2006 from http://www.ojp.usdoj.gov/bjs/abstract/ecp.htm.

Bureau of Justice Statistics. (2004a). Crime characteristics. Retrieved June 15, 2006, from: http://www.ojp.usdoj.gov/bjs/cvict_c.htm.

Bureau of Justice Statistics. (2004b). State prison expenditures, 2001. Retrieved January 9, 2006, from Bureau of Justice Statistics Web site: http://www.ojp.usdoj.gov/bjs/pub/pdf/spe01.pdf.

Bureau of Justice Statistics. (2006). Criminal offenders statistics. Retrieved February 5, 2006, from Criminal Offenders Statistics Web site: http://www.ojp.usdoj.gov/bjs/crimoff.htm#sex.

Butler, J. (2000). *Antigone's Claim: Kinship Between Life and Death*. New York: Columbia University Press.

Califone International Research. (2006, July/August). Clearinghouse, No. 91, 64(6), 362, 3. Retrieved August 21, 2006, from: http://www.califone.com/research.php.

California Department of Corrections and Rehabilitation. (2006). *Ward Per Capita Cost Fiscal Year 2002/2003*. Retrieved June 15, 2006, from the California Department of Corrections and Rehabilitation Web site: http://www.cya.ca.gov/ReportsResearch/wardcost.html.

California Youth Authority. (2000). *About the CYA: Ward per Capita Cost Fiscal Year 2002/2003*. Retrieved January 09, 2006, from California Department of Corrections and Rehabilitation Web site: http://www.cya.ca.gov/About/wardcost.html.

Castles, S. & Davidson, A. (2000). *Citizenship and Migration: Globalization and the Politics of Belonging*. New York: Routledge.

Chaloupka, W. (1996). Forgetting a life: Testimony, identity, and power. In. S. Smith & J. Watson (Eds.), *Getting a Life: Everyday Uses of Autobiography*. Minneapolis: University of Minnesota Press.

Chasnoff, S. (Director). (2006). *Turning a Corner* [Documentary]. Chicago: Beyondmedia Education.

Chevigny, B.G. (2000, July 24). Prison Activists Come of Age: In California, Resistance to Prison Expansion Builds on the Past. *The Nation*.

Civil Rights Project Harvard University. (2003). *School to Prison Pipeline: Charting Intervention Strategies of Prevention and Support for Minority Children*. Retrieved October 24, 2006 from http://www.civilrightsproject.harvard.edu/convenings/schooltoprison/synopsis.php.

Clifford, J. (2003, October 1). *On the Edges of Anthropology: Interviews*. Chicago: Prickly Paradigm Press.

Conover, T. (2001). *Newjack: Guarding Sing Sing*. New York: Vintage Books.

Cooper, C. (2002). A Cancer Grows. *The Nation*. May 6. Retrieved June 15, 2005 from http://www.thenation.com/doc/20020506/cynthiacooper.

Cowrie, E. (1999). The spectacle of actuality. In J. Gaines & M. Renov (Eds.), *Collecting Visible Evidence*. Minneapolis: University of Minnesota Press.

Crenshaw, K.W. (1994). Mapping the margins: Intersectionality, identity politics, and violence against women of color. In M.A. Fineman & R. Mykituk (Eds.), *The Public Nature of Private Violence*. New York: Routledge.

Critical Resistance Publications Collective. (2000). Critical resistance to the prison-industrial complex. Special issue. *Social Justice: A Journal of Crime Conflict and World Order*, 27, 1–5.

Cummins, J. (1988). Empowering minority students: A framework for intervention. *Harvard Educational Review*, 58(1), 50–68.

Cypser, R.J. (1997). *The Pay Back*. CURE-NY Report. Retrieved September 30, 2003, from the CURE Web site: http://www.curenational.org.

Dannenberg, J. (2005). Education Not Incarceration: Action Starts at Home. Retrieved August 1, 2006, from the National Education Association Web site: http://www.nea.org/lessons/2005/jd050318.html.

Danylewycz, M., Light, B., & Prentice, A. (1991). The evolution of the sexual division of labor in teaching: A nineteenth century Ontario and Quebec case study. In J. Gaskell & A. McLaren (Eds.), *Women and Education*. Calgary, Alberta, Canada: Detselig Enterprises.

Darder, A., Torres, R.D., & Gutierrez, H. (Eds.). (1997). *Latinos and Education: A Critical Reader*. New York: Routledge.

Davis, A. (1998). Masked racism: Reflections on the prison industrial complex. *Colorlines*, 1(2). Special Section: The Prison Industrial Complex.

Davis, A. (1999, December 14). *Prison Industrial Complex*. Audio CD Alternative Tentacle.

Davis, A. (2000). From the convict lease system to the super max prison. In J. James (Ed.), *States of Confinement: Policing, Detention and Prison*. New York: St. Martin's Press.

Davis, A. (2003). *Are Prisons Obsolete?* New York: Seven Stories Press.

Davis, A. (2005). *Abolition Democracy: Prisons, Democracy, and Empire*. New York: Seven Stories Press.

Davis, A. & Rodriguez, D. (2000). The challenge of prison abolition: A conversation. *Social Justice*, 27(3), 212–218.

Diaz-Cotto. J. (2005). Latinas and the War on Drugs in the United States, Latin America, and Europe. In J. Sudbury (Ed)., *Global Lockdown: Race, Gender and the Prison Industrial Complex*. New York: Routledge. 137–154.

Diaz-Cotto, J. (2006). *Chicana Lives and Criminal Justice: Voices from El Barrio*. Austin: University of Texas Press.

Dohrn, B. (2000). Look out, kid, it is something you did: The criminalization of children. In V. Polakow (Ed.), *The Public Assault on America's Children: Poverty, Violence, and Juvenile Injustice*. New York: Teachers College Press, 89–113.

Duncan, G.A. (2000). Urban pedagogies and the celling of adolescents of color. *Social Justice: A Journal of Crime Conflict and World Order*, 27, 29–42.

Duncan, G.A. (2004). Urban Pedagogies and the Celling of Black Youth: The Construction of a Superfluous Population in Postindustrial America. Paper presented at the January 2004 Education or Incarceration: Schools and Prisons in a Punishing Democracy, sponsored by the Center for Democracy in a Multiracial Society, University of Illinois at Champaign–Urbana.

Dwyer, J., Neufeld, P., & Scheck, B. (2000). When Justice Lets Us Down. *Newsweek*, 135(7), Society Section.

Eby, C. (2005, July 30). Court upholds housing restrictions for sex offenders. *Sioux City Journal*.

The Economist. (2002, August 8). A stigma that never fades, 25–27.

Edsource. (2003). How California Ranks: The State's Expenditures for k–12 Education. Retrieved January 9, 2006, from Edsource Online Web site: http://www.edsource.org/pdf/RankingsFinal03.pdf .

Education as Crime Prevention: Providing Education to Prisoners. (1997). Research Brief No. 2. The Center on Crime, Communities and Culture. Soros Foundation, New York.

Education Commission of the States. (2005, September). ECS Teaching Quality Research Reports: Eight Questions on Teacher Recruitment and Retention. Retrieved July 15, 2006, from the Education Commission of the States Web site: http://www.ecs.org/.

Eggers, D., Vollen, L., & Turow, S. (2005). *Surviving Justice: America's Wrongfully Convicted and Exonerated*. San Francisco: McSweeny's.

81 Reasons. (2006). Retrieved April 20, 2006, from 81 Reasons Campaign Web site: http://81reasons.revolt.org/node/16.

Elsner. A. (2004). *Gates of Injustice: The Crisis in America's Prisons*. New York: Prentice Hall.

Esser, J. & Hirsch, J. (1994). The crisis of Fordism and the dimensions of a post-Fordist regional and urban structure. In A. Amin (Ed.), *The Post-Fordist Reader*. Oxford, England: Blackwell, 71–98.

Evans, L. (2005). Playing Global Cop: U.S. Militarism and the Prison Industrial Complex. In J. Sudbury (Ed)., *Global Lockdown: Race, Gender and the Prison Industrial Complex*. New York: Routledge. 215–230.

Excerpt from Santorum interview. (2003, April 23). Associated Press, USA TODAY. Retrieved August 22, 2006, from: http://www.usatoday.com/news/washington/2003-04-23-santorumexcerpt_x.htm.

Faith, K. (2000). Reflections on inside/out organizing. *Social Justice: A Journal of Crime Conflict and World Order*, 27, 158–167.

Fazal, S. & Meiners, E. (2005). Letter to the Editor: Prison Break Misrepresents U.S. Incarceration. Unpublished letter to *Chicago Tribune*.

Federal Bureau of Investigation. (n.d.). National Sex Offender Registry. Retrieved February 5, 2006, from Investigative Programs: Crimes Against Children Web site: http://www.fbi.gov/hq/cid/cac/registry.htm.

Federal Bureau of Investigations. National Sex Offender Registry Information. Retrieved October 2, 2006 from http://www.fbi.gov/hq/cid/cac/registry.htm.

Ferak, J. (2006, February 12). What Is a Civil Commitment? Pedophile case brings reform call. A bill seeks to ensure that mentally ill sex offenders at risk to reoffend will be committed for treatment after prison. *Omaha World-Herald* (Nebraska), News Section, 1A.

Ferguson, A.A. (2000). *Bad Boys: Public Schools in the Making of Black Masculinity*. Ann Arbor: University of Michigan Press.

Feuer, A. (2005, October 4). Pataki uses state law to hold sex offenders after prison. *The New York Times*, B4.

Fine, M. (1997). Witnessing whiteness. In L. Fine, L. Weis, L. Powell, & L. Wong (Eds.), *Off-White: Readings on Race, Power and Society*. New York: Routledge.

Fine, M., Weis, L., Powell, L. & Wong, L. M. (Eds.). (1997). *Off-White: Readings on Race, Power, and Society* . New York: Routledge.

Fine, M., Torre, M., Boudin, K., Bowen, I., Clark, J., Hylton, D., Martinez, M. "Missy," Roberts, R., Smart, P., & Upegui, D. (2001, September). *Changing Minds: The Impact of College in a Maximum Security Prison*. Collaborative research by the Graduate Center of the City University of New York and women in prison at the Bedford Hills Correctional Facility. Retrieved August 21, 2006, from: http://www.changingminds.ws/.

Fishman, T. (2000). The joys of global investment. In F. Lechner & J. Boli (Eds.), *The Globalization Reader*. Malden, MA: Blackwell, 167–171.

Food and Agriculture Organization of the United Nations. (2005). USA Agricultural Census 1987—Main Results. Retrieved January 9, 2006, from World Census of Agriculture—Results by Country Web site: http://www.fao.org/es/ess/census/wcares/USA_1987.pdf.

Foucault, M. (1977). *Discipline and Punish: The Birth of the Prison*. Translated From the French by Alan Sheridan. New York: Pantheon Books.

Frankenberg, R. (1993). *White Women, Race Matters: The Social Construction of Whiteness*. Minneapolis: University of Minnesota Press.

Fuentes, A. (2003, December 15). Discipline and Punish. *The Nation*. Retrieved July 15, 2006, from http://www.thenation.com/doc/20031215/fuentes.

Gaines, J. (1999). Political mimesis. In J. Gaines & M. Renov (Eds.), *Collecting Visible Evidence.* Minneapolis: University of Minnesota Press, 84–102.

GAO Month in Review. (2005, September 26). Drug Offenders: Various factors may limit the impacts of federal laws that provide for denial of selected benefits: GAO-05-238. Retrieved July 15, 2006, from the GAO Web site: http://www.gao.gov/review/emir2005/emirseptember2005.html.

Gaskell, J. & McLaren, A. (Eds.). (1991). *Women and Education: A Canadian Perspective.* Calgary: Detselig Enterprises.

Gilbert, D. (2005). Attica—thirty years later. In J. James (Ed.), *The New Abolitionists: (Neo)slave Narratives and Contemporary Prison Writings.* New York: State University of New York Press, 313–316.

Gilliam, W. (2005). Prekindergarteners Left Behind: Expulsion Rates in State Pre-Kindergarten Programs. FCD Brief Series, No. 3. Retrieved August 10, 2005, from Family Child Development Foundation Web site: www.fcd-us.org/PDFs/ExpulsionFinalProof.pdf.

Gilliam, W. & Shahar, G. (2006). Preschool and child care expulsion and suspension: Rates and predictors in one state. *Infants & Young Children,* 19(3), 228–245.

Gilligan, J. (1998). Reflections from a life behind bars: Build colleges, not prisons. *Chronicle of Higher Education,* 45(8), B7–B9.

Gilmore, R.W. (1998–1999). Globalisation and U.S. prison growth: From military keynesianism to post-keynesian militarism. *Race & Class,* 40(2/3), 171–188.

Gilmore, R. (2002). Fatal couplings of power and difference: Notes on racism and geography. *The Professional Geographer,* 54(1), 15–24.

Gilmore, R.W. (2004). Education or Incarceration: Schools and Prisons in a Punishing Democracy. Keynote Address presented at the Center for Democracy in a Multiracial Society, University of Illinois at Champaign–Urbana.

Goffman, E. (1961). *Asylums: Essays on the Social Situation of Mental Patients and Other Inmates.* New York: Doubleday.

Goldfarb, Z. (2006, January 29). Census Bureau, Activists Debate How and Where to Count People Who Are Incarcerated. *The Washington Post.*

Goldstein, R. (2002, July 1). Fighting the Gay Right. *The Nation.* Retrieved July 13, 2002, from: http://www.thenation.com/doc/20020701/goldstein.

Goode, V. & Goode, J. (2003). The Toledo Safe School Ordinance: A Preliminary Analysis of Race and Juvenile Court Cases. Paper presented at the January 2004 Education or Incarceration: Schools and Prisons in a Punishing Democracy, sponsored by the Center for Democracy in a Multiracial Society, University of Illinois at Champaign–Urbana.

Goodman, A. (2006, July 3). Access of Evil. *The Nation.* Retrieved August 22, 2006, from: http://www.thenation.com/doc/20060703/goodman.

Gordon, R., Piana, L.D., & Keleher, T. (2000). Facing the Consequences: An Examination of Racial Discrimination in U.S. Public Schools. ERASE Initiative. Applied Research Center, Ford Foundation, New York.

Gordon, R., Della Piana, L., & Keleher, T. (2001). Zero tolerance: A basic racial report card, in *Zero tolerance: Resisting the Drive for Punishment in Our Schools.* In W. Ayers, B. Dohrn, & A. Rick (Eds.). New York: New Press.

Goswani, S. & Schervish, A. (2002). Unlocking Options for Women: A Survey of Women in Cook County Jail: The Facts Behind the Faces. Policy paper from the Chicago Coalition for the Homeless.

Gramsci, A. (1971). *Selections from the Prison Notebooks*. London: Lawrence and Wishart.

Greene, J., Pranis, K., & Ziedenberg, J. (2006, March). Disparity by Design: How Drug-Free Zone Laws Impact Racial Disparity—And Fail to Protect Youth. A Justice Policy Institute Report. Retrieved August 21, 2006, from the Justice Policy Institute Report Web site: http://www.justicepolicy.org/reports/SchoolZonesReport306.pdf.

Guarino, D.R. (2003, January 8). Profiles in Oz, Part One. Behind the Bars: This Is No Fairy Tale! *Windy City Times*.

Haig Brown, C. (1988). *Resistance and Renewal: Surviving the Indian Residential School*. Vancouver, British Columbia, Canada: Arsenal Pulp Press.

Hancock, A. (2004). The Politics of Disgust and the Public Identity of the "Welfare Queen." New York: New York University Press.

Haraway, D. (2003). *The Companion Species Manifesto: Dogs, People and Significant Otherness*. Chicago: Prickly Paradigm Press.

Harper, H. (2000). White women teaching in the North: Problematic identity on the shores of Hudson Bay. In N. Rodriguez & L. Villaverde (Eds.), *Dismantling White Privilege: Pedagogy, Politics, and Whiteness*. New York: Peter Lang.

Harper, H. & Cavanaugh, S. (1994). Lady bountiful: The white woman teacher in multicultural education. *Women's Education*, 11(2), 27–33.

Harpo Productions, Inc. (2006). Oprah's Child Predator Watch List. Retrieved February 5, 2006, from OPRAH.com Web site: http://www2.oprah.com/presents/2005/predator/predator_main.jhtml.

Harris, C. (1993). Whiteness as property. *Harvard Law Review*, 106, 1709–1791.

Harry, B. & Klingner, J.K. (2005). *Why Are So Many Minority Students in Special Education? Understanding Race and Disability in Schools*. New York: Teachers College Press.

Harvey, D. (2005). The political economy of the public sphere. In S. Low & N. Smith (Eds.), *The Politics of Public Space*. New York: Routledge.

Herivel, T. & Wright, P. (Eds.). (2003). *Prison Nation: The Warehousing of America's Poor*. New York: Routledge.

Hermes, M. (2002, April). Research That Works: Native Language in a Reservation Community. Paper presented at the annual meeting of the American Educational Research Association, New Orleans, LA.

Heyer, R. & Wagner, P. (2004, April). Too big to ignore: How counting people in prisons distorted Census 2000. Retrieved October 1, 2006, from http://www.prisonersofthecensus.org/toobig/toobig.shtml.

Hill, I. (n.d.). Interview with Iyrania Hill. Retrieved July 1, 2006, from the Beyondmedia Education Web site: http://www.womenandprison.org/interviews/iyrania-hill.html.

Hirsch, M. (1999). Project Memory: Holocaust photographs in personal and public fantasy. In M. Bal, J. Grewe, & L. Spitzer (Eds.), *Acts of Memory: Cultural Recall in the Present*. Hanover, NH: University Press of New England, 3–23.

Hoeschsmann, M. (2004). Write it, get it: Motivating youth writers. In F. Ibanez-Carrasco & E. Meiners (Eds.), *Public Acts: Disruptive Readings on Making Curriculum Public*. New York: Routledge.

Hosp, J.L. & Reschly, D.J. (2004). Disproportionate representation of minority students in special education: Academic, demographic, and economic predictors. *Exceptional Children*, 70(2), 185–199.

Hoyt, E., Schiraldi, V., Smith, B., & Zeindenberg, J. (2002). *Reducing Racial Disparities in Juvenile Detention*. Baltimore: Annie E. Casey Foundation.

Hughes, J. (1999, April 21). Opinions Run Gamut on Suspects Among Neighbors, Friends. *Denver Post*, A17.

Huling, T. (2002). Building a prison economy in rural America. In M. Mauer & M. Chesney-Lind (Eds.), *Invisible Punishment: The Collateral Consequences of Mass Imprisonment*. New York: New Press, 197–213.

Human Rights Watch. (1996, December). All Too familiar: Sexual Abuse of Women in U.S. State Prisons.

Human Rights Watch. (1997, October). Cold Storage: Super-Maximum Security Confinement in Indiana.

Human Rights Watch. (1998, July). Nowhere to Hide: Retaliation Against Women in Michigan State Prisons.

Human Rights Watch. (2001). No Escape: Male Rape in U.S. Prisons. Retrieved August 21, 2006, from http://www.hrw.org/reports/2001/prison/report.html.

Humphreys, L. (1970). *Tearoom Trade*. Chicago: Aldine.

Hussain, R. (2006, August 10). 13-year-old Killer Gets 8 Years. Retrieved August 21, 2006, from *Chicago SunTimes* Web site: http://www.suntimes.com/output/news/cst-nws-dice10.html.

Hyman, I.A., Stefkovich, J.A., & Taich, S. (2002). Paddling and pro-paddling polemics: Refuting nineteenth century pedagogy. *Journal of Law & Education*, 31, 74–84.

Ibanez-Carrasco, F. & Meiners, E. (2004). *Public Acts*. New York: Routledge Falmer.

Illinois Department of Corrections (IDOC). (2003). Financial Impact Statement FY03. Retrieved June 15, 2006, from the Illinois Department of Corrections Web site: http://www.idoc.state.il.us/subsections/reports/financial_impact_statements/2003_Financial_Impact_Statement.pdf.

Illinois Department of Corrections. (2006). Facilities. Retrieved October 2, 2006 from www.idoc.state.il.us/subsections/facilities/default.shtml.

Illinois Department of Corrections (IDOC). (2004). Reports and Stats. Retrieved January 9, 2006, from the Illinois Department of Corrections Web site: http://www.idoc.state.il.us/subsections/reports/department_data/department%20Data%202004.pdf.

Illinois State Board of Education. (2003–2006). eReport Card Public Site. Retrieved April 9, 2006, from Data Analysis and Progress Reporting Web site: http://webprod1.isbe.net/ereportcard/publicsite/getSearchCriteria.aspx.

Illinois State Board of Education. (2005). 2004 Annual Report. Retrieved January 9, 2006, from Illinois State Board of Education Agency Budget Information Web site: http://www.isbe.state.il.us/budget/annual_report_04.pdf.

Illinois State Police. (2004). The Law on Domestic Violence. Retrieved April 9, 2006, from Domestic Violence Web site: http://www.isp.state.il.us/crime/domesticvio.cfm.

Illinois State Police. (2005). Illinois Sex Offender Frequently Asked Questions. Retrieved January 16, 2006, from Illinois Sex Offender Information Web site: http://www.isp.state.il.us/sor/faq.cfm?CFID=6634243&CFTOKEN=32 193595&jsessionid=0830335d81c5Ugg$9E$F#register.

Illinois State Police. (February 1, 2004). Study: Sex Offender Registration in Illinois. Retrieved October 2, 2006 from http://www.isp.state.il.us/docs/5-622.pdf.

Illinois State Police. Illinois Sex Offender Frequently Asked Questions. Retrieved October 2, 2006 from http://www.isp.state.il.us/sor/faq.cfm?CFID=45276 &CFTOKEN=71936591.

Illinois State Police. Illinois Sex Offender Registry. Retrieved October 2, 2006 from http://www.isp.state.il.us/sor/.

Illinois State Police. (2006). A Guide to Sex Offender Registration and Community Notification in Illinois [Brochure]. State of Illinois.

Innocent. (1989). In *OED* online (2nd ed.). Oxford, England: Oxford University Press. Retrieved February 20, 2001.

Jacobsen, R. (1999). "Megan's Laws" Reinforcing Old Patterns of Anti-Gay Police Harassment. *Georgetown Law Journal, 87*(7), 2431–2473.

Jaggar, A. (1989). Love and knowledge: Emotion in feminist epistemology. In A. Garry & M. Pearsall (Eds.), *Women, Knowledge and Reality* (2nd ed.). London: Routledge.

James, J. (Ed.). (2000). *States of Confinement: Policing, Detention and Prison.* New York: St. Martin's Press.

James, J. (Ed.). (2005). *The New Abolitionists: (Neo)Slave Narratives and Contemporary Prison Writings.* Albany: State University of New York Press.

Jensen, J. (2004). *"When I Close My Classroom Door..."*: Private places in public spaces. In Ibanez-Carrasco & Meiners (Eds.), *Public Acts: Disruptive Readings on Making Curriculum Public.* New York: Routledge.

Johnson, P. (2004). *Inner Lives: Voices of African American Women in Prison.* New York: New York University Press.

Kane-Willis, K., Janichek, J., & Clark, D. (2006). Intersecting Voices: Impacts of Illinois' Drug Policies. The Illinois Consortium on Drug Policies. Retrieved August 20, 2006, from the Institute for Metropolitan Affairs Web site: http://www.roosevelt.edu/ima/pdfs/intersectingVoices.pdf.

Karp S. (2000, May). State drug law targets city teens, minorities. *Chicago Reporter.* Retrieved August 1, 2006, from *Chicago Reporter* Web site: http://www.chicagoreporter.com/2000/5-2000/TJ/TJprint.htm

Katz, C. (2005). Power, space, and terror: Social reproduction and the public environment. In S. Low & N. Smith (Eds.), *The Politics of Public Space.* New York: Routledge.

Kaufman, P. (1984). *Women Teachers on the Frontier.* New Haven, CT: Yale University Press.

Kincaid, J.R. (1998). *Erotic Innocence: The Culture of Child Molesting.* Durham, NC: Duke University Press.

Kincheloe, J., Steinberg, S., Rodriguez, N. & Chennault, R. (1998). *White Reign: Deploying Whiteness in America.* New York: St. Martin's Press.

Kocal, L. (2003, May 30). Why Build a Prison and Not Use It? (Letter to the Editor). *Chicago SunTimes,* 42.

Kozol, J. (1991). *Savage Inequalities: Children in America's Schools*. New York: Crown.

Kozol, J. (2005). *Shame on the Nation: The Restoration of Apartheid Schooling in America*. New York: Crown.

Ladson-Billings, G. (2004). Landing on the wrong note: The price we paid for Brown. *Educational Researcher*, 33(7), 3–13.

Lane, C. (2005, March 2). 5-4 Supreme Court Abolishes Juvenile Executions. *Washington Post*, A1.

La Vigne, N.G., Mamalian, C.A., Travis, J., & Visher, C. (2003). *A Portrait of Prisoner Reentry in Illinois*. Urban Institute Report. Retrieved April 17, 2003, from http://www.urban.org/url.cfm?ID=410662.

Lesko, N. (2000). *Act Your Age: A Cultural Construction of Adolescence*. New York: Routledge Falmer.

Levine, J. (2002). *Harmful to Minors: The Perils of Protecting Children From Sex*. Minneapolis: University of Minnesota Press.

Levy, E. & Levine, R. (1983). The child's right to corporal integrity in the school setting: A right without a remedy under the Constitution. *Journal of Clinical Child Psychology*, 12(3), 261–265

Lindsley, S. (2002). The gendered assault on immigrants. In J. Silliman & A. Bhattacharjee (Eds.), *Policing the National Body: Race, Gender and Criminalization*. Cambridge, MA: South End Press, 175–196.

Lipsitz, G. (1998). *The Possessive Investment in Whiteness: How White People Profit From Identity Politics*. Philadelphia: Temple University Press.

Lochner, L. (2004). Education, work and crime: A human capital approach. *International Economic Review*, 45, 811–844.

Lochner, L. & Moretti, E. (2004). The effect of education on crime: Evidence from prison inmates, arrests, and self-reports. *American Economic Review*, 94, 155–189.

Lock, M. & Scheper-Hughes, N. (1990). A critical interpretive approach in medical anthropology: Rituals and routines of discipline and dissent. In T. Johnson & C. Sargent (Eds.), *Medical Anthropology: A Handbook of Theory and Method*. Westport, CT: Greenwood Press, 47–73.

Loewen, J.W. (1995). *Lies My Teacher Told Me: Everything Your American History Textbook Got Wrong*. New York: Touchstone.

Lorde, A. (1984). *Sister Outsider: Essays and Speeches*. Berkeley, CA: Crossing Press.

Losen, D. & Orfield, G. (2002). Racial Inequity in Special Education. Retrieved August 22, 2006, from Harvard Graduate School of Education Web site: http://www.gse.harvard.edu/hepg/introduction.html.

Low, S. (2005). How private interests take over public space: Zoning, taxes, and incorporation of gated communities. In S. Low & N. Smith (Eds.), *The Politics of Public Space*. New York: Routledge, 81–104.

Lubiano, W. (1992). Black Ladies, Welfare Queens, and State Minstrels: Ideological War by Narrative Means. In T. Morrison (Ed). *Race-ing Justice, En-Gendering Power: Essays on Anita Hill, Clarence Thomas, and the Construction of Social Reality*. New York: Pantheon Books. 323–363.

Lyman, R. (2006, September 30). In Many Public Schools, the Paddle Is No Relic. *New York Times*, p. A1.

Makela, K. (1996). *Alcoholics Anonymous as a Mutual Help Movement: A Study in Eight Societies.* Madison: University of Wisconsin Press.

Mann, C.R. & Zatz, M. (Eds). (1998). *Images of Color, Images of Crime.* Los Angeles: Roxbury.

Mar, E. & Williams, D.L. (2005). Open forum: Why open prisons and close schools? *San Francisco Chronicle.* Retrieved January 09, 2006, from: http://www.sfgate.com/cgi-bin/article.cgi?file=/chronicle/archive/2005/06/01/EDGSED1AT71.DTL.

Marano, L. (2003, September 10). Analysis: Prison education cuts recidivism. *The Washington Post: United Press International.* Retrieved October 13, 2003, from: http://washingtontimes.com/upi-breaking/20030903-070918-8804r.htm.

Marika. (2006, April 15). Together We Can Stop This Super Jail. 81 Reasons. Retrieved April 20, 2006, from 81 Reasons Campaign Web site: http://81reasons.revolt.org/node/16.

Marlan, T. (2005, April 8). Prisoner of the Past. *Chicago Reader.*

Marshall, L. (2002). *Death Penalty Symposium.* Chicago: Northeastern Illinois University.

Martin, E. (1994). *Flexible Bodies: The Role of Immunology in American Culture From the Days of Polio to the Age of AIDS.* Boston: Beacon Press.

Martin, P., Lowell, B.L., & Taylor, E. (2000). Migration outcomes of guest worker and free trade regimes: The case of Mexico–U.S. migration. In B. Ghosh (Ed.), *Managing Migration: Time for a New International Regime.* Oxford, England: Oxford University Press.

Martusewicz, R. (1994). Guardians of childhood. In W. Reynolds & R. Martusewicz (Eds.), *Inside/Out: Contemporary Critical Perspectives in Education.* New York: St. Martin's Press.

Martusewicz, R. & Reynolds, W. (Eds.). (1984). *Inside/Out: Contemporary Critical Perspectives in Education.* New York: St. Martin's Press.

Maschi, P. (2004, March, 19). Forms of Resistance to the Prison Industrial Complex. Retrieved July 1, 2006, from the Beyondmedia Education Web site: http://womenandprison.org/social-justice/pilar-maschi.html.

Massachusetts Coalition for Adult Education. (2001, November 23). Massachusetts Adult Basic Education Factsheet. Retrieved October 13, 2003, from the System for Adult Basic Education Support (SABES) Web site: http://www.sabes.org/resouces/abestats.htm.

Mauer, M. (1999). *A Race to Incarcerate.* New York: New Press.

Mauer, M. & Chesney-Lind, M. (Eds.). (2002a). Introduction. *Invisible Punishment: The Collateral Consequences of Mass Imprisonment.* New York: New Press.

McBride, D. (2001). *Truth, Abolition and Slave Testimony: Impossible Witness.* New York: New York University Press.

McCarthy, C. & Crichlow, W. (Eds.). (1993). *Race, Identity, and Representation in Education.* New York: Routledge.

McCarthy, M.M. (2005). Corporal punishment in public schools: Is the United States out of step? *Educational Horizons,* 83(4), 235–240.

McDermott, R., Goldman, S. & Varenne, H. (2006). The Cultural Work of Learning Disabilities. *Educational Researcher,* 35(6), 12–17.

McGruder, A. (2003). *A Right to Be Hostile: The Boondocks Treasury.* New York: Three Rivers Press.

McNally, J. (2003a). A ghetto within a ghetto: African-American students are over-represented in special education programs. *Rethinking Schools Online,* 17(3). Retrieved January 30, 2004, from: http://www.rethinkingschools.org/archive/17_03/ghet173.shtml.

McNally, J. (2003b). Black over-representation in special education not confined to segregated states. *Rethinking Schools Online,* 17(3). Retrieved February 10, 2004, from: http://www.rethinkingschools.org/archive/17_03/over173.shtml.

McRobbie, A. (2000). *Feminism and Youth Culture* (2nd ed.). London: Routledge.

Mears, D. (2006, March). Evaluating the Effectiveness of Supermax Prisons, Retrieved May 15, 2006, from the Urban Institute Web site: www.urban.org/uploadedPDF/411326_supermax_prisons.pdf.

Medina, J. (2006, February 6). As Albany Weighs Confinement of Sex Offenders, Some Fear a Threat to Civil Liberties. *New York Times,* B4.

Mills, C. (1997). *The Racial Contract.* Ithaca, NY: Cornell University Press.

Mills, C. (2003). *From Class to Race: Essays in White Marxism and Black Radicalism.* Lanham, MD: Rowman & Littlefield.

Moore, K. & Redd, Z. (2002). Children in Poverty: Trends, Consequences, and Policy Options. Retrieved November 11, 2005, from Child Trends Research Center Web site: http://www.childtrends.org/Files/PovertyRB.pdf.

Morrison, T. (Ed.) (1993). *Race-ing Justice, En-Gendering Power: Essays on Anita Hill, Clarence Thomas and the Construction of Social Reality.* New York: Chatto & Windus.

Muntaquim. J. (2005). The Criminalization of Poverty in America (Abridged) in. J. James. *The New Abolitionists: (Neo) Slave Narratives and Contemporary Prison Writings.* Albany, NY: SUNY Press. 29–36.

Nader, L. (1972). Up the Anthropolgist. In D. Hymes (Ed.), *Reinventing Anthropology.* New York: Pantheon Books.

Nader, L. (2005). *Life of the Law.* Berkeley: University of California Press.

Naples, N. (2003). *Feminism and Method: Ethnography, Discourse Analysis and Activist Research.* New York: Routledge.

National Center for Education Statistics (NCES). (1998). The Condition of Education 1998. Retrieved October 27, 2005, from the NCES Web site: http://nces.ed.gov/pubs98/98013.pdf.

National Center for Education Statistics (NCES). (2003a). Status and Trends in the Education of Blacks: 2003. Retrieved November 11, 2005, from the NCES Web site: http://nces.ed.gov/pubs2003/2003034.pdf.

National Center for Education Statistics (NCES). (2003b). Indicators of School Crime and Safety Report 2003. Retrieved June 15, 2006, from the NCES Web site: http://nces.ed.gov/pubs2004/crime03/.

National Center for Education Statistics (NCES). (2004). Indicators of School Crime and Safety: 2004. Retrieved October 27, 2005, from the NCES Web site: http://nces.ed.gov/pubs2005/crime_safe04/.

National Center for Education Statistics (NCES). (n.d.). Digest of Education Statistics Tables and Figures 1999: Table 72. Retrieved January 9, 2006, from the NCES Web site: http://nces.ed.gov/programs/digest/d99/d99t072.asp.

National Center for Higher Education Management Systems (NCHEMS). (2006). Finance: State and Local Public Higher Education Support Per Full-Time Equivalent Student. Retrieved July 15, 2006, from the NCHEMS Web site: http://www.higheredinfo.org/dbrowser/index.php?submeasure=67&year =2005&level=nation&mode=data&state=0.

National Clearinghouse on Child Abuse and Neglect Information. (2004). Child Abuse and Neglect Fatalities: Statistics and Interventions. Retrieved July 15, 2006, from the U.S. Department of Health and Human Services Web site: http://nccanch.acf.hhs.gov/index.cfm.

National Council for Accreditation of Teacher Education (NCATE). (2001). Standards for Professional Development Schools. Retrieved August 20, 2006, from the NCATE Web site: http://www.ncate.org/documents/pdsStandards.pdf.

National Fair Housing Alliance. (2006). Unequal Opportunity—Perpetuating Housing Segregation in America Report. Retrieved October 20, 2006 from http://www.nationalfairhousing.org/resources/newsArchive/resource_ 20628126054870386567.pdf.

New York State Education Department: Elementary, Middle, Secondary and Continuing Education. (n.d.). The New York State School Report Card 2003–2004 Fiscal Accountability Supplement. Retrieved January 9, 2006, from the University of the State of New York State Education Department Web site: http://www.emsc.nysed.gov/repcrd2004/supplement/280402030000.pdf.

Ninny. (1989). OED online (2nd ed.). Oxford: Oxford University Press. Retrieved February 20, 2001.

Noguera, P. (2003, October 19). Schools, prisons, and social implications of punishment: Rethinking disciplinary practices. *In Motion Magazine.*

Oakes, J. (1985). *Keeping Track: How Schools Structure Inequality.* New Haven, CT: Yale University Press.

O'Brien, P. (2002, June). Reducing Barriers to Employment for Women Ex-Offenders: Mapping the Road to Reintegration. Retrieved June 15, 2006, from the Safer Foundation Web site: http://www.saferfoundation.org/docs/womens-policypaper.pdf.

O'Connor, C. & Fernandez, S.D. (2006). Race, Class, and Disproportionality: Reevaluating the Relationship Between Poverty and Special Education Placement. *Educational Researcher, 35*(6), 6–11.

OCR Elementary and Secondary School Survey. (2002). Retrieved August 15, 2006, from the U.S. Department of Education Web site: http://vistademo.beyond2020.com/ocr2002r/wdsdata.html.

Office of Special Education Programs (1999). Special Education in Correctional Facilities, II. Student Characteristics. Retrieved October 2, 2006 from U.S. Department of Education Web site: www.ed.gov/about/reports/annual/osep/1999/ch2.doc.

Office of the Governor. (2005, September 14). For Immediate Release. Retrieved August 22, 2006, from the Press Release Web site: http://www.amberillinois.org/PDF/PressReleases/release091405.pdf.

Office of the Governor Rick Perry. (2006). Governor's Advisory Council Recommends Changes to Criminal Justice System. Retrieved April 9, 2006, from the Press Release Web site: http://www.governor.state.tx.us/divisions/press/pressreleases/PressRelease.2006-02-07.5221.

Ogden, S. (2005). The prison industrial complex in indigenous California. In *Global Lockdown: Gender, Race, and the Rise of the Prison Industrial Complex*. New York: Routledge, 57–66.

Ogunnaike, L. (2005, October 30). Aaron McGruder. *New York Times*, Arts & Leisure Section, 29.

Ogletree, C. & Sarat, A. (2006). *From Lynch Mobs to the Killing State: Race and the Death Penalty in America*. New York: New York University Press.

Ohlemacher, S. (2006, January 28). Where's Home for Prison Inmates? Answer Could Mean Dollars for Communities. *Newsday*.

Opportunities Suspended: The Devastating Consequences of Zero Tolerance and School Discipline Policies. (2000). Advancement Project & the Civil Rights Project, Harvard University. Retrieved July 15, 2006, from the Civil Rights Project Web site: http://www.civilrightsproject.harvard.edu.

Oprah's Child Predator Watch List. Retrieved April 20, 2006 from http://www2.oprah.com/presents/2005/predator/predator_main.jhtml.

Orfield, G. (2001, July 17). Schools More Separate: Consequences of a Decade of Resegregation. Retrieved August 1, 2006, from the Civil Rights Project Web site: http://www.civilrightsproject.harvard.edu/research/deseg/separate_schools01.php.

Page, J. (2004). Eliminating the enemy: The import of denying prisoners access to higher education in Clinton's America. *Punishment & Society*, 6(4), 357–378.

Paintal, S. (1999). Banning corporal punishment of children. *Childhood Education*, 76, 36–39.

Paley, V. (1979). *White Teacher*. Cambridge: Harvard University Press.

Parenti, C. (2004). *The Soft Cage: Surveillance in America From Slavery to the War on Terror*. New York: Basic Books.

Pateman, C. (1988). *The Sexual Contract*. Stanford: Stanford University Press.

Petit, B. & Western, B. (2004). Mass imprisonment and the life course: Race and class inequality in U.S. incarceration. *American Sociological Review*, 69, 151–169.

Pewewardy, C.D. (1999). From La Belle Sauvage to the Noble Savage: The deculturalization of Indian mascots in American culture. *Multicultural Education*, 6(3), 6–11.

Pintado-Vertner, R. (2002). From Sweatshop to Hip-Hop. *Colorlines*, Summer. Retrieved June 2005 from http://www.colorlines.com/article.php?ID=92.

Polakow, V. (Ed.). (2000). *The Public Assault on America's Children: Poverty, Violence, and Juvenile Injustice*. New York: Teachers College Press.

Polakow, V., Butler, S.S., Stormer Deprez, L., & Kahn, P. (Eds.). (2004). *Shut Out: Low Income Mothers and Higher Education in Post-Welfare America*. Albany: State University of New York Press.

Postman, N. (1994). *The Disappearance of Childhood*. Reprint. New York: Vintage Books.

Quadagno, J. (1994). *The Color of Welfare: How Racism Undermined the War on Poverty*. New York: Oxford University Press.

Rapping, E. (1997). *The Culture of Recovery: Making Sense of the Self-Help Movement*. Boston: Beacon Press.

Rapping, E. (2003). *Law and Justice as Seen on TV.* New York: New York University Press.

Reagan, R. (1986, October 27). Remarks on Signing the Anti-Drug Abuse Act of 1986. Retrieved August 23, 2006, from the Reagan Archives at the University of Texas Web site: http://www.reagan.utexas.edu/archives/speeches/1986/102786c.htm.

Reid, D. K., Knight, M. G. (2006). Disability Justifies Exclusion of Minority Students: A Critical History Grounded in Disability Studies. *Educational Researcher,* 35(6), 18–23.

Report Finds Zero Tolerance Needlessly Tracks Illinois Students from Schools to Jails. (n.d.). Stop the Schoolhouse to Jailhouse Track. Retrieved April 10, 2006, from Schools Not Jails Web site: http://www.stopschoolstojails.org/chicago/default.asp.

Rhodes, L.A. (2001). Toward an anthropology of prisons. *Annual Review of Anthropology,* 30, 65–83, 1163.

Rhodes, L. (2004). *Total Confinement: Madness and Reason in the Maximum Security Prison.* California Series in Public Anthropology. Berkeley: University of California Press.

Rhodes, L.A. (2005, August). Changing the subject: Conversation in supermax. *Cultural Anthropology,* 20(3), 388–411, 526.

Richie, B. (1996). *Compelled to Crime: The Gender Entrapment of Battered Black Women.* New York: Routledge.

Ritchie, B. (2005). Queering Antiprison Work: African American Lesbians in the Juvenile Justice System. In J. Sudbury (Ed). *Global Lockdown: Race, Gender and the Prison Industrial Complex.* New York: Routledge. 73–86.

Rios, V. (2006). "Deviant Politics: Identity Formation Among Criminalized Urban Male Youth." Paper presented at the Latinos and Incarceration conference at the University of Illinois at Chicago, October 20, 2006.

Roberts, D. (1997). *Killing the Black Body: Race, Reproduction, and the Meaning of Liberty.* New York: Vintage Books.

Rodriguez, D. (2004). Paper presented at the conference on Education or Incarceration: Schools and Prisons in a Punishing Democracy, sponsored by the Center for Democracy in a Multiracial Society, January, University of Illinois at Champaign–Urbana.

Rodriguez, N. & Villaverde, L. (Eds.). (2000). *Dismantling White Privilege: Pedagogy, Politics and Whiteness.* New York: Peter Lang.

Roediger, D. (1991). *Wages of Whiteness: Race and the Making of the American Working Class.* London: Verso Press.

Rogoff, B. (2003). *The Cultural Nature of Human Development.* Oxford, England: Oxford University Press.

Rojas, P. (1998).Complex facts. *Colorlines,* 1(2). Special Section: The Prison Industrial Complex.

Rose, J. (1992). *The Case of Peter Pan: Or the Impossibility of Children's Fiction.* New Cultural Studies Series. Philadelphia: University of Pennsylvania Press.

Rose, T. (1994). *Black Noise: Rap Music and Black Culture in Contemporary America.* Hanover, NH: University Press of New England.

Rothstein, M.A. (2005). Genetic justice. *The New England Journal of Medicine,* 352(26), 2667–2668.

Roy, L. (2001). Corporal punishment in American public schools and the rights of the child. *Journal of Law & Education*, 30, 554–563.

Royse, D. (2004, September 28). Family: 7-year-old too young to be arrested. Associated Press.

Salazar-Parrenas, R. (2001). *Servants of Globalization: Women, Migration and Domestic Work*. Stanford, CA: Stanford University Press.

Saltman, K.J. & Gabbard, D.A. (Eds.). (2003). *Education as Enforcement: The Militarization and Corporatization of Schools*. New York: Routledge Falmer.

Sandoval, C. (2000). *Methodology of the Oppressed*. Minneapolis: University of Minnesota Press.

San Miguel, G., Jr. (1985). Roused from our slumbers. In A. Darder (Ed.), *Latinos and Education*. New York: Routledge.

Savage, D. & Warren, J. (2005, February 24). Justices Reject Segregation in State's Prisons. *Los Angeles Times*. Retrieved May 15, 2006, from the *Los Angles Times* Web site: http://www.latimes.com/news/nationworld/nation/la-na-scotus24feb24,0,4590196.story?coll=la-home-nation.

Schiraldi, V. and Ziedenberg, J. (2001) How Distorted Coverage of Juvenile Crime Affects Public Policy. In W. Ayers, B. Dohrn, and R. Ayers (Eds.) *Zero Tolerance: Resisting the Drive for Punishment in our Schools*. New York: The New Press. 113–126.

Schor, N. & Weed, E. (Eds.). (1994). *The Essential Difference*. Bloomington: Indiana University Press.

Scott, J. (1999). The Evidence of Experience. In S. Hesse-Biber, C. Gilmartin and R. Lydenberg (Eds.), *Feminist Approaches to Theory and Methodology*. Oxford: Oxford University Press. 79–99.

Sedgwick, E. (1990). *The Epistemology of the Closet*. Berkeley: University of California Press.

Sentencing Project. (2002). *Mentally Ill Offenders in the Criminal Justice System*. Retrieved May 5, 2006, from the Sentencing Project Web site: http://www.sentencingproject.org.

Shahar, S. (1990). *Childhood in the Middle Ages*. New York: Routledge.

Shuler, P. (2002, April 4). Educating prisoners is cheaper than locking them up again. *City Beat: Statehouse*, 8(21). Retrieved September 30, 2003, from: http://www.citybeat.com/2002-04-04/statehouse.shtml.

Silko, L.M. (1996). *Yellow Woman and a Beauty of the Spirit: Essays on Native American Life Today*. New York: Simon & Schuster.

Silliman, J. & Bhattacharjee, A. (Eds.). (2002). Introduction. *Policing the National Body: Race, Gender and Criminalization*. Cambridge, MA: South End Press.

Simkins, S., Hirsch, A., & Horvat, E. (2003). The School to Prison Pipeline for Girls: The Role of Physical and Sexual Abuse. Paper presented at the conference on the School to Prison Pipeline: Charting Intervention Strategies of Prevention and Support for Minority Children, May 16–17, Northeastern University, Boston. Retrieved October, 20, 2006 from: http://www.civilrightsproject.harvard.edu/research/pipeline03/Hirsch.pdf.

Simmons, L. (2004, November). Urban Education and the Prison Industrial Complex. Paper presented at the Council on Anthropology and Education Meetings, San Francisco CA.

Simpson, K. & Blevins, J. (1999, April 23). Mystery How Team Players Became Loners: Friends Remember Two Suspects as Bashful, Ordinary Children. *Denver Post*, A4.

Skiba, R. (2000). *Zero Tolerance, Zero Evidence: A Critical Analysis of School Disciplinary Practice*. Bloomington: Indiana University Press.

Skiba, R. (2001). When is disproportionality discrimination? The overrepresentation of black students in school suspension. In W. Ayers, B. Dohrn, & R. Ayers (Eds.), *Zero Tolerance: Resisting the Drive for Punishment in Our Schools: A Handbook for Parents, Students, Educators, and Citizens*. New York: New Press.

Skiba, R., Michael, R.S., Nardo, A.C., & Peterson, R. (2000). *The Color of Discipline: Sources of Racial and Gender Disproportionality in School Punishment*. Bloomington: Indiana University, Education Policy Center. Policy Research Report #SRS1.

Skiba, R., Peterson, R., & Williams, T. (1997). Office referrals and suspension: Disciplinary intervention in middle schools. *Education and Treatment of Children*, 20(3), 295–315.

Slate, J & Perez, E. (n.d.). Corporal Punishment: Used in a Discriminatory Manner? Retrieved August 21, 2006, from: http://www.ctserc.org/library/bibfiles/discipline.pdf.

Sleeter, C. (1993). How white teachers construct race. In C. McCarthy & W. Crichlow (Eds.), *Race, Identity, and Representation in Education*. New York: Routledge.

Smith, A. (2005). *Conquest: Sexual Violence and American Indian Genocide*. Cambridge, MA: South End Press.

Smith, A. (2006). Soul Wound: The Legacy of Native American Schools. Retrieved August 15, 2006, from the Amnesty International Web site: http://www.amnestyusa.org/amnestynow/soulwound.html.

Smith, D.E. (2005). *Institutional Ethnography: A Sociology for People*. Walnut Creek, CA: Alta Mira Press.

Smith, D.E. & David, S.J. (Eds.). (1975). *Women Look at Psychiatry*. Vancouver, British Columbia, Canada: Press Gang.

Smith, K. (2005). Modern day slavery: Inside the prison industrial complex. In *Global Lockdown: Gender, Race, and the Rise of the Prison Industrial Complex*. New York: Routledge.

Smith, L.T. (1999). *Decolonizing Methodologies: Research and Indigenous Peoples*. New York: Zed Books.

Smith, S. & Watson, J. (Eds.). (1996). *Getting a Life: Everyday Uses of Autobiography*. Minneapolis: University of Minnesota Press.

Sommer, D. (1999). *Proceed With Caution, When Engaged by Minority Writing in the Americas*. Cambridge, MA: Harvard University Press.

Sommer, D. (2004). *Bilingual Aesthetics: A New Sentimental Education*. Durham, NC: Duke University Press.

Spousal Rape Laws: 20 Years Later. (2004). Retrieved June 15, 2006, from the National Center for Victims of Crime Web site: http://www.ncvc.org/ncvc/main.aspx?dbName=DocumentViewer&DocumentID=32701.

Spring, J. (2001). *The American School: 1642–1996*. New York: McGraw-Hill, 5th Ed.

Sproul, K. (1997). California's Response to Domestic Violence. Retrieved April 09, 2006, from Senate Office of Research Web site: http://www.sen.ca.gov/sor/reports/reports_by_year/1997/9711dmv.txt.

Stacey, J. (1988). Can there be feminist ethnography? *Women's Studies International Forum*, 11, 21–27.

Steelwater, E. (2003) *The Hangman's Knot*. Boulder, CO: Westview Press.

Stevenson, R.D. & Ellsworth, J. (1993). Dropouts and the silencing of critical voices. In L. Weis & M. Fine (Eds.), *Beyond Silenced Voices: Class, Race, and Gender in United States Schools*. Albany: State University of New York Press.

Stop Schools to Jails. (2006). Retrieved April 10, 2006, from the Schools Not Jails Web site: http://www.stopschoolstojails.org/chicago/default.asp.

Stoskepf, A. (1999). The forgotten history of eugenics. *Rethinking Schools*, 13(3). Retrieved August 15, 2006, from the Rethinking Schools Web site: http://www.rethinkingschools.org/archive/13_03/eugenic.shtml.

Sudbury, J. (2004). A world without prisons: Resisting militarism, globalized punishment, and empire. *Social Justice*, 31(1/2), 9–30.

Sudbury, J. (Ed.) (2005). *Global Lockdown*. New York: Routledge.

Sudbury, J. (2005). Introduction: Feminist Critiques, Transnational Landscapes, Abolitionist Visions. In J. Sudbury (Ed). *Global Lockdown: Race, Gender and the Prison Industrial Complex*. New York: Routledge. xi–xxvviii.

Taylor, J.M. (1992). Post secondary correctional education: An evaluation of effectiveness and efficiency. *Journal of Correctional Education*, 43(3), 132–141.

Taylor, J.M. (1993, January 25). Pell Grants for prisoners. *The Nation*.

Taylor, J.M. (1995). It's Criminal to Deny Pell Grants to Prisoners. *The World and I* [Special Report]. Retrieved September 30, 2003, from: http://www.world-andi.com/specialreport/1995/March/Sa13525.htm.

Thomas, P. (n.d.). Interview with Pamela Thomas. Retrieved July 1, 2006, from the Beyondmedia Education Web site: http://www.womenandprison.org/interviews/pamela-thomas.html.

Toppo, G. (2003). The Face of the American Teacher: White and Female While Her Students Are Ethnically Diverse. *USA Today*. Retrieved January 09, 2006, from: http://www.usatoday.com/educate/college/education/articles/20030706.htm.

Townsend, B. (2000). The disproportionate discipline of African American learners: Reducing school suspensions and expulsions. *Exceptional Children*, 66(3), 381–391.

Travis, H. (2006, February 4). Pickton Trial: Who Were the Victims? Retrieved August 22, 2006, from: http://thetyee.ca/Mediacheck/2006/02/04/Pickton Trial/.

Travis, J. (2002). Invisible Punishment: An Instrument of Social Exclusion. In M. Mauer and M. Chesney-Lind (Eds) *Invisible Punishment: The Collateral consequences of Mass Imprisonment*. New York: New Press. 15-36.

Two Million and Counting. (2003, April 09). *New York Times*, A20.

Tyrnauer, M. (2005, August). The Prisoner of Bedford. *Vanity Fair*, 110–119, 176–180.

U.S. Department of Agriculture. (n.d.). 2002 Census of Agriculture. Retrieved January 9, 2006, from the National Agricultural Statistics Service Web site: http://www.nass.usda.gov/Census_of_Agriculture/index.asp.

U.S. Department of Education. (2002). Education department submits 23rd annual report to Congress on special education: Graduation rates up, dropout rates down, inclusion at record level. Retrieved November 11, 2005, from U.S. Department of Education Web site: http://www.ed.gov/news/pressreleases/2002/05/05102002.html.

U.S. Department of Education. (n.d.). Gun Free Schools Act of 1994. Retrieved October 27, 2005, from Improving America's Schools Act of 1994 Web site: http://www.ed.gov/legislation/ESEA/sec14601.html.

U.S. Department of Education, Office for Civil Rights. (2002). Elementary and Secondary School Survey: State and National Projections for Enrollment and Selected Items by Race/Ethnicity and Sex. Retrieved August 22, 2006, from the Washington, D.C., U.S. Government Printing Office Web site: http://vistademo.beyond2020.com/ocr2002r.

U.S. Department of Justice. (1994, October 24). *Fact Sheet*. Retrieved August 22, 2006, from the National Criminal Justice Web site: http:// www.ncjrs.org/ txtfiles/billfs.txt.

U.S. Department of Justice. (1998a, March). *Violence by Intimates: Analysis of Data on Crimes by Current or Former Spouses, Boyfriends, and Girlfriends.* Retrieved July 20, 2006, from the U.S. Department of Justice Web site: www. ojp.usdoj.gov/bjs/pub/pdf/ipv.pdf.

U.S. Department of Justice. (1998b, November). *Prevalence, Incidence, and Consequences of Violence Against Women: Findings From the National Violence Against Women Survey.* Retrieved June 20, 2006, from the National Criminal Justice Reference Service Web site: www.ncjrs.gov/pdffiles/172837.pdf.

U.S. Department of Justice. (2001). Audit Report: Combined DNA Index System. Retrieved April 9, 2006, from the United States Department of Justice Web site: http://www.usdoj.gov/oig/reports/FBI/a0126/final.pdf.

U.S. Department of Justice. (2006). Retrieved February 5, 2006, from the National Sex Offender Public Registry Web site: http://www.nsopr.gov/.

U.S. House of Representatives. (2000). Innocence Protection Act of 2000. Retrieved April 9, 2006, from the Committee Hearings Web site: http://commdocs. house.gov/committees/judiciary/hju66013.000/hju66013_0.HTM.

Varenne, H. & McDermott, R. (1998). *Successful Failure: The School America Builds.* Boulder, CO: Westview Press.

von Zielbauer, P. (2005, February 27). As Health Care in Jails Goes Private, 10 Days Can Be a Death Sentence. *New York Times*, 1:1.

Wacquant, L. (2000). Deadly symbiosis: When ghetto and prison meet and mesh. *Punishment and Society*, 3(1), 95–134.

Wacquant, L. (2002). From slavery to mass incarceration: Rethinking the "race question" in the U.S. *New Left Review*, 13, 41–60.

Wagner, P. (2003). *The Prison Index: Taking the Pulse of the Crime Control Industry.* Published by the Western Prison Project and the Prison Policy Initiative. Retrieved June 15, 2006, from the Prison Policy Initiative Web site: http://www.prisonpolicy.org/prisonindex/rootsofcrime.shtml.

Wald, J. & Losen, D. (2003). Defining and Redirecting a School-to-Prison Pipeline. Paper presented at the conference on the *School to Prison Pipeline: Charting Intervention Strategies of Prevention and Support for Minority Children*, May 16–17, Northeastern University, Boston. Retrieved August 22, 2006, from: http://media.wiley.com/product_data/excerpt/74/07879722/0787972274. pdf.

Walkerdine, V. (1988). *The Mastery of Reason: Cognitive Development and the Production of Rationality*. Critical Psychology Series. New York: Routledge.

Walkerdine, V. (1990). *Schoolgirl Fictions*. London: Verso.

Warhol, R., and Michie, H. (1996). Twelve-Step Teleology: Narratives of Recovery/Recovery as Narrative. In S. Smith and J. Watson (Eds.) *Getting a life: everyday uses of autobiography*, Minneapolis and London: University of Minnesota Press.

Weis, L. & Fine, M. (Eds.). (1993). *Beyond Silenced Voices: Class, Race, and Gender in United States Schools*. Albany: State University of New York Press.

Wells-Barnett, I. (2002). *On Lynchings*. Amherst, NY: Humanity Books.

West, E. (1996). *Growing Up in Twentieth-Century America*. Westport, CT: Greenwood Press.

Western, B., Pettit, B., & Guetzkow, J. (2002). Black economic progress in the era of mass imprisonment. In M. Mauer & M. Chesney-Lind (Eds.), *Invisible Punishment: The Collateral Consequences of Mass Imprisonment*. New York: New Press.

Whitehorn, L. (1997, March 21). *Surviving Solitary*. Retrieved August 23, 2006, from the Women and Prison Web site: http://womenandprison.org/violence/laura-whitehorn.html.

Winant, H. (2004). *The New Politics of Race: Globalism, Difference, Justice*. Minneapolis: University of Minnesota Press.

Wolch, J. R. (1990). *The shadow state: Government and voluntary sector in transition*. New York: The Foundation Center.

Wolff, J. (1994). Opening Up, Online: What Happens When the Public Comes at You From Cyberspace. *Columbia Journalism Review*. November/December 1994, 62–65. Retrieved Ocotoer 1, 2006 from http://archives.cjr.org/year/94/6/online.asp.

Women and Prison: A Site for Resistance. (2006). Retrieved October 1, 2006, http://www.womenandprison.org.

Wright, G. & Millar, S. (1999, April 22). A Clique Within a Clique, Obsessed With Guns, Death and Hitler. *The Guardian*, 3.

Yoon-Louie, M.C. (2001). *Sweatshop Warriors*. Cambridge, MA: South End Press.

Yoon-Louie, M.C. (2001–2002). Sweatshop warriors. *Colorlines*, 4(4), 40–42.

Zook, J. (1994). Crime bill would bar Pell grants to federal and state prisons. *Chronicle of Higher Education*, 41(11), A24.

Zucchino, D. (1999). *The Myth of the Welfare Queen: A Pulitzer Prize-Winning Journalist's Portrait of Women on the Line*. New York: Touchstone.

Index

H

Hancock, A., 84
Haraway, D., 21, 24
Harmful to Minors, 138
Harry, B., 3, 37–38, 49, 145, 148
Harvey, D., 62
Herivel, T., 82
Heyer, R., 76
Hill, L., 163
Hirsch
    J., 67–69
    M., 125–126
Hoeschsmann, M., 110
Huling, T., 76
Human Rights Watch, 85, 92, 162
Humphreys, L., 132
Hurricane film, 82
Hurricane Katrina, 66, 96
Hussain, R., 130
Hyman, L.A., 171, 173

I

Ignorance, epistemology of, 19–25
In loco parentis responsibility, 172
Incarceration rates, 98–109
Informed consent, 13
Ingraham v Wright, 173
Inner Lives: The Voices of African-
    American Women in Prison,
    15, 35
Innocence Project, 175–181
Interviews, surveys, utilization of, 13

J

Jacobsen, R., 132–134
Jaggar, A., 6, 29
James, J., 20
Janichek, J., 5
Johnson, P., 35, 40, 72, 74, 86, 90, 104
Justice Policy Institute, 59

K

Kahn, P., 87
Kane-Willis, K., 5, 57–58, 60, 86, 98–99,
    104

Karp S., 129–130
Katz, C., 75
Kaufman, P., 47
Keleher, T., 32–34
Kilgore, D., 87, 152
Kincaid, J.R., 128
Kind and Unusual Punishment, 182
Klingner, J.K., 3, 37–38, 49, 145, 148
Knight, M.G., 38, 145–146
Kocal, L., 75

L

La Vigne, N.G., 58, 76
Ladson-Billings, G., 182
Lady Bountiful concept, 43–56
Lane, C., 129
Language, 19–20
Larry v. Riles, 37
Law and Order, television series, 16, 82,
    93
Lawrence & Garner v. State of Texas,
    132–133
Le Monde, 183
Leistyna, P., 108
Lesko, N., 5, 126, 144, 172
Levine
    J., 138
    R., 173
Levy, E., 173
Light, B., 47
Lochner, L., 59, 104
Lock, M., 150
Loewen, J.W., 5
Lorde, A., 29
Losen, D., 3, 31, 36, 38
Loving v. State of Virginia, 132
Low, S., 69–70
Lowell, B.L., 70
Lyman, R., 171

M

Macroeconomic mandates, *vs.* urban
    educational policy, 77
Makela, K., 151–153
Mamalian, C.A., 58, 76
Management of outlaw emotions, 27–56
Marlan, T., 4

CPSIA information can be obtained at www.ICGtesting.com
Printed in the USA
LVOW071407010212

266413LV00005B/201/P

9 780415 957120